Survival Guide to Computer Systems

Survival Guide to Computer Systems

WILLIAM E. PERRY

CBI

CBI Publishing Company, Inc.
51 Sleeper Street
Boston, Massachusetts 02210

Production Editor/Becky Handler
Text Designer/Becky Handler
Compositor/Commonwealth Graphics
Jacket Designer/Deborah Flynn

Library of Congress Cataloging in Publication Data

Perry, William E.
Survival guide to computer systems.

Includes index.
1. Computers. 2. Electronic data processing.
I. Title.
QA76.P426 001.64 81-18027
ISBN 0-8436-0880-3 AACR2

Printed in the United States of America

Printing (last digit): 9 8 7 6 5 4 3 2 1

Contents

Preface

The success of certain people is frequently tied to their ability to interact with computer systems. These systems are written in languages that are foreign to most managers and are formulated by people who possess unique and sometimes mystifying skills. The failure to understand and communicate with computer people and their systems may be reflected in missed opportunity and frustration. This book is designed to demystify the black box and to put it in its proper perspective—that of running the organization. The computer process will be segmented and explained in lay terms, enabling you to stay in charge of your operation. This is the one book that everybody should read before they fight, support, attempt to modify, or use the results produced by computer systems, or merely converse with computer professionals.

1/ How a computer does its thing

"If computers are so great, why do they give me the blahs?"—wonders a frustrated computer user.

So you need help with the computer

Visualize a large auditorium filled with people. The performance ends. Instead of the usual mass exodus, the people in the first row get up and leave, followed by those in the second row, the third row, and so on. The process is orderly. People know when they are to leave and approximately how long it will take them to get out of the auditorium. There is virtually no shoving or pushing. Because the process is orderly and systematic, the auditorium empties quickly.

Visualize the same full auditorium under "normal" circumstances. When the performance ends, everyone heads for the exits at the same time. The aisles are clogged and the people move slowly through the crowded doorways. This disorderly process causes tempers to flare, and the auditorium empties slowly.

These examples illustrate two approaches to emptying a full auditorium. The first approach is systematic; the second is chaotic. Systems of any kind are designed to bring order out of chaos, to find a simple, efficient, routine way of doing a task. In organizations, systems are designed to process great amounts of data and information—whether for accounting, personnel, or production purposes—in an orderly, controlled manner. Systems make for smoothly running organizations. Good systems are essential if an organization is to survive.

Good systems don't just happen. Before their implementation, they must be planned in detail so that each procedure in the system is defined clearly. Also, because systems are designed to perform the same tasks repeatedly, the rules must be understood and executed consistently.

In today's world, most systems are computerized. The computer is a tool used by people to help people do their work more efficiently, effectively, and economically. Because the computer interacts so closely with most of our day-to-day life, we need to understand how this "black box" works.

This book explains how computer systems are conceived, implemented, and operated. It not only discusses the mechanics and the concepts of computer systems, but it also emphasizes the role of people in these systems. To leave out this aspect would be to speak abstractly rather than realistically. In fact, learning how people fit into systems is the key to understanding how systems work.

Successful systems facilitate work. As new processes develop or existing processes change, systems must be either created or revised to support these processes. For example, information systems do the paperwork and provide accounting data that make it easier for organizations to conduct a profitable business in an orderly way. Management can use accounting information provided through systems to measure effectiveness without great effort.

Let's first see how a computer works and then review how a system is designed and operated with a computer.

How a computer works

The computer has been described in many terms, some eloquent and some vulgar. At the same time as the computer has been called the dominant advance of the twentieth century, it has been compared in intelligence to a two-year-old child. It's no wonder that so many people are confused about the capabilities of computers and how they work.

Let's explore for a moment some of the common misconceptions about computers:

- *Computers can think.* Not true! Computers do what they are instructed to do, no more and no less. A computer can be taught some intricate tasks, such as playing chess, but to do so it must be preinstructed regarding each type of move to make on the basis of the situation on the playing board. If a situation should occur for which the computer has not been instructed, it will fail.

- *It requires a mathematical genius to instruct a computer.* Not true! With three to four hours of instruction, most people can perform elementary tasks on a computer. This is not to say that in three to four hours you will know all that must be known about a computer. However, you will have enough information to give you the confidence to do things and to learn more.
- *Computers make mistakes.* Not true! People, not computers, make mistakes. Computers don't embezzle, computers don't lose information, and computers don't do anything except what they are instructed to do.

What can computers do?

Computers are machines. As such, they have finite capabilities. For example, an electric saw is designed to cut wood. The saw is not an effective tool for sanding wood or for drilling holes in it. However, as long as you understand the capabilities of the electric saw and use it in accordance with the instructions, it should perform well if it is not pushed beyond its limited capabilities.

Computers are no different from other pieces of machinery. Computers are constructed with predetermined capabilities. Thus, the limits of what a computer does are dictated by the capabilities built into the computer. These capabilities vary from vendor to vendor, but all offer only limited capabilities.

Most computers are restricted to the following three capabilities (see Figure 1-1):

- *Move data.* Data is the information used by computers. For example, data in a payroll system would be an employee's name or identification, the number of hours worked, and the hourly pay rate. The computer can move data from an external source, such as a punched card, into computer memory (i.e., that segment of the computer where data are stored), or from memory to an external medium such as a paycheck. The process is similar to hearing a question and providing an answer. Our ears receive information from an external source (i.e., the question). The information moves into our brain through our ears (i.e., into memory) and then from our brain to our vocal cords, where it becomes an external response (i.e., the answer to the question).
- *Compute data.* Computers can perform mathematical functions on data. The mathematical functions normally include

Figure 1-1. Three Computer Capabilities

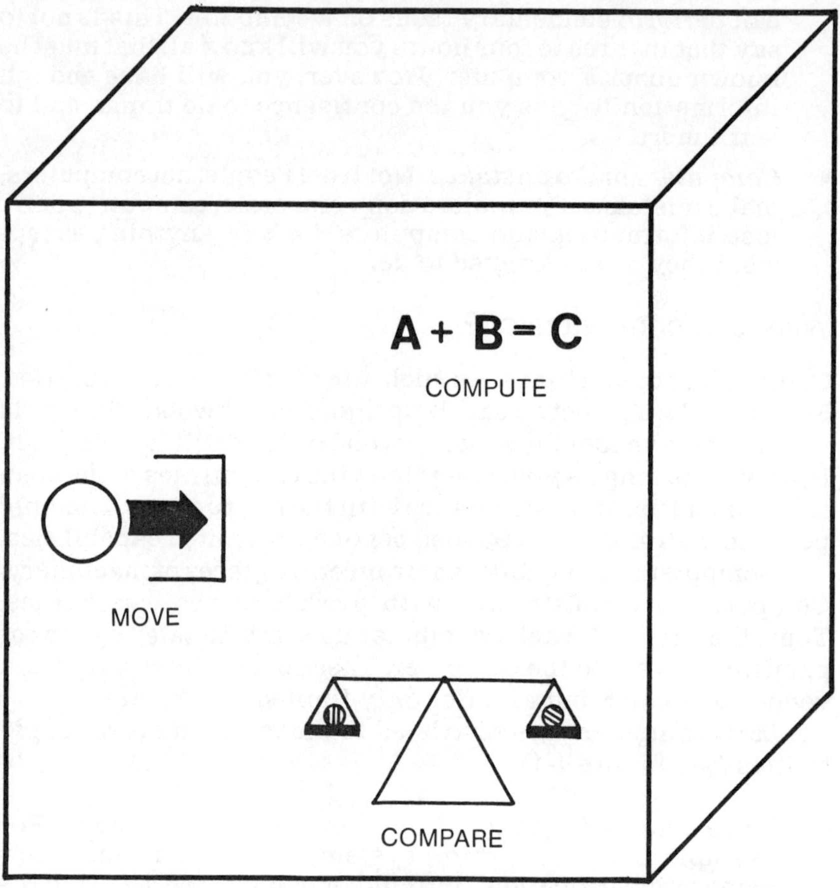

addition, subtraction, multiplication, and division. With these basic mathematical functions, many computers also offer more complex functions, such as square root and regression analysis.

- *Compare data.* The computer assigns values to data. Each value is different and can be ranked. We can understand readily some of these mathematical values, such as a nine being higher than one. However, the computer also assigns values to alphabetic characters and to other, special characters that the computer recognizes. The computer then can determine whether two values, such as two personal names, are equal or whether one name value is higher or lower than the other. This enables the computer to perform tasks such as putting all the names in a telephone book in the proper sequence.

That's it. There is no more. These are the capabilities of the computer, and all the wonderful things you have heard about computers must be accomplished using these three simple instructions. Hence you hear the intelligence of a computer being compared to that of a two-year-old child.

How, then, you might ask, can the computer do all these wonderful things with three simple instructions? The answer is to break tasks into small enough components to accomplish the desired goal.

A common mistake that people make in conceptualizing the computer's capability is that they assume that the computer performs tasks in the same way that people do. This is not true. Human intelligence provides far greater capabilities than those of a computer. Let's look at a simple example.

You are in a department store and are attempting to buy some merchandise. You present your credit card to the sales clerk, who, using a computer, will determine whether or not your credit is good. Using a piece of machinery, the sales clerk moves your customer number from an external source (your credit card) to computer memory. There, using the instructions available, the computer first must determine your customer number before it can search for your name to verify credit. Let's evaluate how the computer reads and recognizes your customer number.

A person who looks at your customer number on the credit card can quickly say it is, for example, number 123456. Unfortunately, the computer cannot perform the task in this simple manner. It must do so with its compare command. If we look at two of the options available to the computer for identification of your customer number, you will get a better feel for the way the computer operates.

Option 1 allows the computer to compare your number sequentially against every valid customer number. If there are 50,000 customers in the store, the computer will compare your number against each of the 50,000 valid customer numbers to determine whether it is equal. The computer begins the task by determining whether your number is equal to the first customer number. If it is not, it will compare your number against the next customer number. If it is not equal, it will compare it against the third customer number, and so on through all 50,000 customer numbers until it finds an equal. This is similar to a child trying to fit a peg into one of many differently shaped holes. The child will keep trying to find the hole that matches the shape of the object.

In option 2, the computer plays a guessing game to narrow the list of 50,000 customer numbers to a small group. For example, in a six-digit customer number, the range of valid numbers is 000001 through 999999. The computer begins the game by comparing your number against the number 500000 to determine whether your number is higher or lower than 500000. If it is lower than 500000, the computer then will compare it against 250000; if it is lower, it will compare it against 125000; if it still is lower, it will compare it against 62500, and so on. Within fifteen comparisons, the computer will have narrowed your number to a relatively small range of customer numbers. The computer then begins a one-by-one comparison, as it did in option 1, until it finds an exact match. However, with this more sophisticated approach it may need only 50 tries, or comparisons, to identify your number positively, as opposed to up to 50,000 questions, or comparisons, as with the first option.

The computer now has identified your customer number. What a lot of work for a small task! Its next task is to find where the information about you is located, move that information into computer memory, and then make more comparisons. You can see that accomplishment of what appears to be a relatively simple task may require thousands of computer instructions.

Computer Survival Rule #1

Even simple tasks are complex for a computer to perform. Don't overestimate the ease with which the computer can perform simple tasks.

Understanding computer systems

Computers are not magic. Computers are machines that operate by very detailed instructions. If there is a magic to the working of computers, it is because people are intelligent enough to break complex tasks into segments small enough to be executed by a computer. We all have witnessed the problem a small child has in tying shoelaces. Try for a moment to visualize how complex the written instructions for a two-year-old to tie shoelaces would be, and you will have some idea of the detail required to instruct a computer.

I hope that this book will put computer systems into the proper perspective for you. However, to understand fully how a system is designed, implemented, and operated, you will need to read and study the entire book. Since many of us are impatient and may not wish to wait until the last chapter to see how the story ends, we need an overview before we learn about all the parts.

Computers are complex machines to understand and use. Each new advance in technology has increased the obstacles to understanding the "nature of the animal." Whether you are discussing power steering in your automobile or the latest electronic computer system, the question inevitably arises: What makes it tick?

If you want to understand the electronic computer system—its functions, capabilities, applications, and limitations—you might decide to rely on manuals and other material published by a computer manufacturer. This approach could be your undoing! In order to understand manuals, you must already have a wealth of background information. Such manuals fairly overflow with technical jargon, such as "inability to execute a predetermined group of instructions in a set sequence," and similar statements that confuse more than they enlighten. The statistics they cite aren't much help either. Although such statistics establish a time perspective and often are interesting, they rarely explain the underlying principles of a system.

For instance, operating cycles expressed in terms of telephone books per minute, multiplications per second, milliseconds per machine cycle, and hundreds of cards per minute conjure images of fantastic speed. However, these measurements tell how fast rather than how a computer works. Even performance figures can be misleading, since the manufacturer cites only the most impressive statistics and omits the unimpressive ones.

Having failed to understand computer systems through manuals, you might decide to watch the computer in operation. Unfortunately, this approach also won't help much, because the important things are happening *inside* the computer. It is interesting, of course, to watch the blinking console lights, see the sporadic movement of magnetic tapes, and read the printout. However, these visual effects tell you little about a computer's performance.

How, then, *can* you understand computer systems? One way is to follow a new systems application from its conception through the various stages to the point where the system can be coded in a language computers can understand. Since this process is time consuming, it is advisable to start with an artificially constructed application that can be subjected to the same detailed analysis as a practical application. An example of this approach is provided in "The Secret Woes of Mr. Knowlittle," which follows.

The secret woes of Mr. Knowlittle

This story tells of the sometimes amusing efforts of a systems analyst who tries to specify in detail the requirements of a simple system: going to work in the morning. This system, widely published and distributed for training purposes, is a classic in its field. Using flowchart symbols, our systems analyst shows how to convert this daily chore into one that can be done by a computer (Figure 1-2). Starting with "Set Alarm" at the top of the diagram and proceeding downward, the step-by-step instructions illustrate the type of logic required to write computer programs for commercial applications. On the basis of this example alone, you will see how much detail is needed to convert a fairly simple manual system into a completely automated computer system. Let us follow Mr. Knowlittle as he proceeds through the agony and the ecstasy of installing a computer system. This example will provide some insight into the importance of people in systems and the various roles that people should play.

Understandably excited, Mr. Knowlittle nervously taps his slide rule on the desk as his department head, I. M. Sharpe, outlines Knowlittle's first project of consequence since the latter joined the ranks of the systems group. Sharpe is saying, "Our systems group has been assigned the vital task of investigating possible machine applications and, if they prove feasible, of preparing the detailed routines necessary to put the resulting programs into operation. In view of your limited experience, Knowlittle, I am assigning you to a project that requires minimal effort—the chore of designing a system to get the family off to work each day."

Figure 1-2. How to Get to Work in the Morning

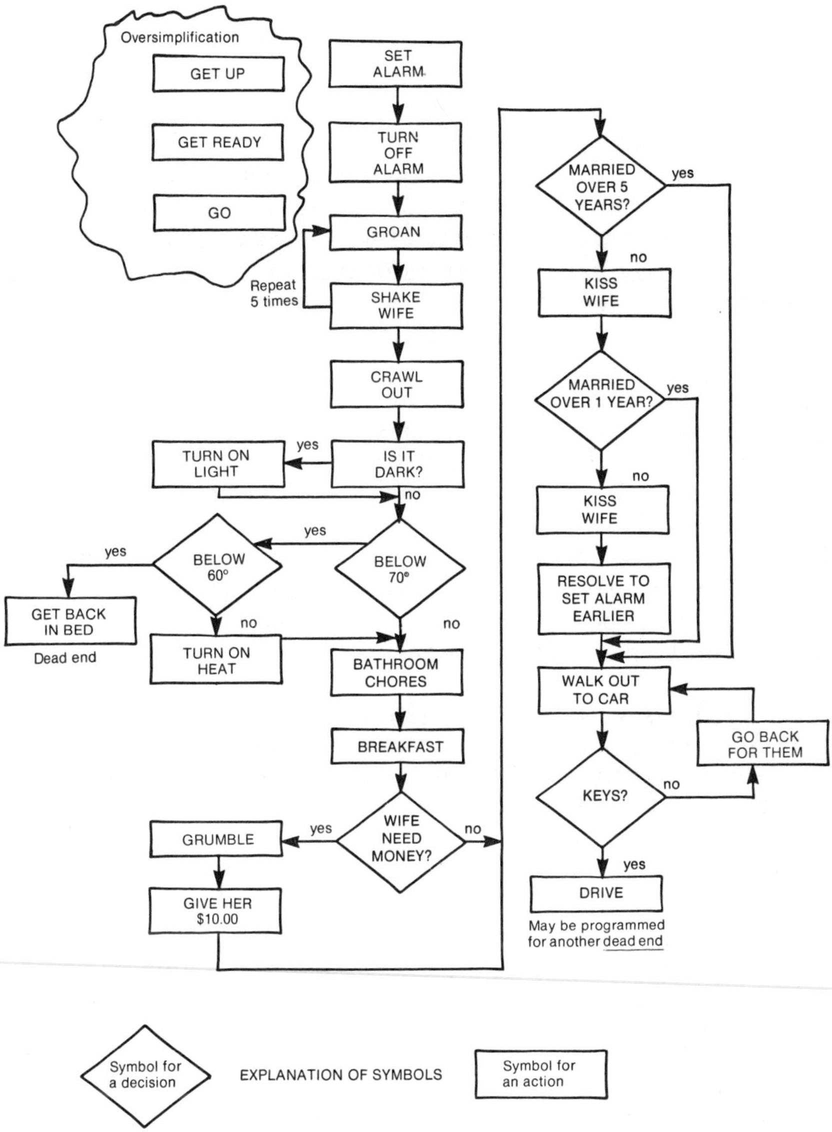

Knowlittle nods in agreement and slides back in his seat as his boss continues: "We don't expect this project to overtax you, Knowlittle, but it should be good experience. The rules and steps necessary to put this program into operation shouldn't be too difficult to work out. After all, the routine itself has been common household practice for centuries. One word of caution, however. We'll expect the customary thoroughness that has become the byword of this department. Check back with me when you have completed the rough drafts. Any questions?"

"No, sir!" says a bewildered Knowlittle.

Determined to impress Sharpe with a skilled effort, Knowlittle begins by reviewing his own experiences in getting to work in the morning. He assembles a rather formidable list of data. "Still," he muses, "I mustn't forget the byword—thoroughness. Do I really have enough information?" While pondering his problem one evening, he hits on the obvious solution. Knowlittle documents his solution quickly in a flowchart entitled, "How to Get to Work in the Morning" (Figure 1-2). His mental processes now attuned keenly to his project, Knowlittle snatches up his prize and heads for the boss's office.

Bolting breathlessly through the door, Knowlittle tosses the masterpiece on Sharpe's mahogany desk, reclines in a comfortable chair, and awaits his reward anxiously. Unfortunately for Knowlittle, Mr. Sharpe's fine reputation in systems circles is due largely to his uncanny ability to define and analyze problems. Under the boss's intense scrutiny, Knowlittle's "masterpiece" crumbles as Sharpe raises such points as:

1. Have the labor laws been changed recently, or is it still possible for women and single people to be gainfully employed? Perhaps Sharpe was a bit blunt, but it is true that Knowlittle's plan was for married men only.
2. Apparently there is no provision for "sleep" in this chart, an oversight that might jeopardize the success of the rest of the routine.
3. It appears rather odd that this worker should be so sensitive to the lower ranges of the thermometer but completely oblivious to the equally uncomfortable higher ranges. Even more important, no consideration has been given to "occupation." What if this worker happens to be a snowplow operator?
4. Does this fellow normally sleep in work clothes, or is "dressing" assumed to be included under "bathroom chores?" If "dressing" is not included, this may partially explain his extreme sensitivity to cold.
5. Attention should be given to the question of how much money is needed.

6. What if the thermometer is broken?
7. Suppose the furnace is malfunctioning?
8. What if the worker's child is hogging the bathroom?
9. What if the ignition keys are lost?

When Mr. Sharpe pauses for a second breath, a soundly whipped Knowlittle scrapes up the remains of his program and heads for the nearest exit. "Just a minute!" orders Sharpe. "Let's try to analyze a few of your major difficulties and formulate a more realistic plan of action. Perhaps the most glaring error in your proposal is the fact that it lacks flexibility to adapt to a wide range of individuals and environments. Using your program, Knowlittle, an Eskimo living in an Arctic igloo might well slumber right through the walrus season before he found out that the program excluded him.

"Your second major difficulty can best be described as lack of completeness. The chain of thought in your proposal contains many weak and broken links. Flaws in logic can be overcome only by splitting an operation into step-by-step detail, pausing after each step to examine, not only the road ahead, but also the impact of the last step on the whole routine. Admittedly, this rule is easier to define than to put into practice, but the task is not impossible. Perhaps I should reiterate a statement from our previous meeting: This project is basically simple—after all, the routine itself has been common household practice for centuries. Any questions? Oh, come now, Knowlittle, I know you can do it!"

When a rehabilitated Knowlittle returns about six months later with a completely revamped system, he is brimming with renewed confidence and declares flatly, "Mr. Sharpe, I have analyzed every detail of the problem. How soon can we put the system into operation?" Sharpe merely smiles, studies the new proposal at some length (Knowlittle has since buttressed the general chart with ten pages of categories and 125 pages of alternatives), then replies, "Very good, we are now about ready to start the *computer system design.*"

Knowlittle's undisguised bewilderment leads Sharpe to elaborate: "The term *computer system design* represents a very important step between the work you have already completed and the actual coding or programming of instructions, a final gesture that constitutes a relatively small part of the total project effort. We must face the fact squarely that a computer is, after all, only an electronic robot that does exactly what it is told. It behooves us, then, to organize details of the desired system into instructions that will be intelligible to a computer and to provide a course of action for any situation that we may encounter. Generally, the best instructions are those that allow performance of a given series of tasks most efficiently."

What does this example teach us?

One glance at Knowlittle convinces Mr. Sharpe that his fledgling hasn't any idea of what he is talking about, so he abruptly changes his approach. "Okay, let's dissect the first block of the diagram that simply states 'Set Alarm.' Although the statement 'Set Alarm' is sufficient for a person to execute the command, it raises many questions for a computer. Let's examine some of the confusion caused by this command and then state some preliminary survival rules that should be followed in designing a computer system to avoid problems or confusion in future systems."

Description of "alarm" needed

The word *alarm* is too vague to distinguish between similar objects. Is it a fire alarm or a burglar alarm?

> **Computer Survival Rule #2**
>
> *Define all terms in such a manner that each term can be distinguished from all others.*

The alarm clock cited in the example might be described as a "time-measuring device that can activate an alarm at a predetermined time, making enough noise to awaken a sleeping person."

Time considerations must be specified

Apparently, the fellow in the example wearily trudges off to work every day, irrespective of weekends, legal holidays, and vacations. Is he a lighthouse keeper? If not, the dates on which this program should be operative must be clearly designed.

Computer Survival Rule #3

Supply the precise times when a given action should be performed, along with any special variations that accompany these times.

Hence, in the example, "Work Day" might be outlined as "Monday through Friday weekly, except the first two full weeks of July (vacation) and eight paid holidays." Furthermore, "Work Day" needs to be defined, and special codes must be devised to identify unforeseeable schedule changes, such as "Strikes" and "Overtime."

Locale should be identified

The example doesn't say where the alarm clock is located. Should the worker place it in the living room, where it probably would frighten the wits out of the goldfish? Or should he place the clock in the bedroom?

Computer Survival Rule #4

Specify exact locations, physical or relative, that are pertinent to a given action.

Accordingly, the example might locate the alarm clock "in the worker's sleeping quarters, within his arm's reach."

Operation of alarm should be analyzed

It appears that the computer is supposed to rely on imagination and experience (neither of which it has) to guide it in setting the alarm. Is the alarm set like arming a hand grenade—just pull the pin—or is this one of those newfangled clock radios?

Computer Survival Rule #5

Explode multistep operations into simplified, step-by-step procedures.

For instance, having agreed on a standard alarm clock, the worker might (1) wind the clock, (2) wind the alarm, (3) turn the alarm dial shaft in a counterclockwise direction until the pointer indicates the waking hour, (4) turn the main shaft in a clockwise direction until the minute and hour hands indicate the current time, and (5) pull the alarm stem to the outward position.

Recovery techniques should be specified

Completely automatic computer systems demand that routines be devised to satisfy even situations that are wholly unanticipated but theoretically possible. Suppose the worker in the example found, to his chagrin, that he doesn't even own an alarm clock. Must he quit his job?

Computer Survival Rule #6

Devise routines that will minimize losses attributable to error conditions and permit completion of the task under any circumstances.

Instead of a literal dead end, the worker may have salvaged the situation simply by telephoning his boss and explaining the predicament. Obviously, he might have resolved the dilemma in numerous ways, the best choice being that which brought him to work on time with the least amount of additional cost or effort. A system cannot be termed complete unless the challenge "What if this condition did not exist?" can be answered satisfactorily.

What are the components of a computer?[1]

A computer is not a single piece of machinery as is sometimes thought, but consists of a number of components that are tied together. A computer usually consists of the following components (see Figure 1-3):

- *CPU.* The central processing unit (CPU), or computer, performs arithmetic, logic, and control functions.
- *Input/Output.* Includes associated peripheral equipment, such as devices for data preparation and input and output.

[1]Reprinted with permission from *EDP Controls and Auditing,* 3rd ed. W. Thomas Porter and William E. Perry, (Boston: Kent Publishing Co., 1981), Appendix G.

Figure 1-3. Components of a Computer

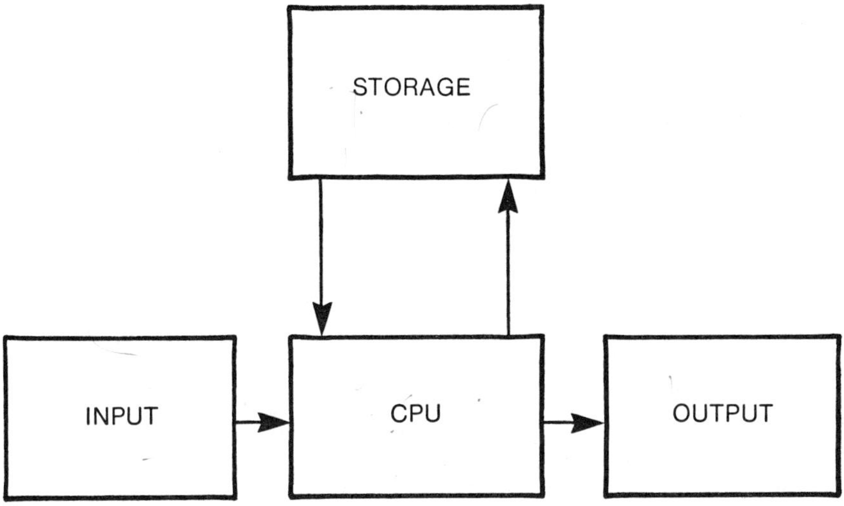

- *Storage.* This is the area where information is retained until needed—sometimes referred to as computer memory.

CPU

The CPU directs and coordinates all electronic data processing (EDP) systems operations. The concept of on-line is related to the CPU control function. All input-output devices, such as the card reader, tape drives, and disk drives, usually are under the control of the CPU, which temporarily is storing the data read from the files on the input devices and writing data onto the files on the output devices. Thus, the control section governs input-output devices, entry and removal of information from storage, and routing of information between storage and the arithmetic/logic unit.

The arithmetic/logic unit of the CPU contains the circuitry for performing arithmetic and logical operations. The arithmetic circuitry performs computations (addition, subtraction, multiplication, division), sets the algebraic sign of results, rounds values, and so on. For example, after reading data from a sales record, a sales program may compute a sales price by multiplying unit price by the number of units sold, rounding the result to the nearest cent; the arithmetic circuitry would perform this computation.

The logic circuitry performs decision-making functions by looking for the presence or absence of certain conditions and executing the set of program instructions associated with a set of conditions. For example, an auditor may wish to print a confirmation request if the receivable balance for a client's customer exceeds a certain dollar value (a constant, such as $5,000). For each record in the receivable file, the program would compare the customer's balance with the constant $5,000 and print a confirmation request if the customer's balance exceeds $5,000 (the presence of the condition).

Storage

The storage used by the CPU is referred to as *main storage,* a term used to designate all internal storage of the CPU. This storage consists of magnetic codes arranged so that numeric and alphabetic characters, such as a comma or a dollar sign, can be represented in storage and be retrieved when needed. As I suggested previously, this main, or core, storage is limited and is used temporarily to store both the data being processed and the stored program used in processing the data; thus, the main storage is also referred to as temporary storage.

Storage is divided into locations, usually consisting of a set of eight on-off conditions. A combination of codes (usually called *bits*) is used to represent the remaining letters, numbers, and special characters. One additional bit is used as a check bit. With this eight-bit code, 256 characters can be represented using both upper- and lowercase alphabetic characters, numbers, and a wide range of special characters.

Each eight-bit set of cores has an address, and the address of the storage location must be known either to the programmer or to a control program in order to store data in and read data from a location. When data are read from an input file or from another location in main storage and stored in a particular location, they replace the previous data in that location. Reading data from a particular location does not alter the contents of the location. Thus, the same data may be used many times once they are written into storage (nondestructive read-out). Data are destroyed only when they are replaced by new data (destructive read-in).

Input-output devices and media

Another major element of an EDP system is the input and output devices that enable data on input files to be read into the CPU and

Table 1-1. Commonly Used Input-Output Devices

Medium	*Device*	*Input*	*Output*	*Unit of Measurement*
Punched cards	Card reader	X		Cards/minute
	Card punch		X	Cards/minute
Paper tape	Tape reader	X		Characters/second
	Tape punch		X	Characters/second
Magnetic ink	Reader	X		Documents/minute
Paper	Optical scanner	X		Documents/minute
	Printer		X	Lines/minute
	Console typewriter	X	X	Characters/second
Cathode-ray tube	Display	X	X	Characters/second
Sound	Audio		X	Words/second
Magnetic tape	Tape drive	X	X	Characters/second
Magnetic disk	Disk drive	X	X	Characters/second
Display/print	Point-of-sale equipment	X	X	Characters/second
Money	Cash-dispensing terminal	X	X	Characters/second
Magnetic disk	Key to disk	X	X	Characters/second

also enable data to be written onto output files. The devices used correspond to the input and output media on which the data are recorded. We have already mentioned the primary input-output media (punched cards, magnetic tapes, magnetic disks). Other types of media include audio, paper tape, magnetic ink, and optically readable characters. Also, data may be introduced into an EDP system through a console typewriter located at or near the console of the CPU and through remote terminals, such as those used in airline reservation systems. The input devices used most widely to process and record data on the various media are summarized in Table 1-1.

The input and output devices in the table often are classified as either high-speed or slow-speed devices. Card readers, card punches, paper-tape readers, printers, and direct-input devices (e.g., console typewriter, cathode-ray tube) are slow-speed devices; magnetic tape units and disk drives are high-speed devices. For example, in one minute a typical magnetic tape unit can read a quantity of data equivalent to that recorded on 25,000 punched cards. Since cards, tapes, and disks are the most widely used input-output media in EDP systems, we shall discuss each of these media in detail.

Cards

The punched card is a common and familiar type of input media. The most common type of card contains twelve horizontal rows and eighty vertical columns. Data are represented by small rectangular holes in specific rows in the columns; only one character can be recorded in each column, as shown in Figure 1-4. Of course, information is read from punched cards by a card reader on-line or under the control of the CPU. The conversion of the twelve-bit code (corresponding to the twelve rows) in the card into the code for internal storage discussed previously (EBCDIC) is performed automatically by the control unit of the card reader as data are read from the card.

Figure 1-4. Example of a Punched Card

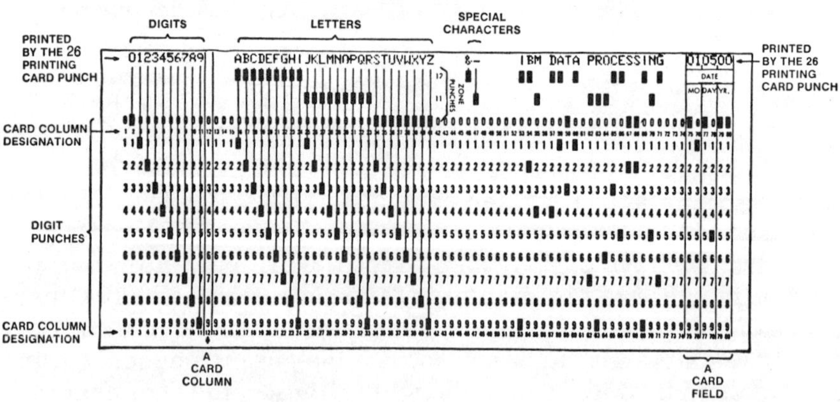

Figure 1-5. Example of an IBM System/3 Card

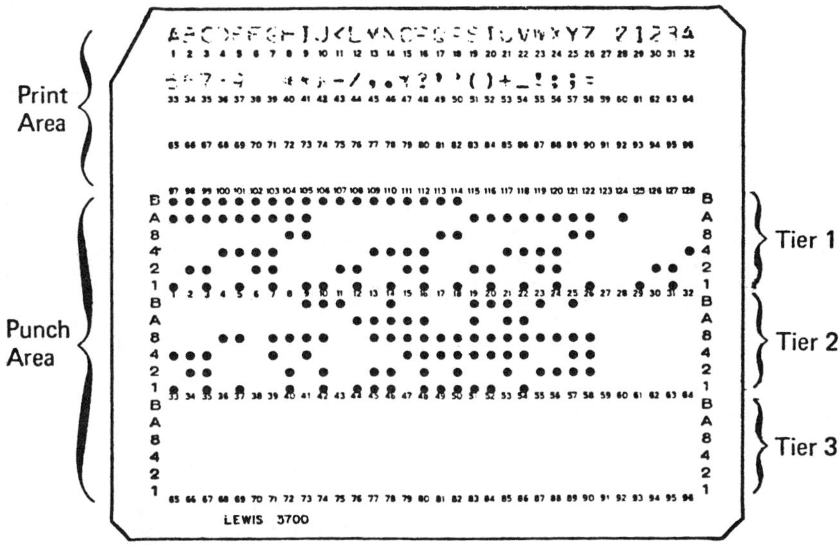

A newer card format is the ninety-six-column card introduced with the IBM System/3 computer. Data are punched in the lower part of the card and printed on the upper part, as shown in Figure 1-5. The punch area is divided into three parts called tiers. Each tier has thirty-two places where characters of data can be punched. These places are called card columns. The card columns have six positions in which punches can be placed. Characters are represented by a combination of zone (B.A.) and numeric punches (8, 4, 2, 1). Sixty-four different characters can be represented by various punch combinations.

Paper tape

Data are recorded as punched holes in paper tape by means of different coding schemes. While paper tape is not used much in commercial data processing, it is used heavily by numerically controlled machine tools to receive input instruction data.

Magnetic ink

Magnetic ink readers use the type font approved by the American Bankers Association, illustrated in Figure 1-6. Today, one of the major uses of magnetic ink characters is on checks.

Figure 1-6. Example of Magnetic Ink Characters

Optical character reader

An emerging group of input devices read handwritten and standard type fonts. Use of such devices eliminates the need for transcribing source data to another medium. Both reduction of input preparation and elimination of transcribing errors are advantages of the optical character reader.

Universal vendor coding, used in supermarkets, is an example of optical characters. This code is a series of bars that can be read by a scanner at the checkout counter to identify each product. The code can be read from either direction. A small computer connected to the checkout cash register can perform a computer lookup to obtain the correct price for the product identified by the scanner.

Cathode-ray tube (terminals)

This is one of the most popular types of computer terminals in use. Both printing and graphics can be displayed on the tube. The system can provide the terminal operator with either a series of questions to answer or forms to complete as a means of communicating with the system. A keyboard is available to the operator to communicate with the system. The data entered via the keyboard can be displayed on the tube.

Sound

Audio response units with a vocabulary of a few hundred words are available for special system uses. The voices of these units can be either male or female. Normally these units are used in conjunction with a system that uses Touch-Tone telephones as input. In such a system, the individual making the input can obtain an audio response from the system.

Magnetic tapes

Magnetic tapes are one of the principal input-output media used in EDP systems. They are similar to the tapes used on a tape recorder. A reel of tape 2,400 feet long can contain as much information as 400,000 fully punched cards (16 million characters). Each reel consists of a long roll of flexible plastic material with a magnetic coating that contains small particles of iron oxide, which provides a ferromagnetic coating on which the data are recorded. Data are recorded on the tape by changing the direction of magnetization in the seven or nine tracks across the tape. The absence of a change of polarity from one vertical column to the next in a horizontal track indicates an "off" position for that bit; in other words, it is sensed as a zero-bit. A change in the direction of magnetization from one vertical column to the next in a horizontal track indicates an "on" condition, which is sensed as a one-bit.

Since one character can be recorded in each vertical column, the next logical question is, "How many vertical columns are there?" Closeness of vertical columns or the number of characters that can be packed into an inch of tape is referred to as density; density varies considerably with different types of tape drives. Densities of 200, 556, 800, 1,600, and 6,250 characters, or bytes, per inch, are common. For descriptive purposes, a byte and a character are considered to be the same unit.

One of the principal differences between punched cards and magnetic tape is that a tape record is not limited to a particular length. A card will have a definite, specific limitation in length, such as eighty characters, while a tape record, with some practical limitations, can be almost any length. Tape records of 300, 500, 800, and 1,000 characters are common; however, the record should not be so long that it cannot be read into core storage. For instance, if the program permits 980 positions in core storage, this should be the maximal length for any tape record.

Disk storage

Another medium commonly used for storing data is magnetic disks. Such a medium is referred to as direct-access storage because any storage position containing data can be read or written directly without sequential location of the record. As mentioned in the discussion of cards and tapes, we do have to process card and tape files sequentially in order to use them. Direct-access devices allow processing to be handled without sorting of input data and without processing of master records that are not related to the transactions. A common disk storage is the removable disk unit (disk pack) with moving read-write heads for each track in the disk.

Point of sale

Point-of-sale units are electronic terminals that are connected to computer processing capabilities. These devices are programmed to search computer storage for predetermined values, such as product prices and validity of credit card numbers. This replaces the cash register with a device that can help the sales clerk price the purchases and, at the same time, enter the sales information for additional processing.

Cash-dispensing terminals

Automatic teller machines (ATM) permit banking to be conducted twenty-four hours a day, seven days a week, without the attendance of bank personnel. Depositors are given magnetically encoded cards and passwords. They conduct their business on the ATM, which is programmed to dispense cash usually in fixed amounts, such as $50 or $100. There is also a maximal withdrawal per day.

Key to disk

Key-to-disk devices are rapidly replacing keypunches as the most common method for entering batched information. Rather than punch information into cards, it is recorded on a magnetic disk. This technique not only eliminates handling and cost of cards, but it also provides the opportunity for the operator to correct errors immediately. This is not possible on a keypunch machine because the card containing the error must be destroyed and a new card entered and punched.

Computer Survival Rule #7

There are a lot of methods for accomplishing the same task. Leave the methods to the data-processing personnel; you concentrate on the tasks.

Conclusion

Systems provide an orderly approach to doing work. Systems imply a repetition of tasks so that the same results will occur each time. In order to do this, the rules of the system must be very detailed. Large and complex systems are usually performed on a computer.

People make systems work. People who need the results of system processing in their work are called users. Users specify what the system is to do. The people that design the system or decide how the needs will be satisfied are called systems analysts. A programmer converts the design into instructions that a computer can understand. The computer is run by a computer operator.

Successful organizations use effective systems. The computer has enabled organizations to build more complex and efficient systems. Complex systems are needed to accommodate increasing competition and government requirements that force organizations to generate data about its operations in greater amounts and at greater speed. The increased use of the computer causes organizations to rely more heavily on systems because tasks previously performed by people are now being done on computer systems.

2/ What's different about a computer system?

The following two laws govern the performance of computer systems:

- *Law 1:* Any computer, regardless of its manufacturer, may be expected to perform at any time in a totally unexpected manner for reasons that are either totally obscure or completely mysterious.
- *Law 2:* When all else fails, read the directions.

The computer must be different—it doesn't smile

Although computers aren't black boxes, many people still perceive them as such (see Figure 2-1). A mystique has been created by the computer profession to dazzle those not invited to their rituals. Computer professionals use secret words and processes to confuse the innocent.

A select group of individuals from science, aviation, and the press corps were invited aboard the inaugural flight of a completely computerized airplane. The computer performed every task previously executed by the pilots and the flight crew. Onboard service was performed by robots moving up and down the aisle and controlled by hidden wiring. The movement of the aircraft was performed completely by computer. Shortly after takeoff, a prerecorded computer message announced, "Welcome aboard a completely computer-controlled aircraft. Every possible condition has been predetermined and you have absolutely nothing to worry about, worry about, worry about, worry about, worry about, worry about..."

We know computer systems are different from manual systems because computer systems don't smile. In addition, they usually don't respond to our oral questions, are frequently not very responsive to our needs, and at times seem to want to do things their own way. If we are going to survive the computer

Figure 2-1. People Perceive Computer Systems as Black Boxes

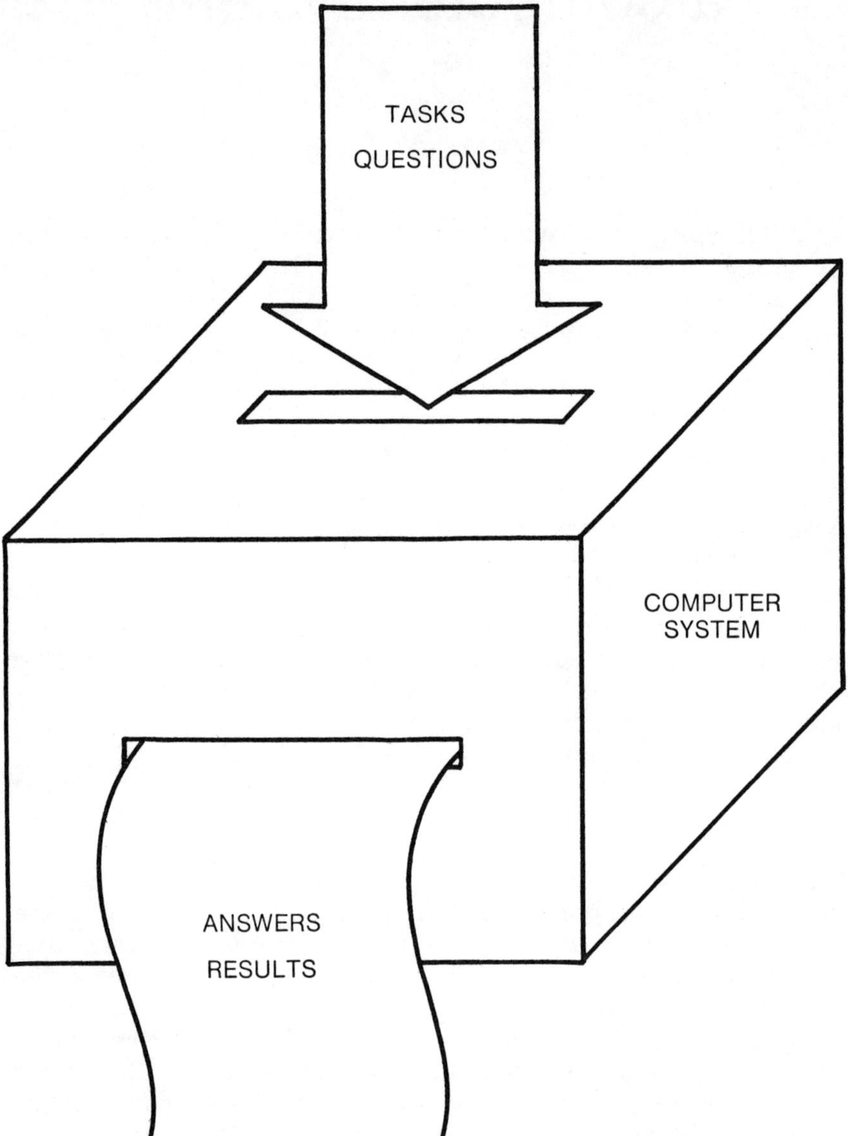

era, we need to know both how computers work and the differences between manual and computerized systems. A simple analogy is moving from a stick-shift automobile to one with an automatic transmission. If you have been driving a stick shift, you must understand the differences between the two transmissions in order to drive the automatic.

Let's examine a system as it might be performed manually and on the computer.

Manual/computerized systems: a comparison

Most of us are familiar with an accounts receivable system. This system is used by a store to account for and control credit purchases. In order to illustrate the differences between systems, we will review how such a system is constructed when the records are maintained manually, and then look at the same system after it has been computerized. However, first we must review the steps that occur in systems processing so we can relate the differences to those steps.

Six system steps

All systems contain the same steps. These steps occur as transaction information flows through the system. The six steps, in their proper sequence, are:

1. *Recording.* Once a transaction is originated, the data must be prepared for processing. This is done by recording transaction data.
2. *Authorization.* This step permits processing to begin. Certain procedures and methods allow only legitimate (authorized) documents to enter the system. Authorization may be as simple as obtaining a customer's name and address or as complex as obtaining several signatures on a form.
3. *Transmitting.* This is the process of entering data into the system. It may be done by delivering input documents personally, sending them through the mail, or transmitting information electronically.
4. *Processing.* In this step, the rules are applied to the data entered according to the predetermined systematic procedures each time a transaction or request for action is received.
5. *Storage.* This step involves retaining the data used by the system, including the input data, the results of processing (historical data), and data used by the system during processing (e.g., lists of prices and product names).
6. *Output.* This step provides the user with the results of processing.

Accounts receivable system example: manual to computerized

Most of us can understand manual systems readily because that's how we maintain our personal records. Our checking account, our income tax records, and the debts we must pay and collect usually are manually maintained systems. Many of us do not write down these items as formally as a business does, but we still keep these records without a computer.

For this reason, many people consider the computer to be a mysterious black box. It is unfamiliar to our daily routine. It is difficult to understand how machines can make decisions that affect our comfort and well-being. However, it can be done. For example, since we need a continuous supply of food and clothing, computers could be programmed to automatically replenish our shelves with food and our closets with clothing when we are in need.

By observing the transformation of a manual system to a computerized system, we can gain some insight into a process that, to the uninitiated, seems almost magical. Once we understand computerized systems, however, they will appear to be very logical and methodical in their approach to problem solving.

Let's examine a manual accounts receivable system. All of us have bought and paid for products using charge accounts. We will follow the manual process step by step as the merchandiser accepts the sale on credit, maintains accounts receivable records, and receives payments to apply against that receivable. Then we will look at the same process as it would be handled using the most modern computer technology. Many retail stores, such as Sears Roebuck and Co., use the same technology that we will be describing.

This section will show that the six system steps described previously are performed in both the manual and the computerized application. From this perspective, we can begin to understand the similarities and differences between manual and computerized systems.

Description

The accounts receivable system we are about to examine is an average system, in an average organization, in an average city. The organization is the Manual Market Co. (2M). The company's most mechanized piece of equipment before they bought a computer was an adding machine. All other tasks were done manually.

2M has issued plastic charge cards to its customers and uses them to imprint the customer's name and charge account number on invoices and credit memos. The account number is the main identifier for each customer; invoices are sent monthly to customers who have made purchases during the month or who have a balance due.

2M uses the following documents for accounts receivable purposes:

- *Customer invoice.* Sales personnel use this document to record an order.
- *Customer credit memo.* This document is used when products are returned to the organization.
- *Accounts receivable journal* (Figure 2-2). The document is used for recording sales invoices and credit memos. Note that the sale and return have now been manually recorded twice.
- *Tub card ledger file* (Figure 2-3). This file contains an individual card on each customer's account. Note that this is the third manual recording for an accounts receivable sale or return.
- *Customer's monthly statement.* This document is sent to customers to bill them for charges made during the last billing period. The customer will pay on the basis of this statement.
- *Manually-produced accounts receivable reports.* The three most common reports are a summary report of accounts receivable, a report of overdue accounts, and a current list of customers' names and addresses.

Manual system

The accounts receivable cycle begins when a customer makes a purchase on credit. (Manual processing of accounts receivable is illustrated in Figure 2-4.)

The sales clerk performs the first two of the six systems steps simultaneously: *recording* and *authorizing* the sale. To perform these steps, the sales clerk fills out an invoice. Some of the *processing* occurs as the sales clerk calculates the price of the purchase. *Output* occurs when the clerk exchanges merchandise for the signed invoice. The customer leaves the store with both the merchandise and a copy of the invoice.

At the end of the day, the sales clerk totals the invoices (another step in processing). The invoices then are hand carried or *transmitted* to the accounts receivable department. The accounts receivable department *stores* the invoices. Note that the flow through the system is not as smooth as is indicated by the six steps in the system. This irregular flow is normal in manual systems.

A process similar to a sale occurs when a customer returns merchandise to the store. Again, the clerk performs the recording and authorizing steps almost simultaneously. This is done according to rules that management has given to the sales clerk. The more valuable the merchandise, the higher level the person must be to authorize credit for the returned merchandise. The sales clerk fills out the credit memo and exchanges it with the customer for the returned merchandise. At the end of the day, the clerk totals the credit memos and hand carries or transmits them through distribution to the accounts receivable department.

At this point, the accounts receivable department has the daily batch of invoices and credit memos. The department in turn posts these to the accounts receivable journal (Figure 2-2). The accounts receivable journal is a listing of the day's transactions for both invoices and credit memos. The accounts receivable department totals the day's transactions. The totals in

Figure 2-2. Accounts Receivable Journal

MANUAL MARKET CO. (2M)
ACCOUNTS RECEIVABLE JOURNAL

Date ____________

ID Number	Account Number	Payments	Charges	Credit	Total

the journal are compared with the totals calculated by the sales clerks. When the grand totals are reconciled, they can be posted to the general ledger.

From the accounts receivable journal each customer's records are posted to a ledger card (Figure 2-3). Invoices and credit memos are recorded on the ledger card. On a monthly basis, the

Figure 2-3. Tub Card Ledger File

Account Number

LEDGER CARD

NAME ______________________________

ADDRESS ______________________________

CITY, STATE ______________________________

DATE	IDENTIFICATION NUMBER	CHARGE	CREDIT PAYMENT	TOTAL

Figure 2-4. Manual Processing of Accounts Receivable

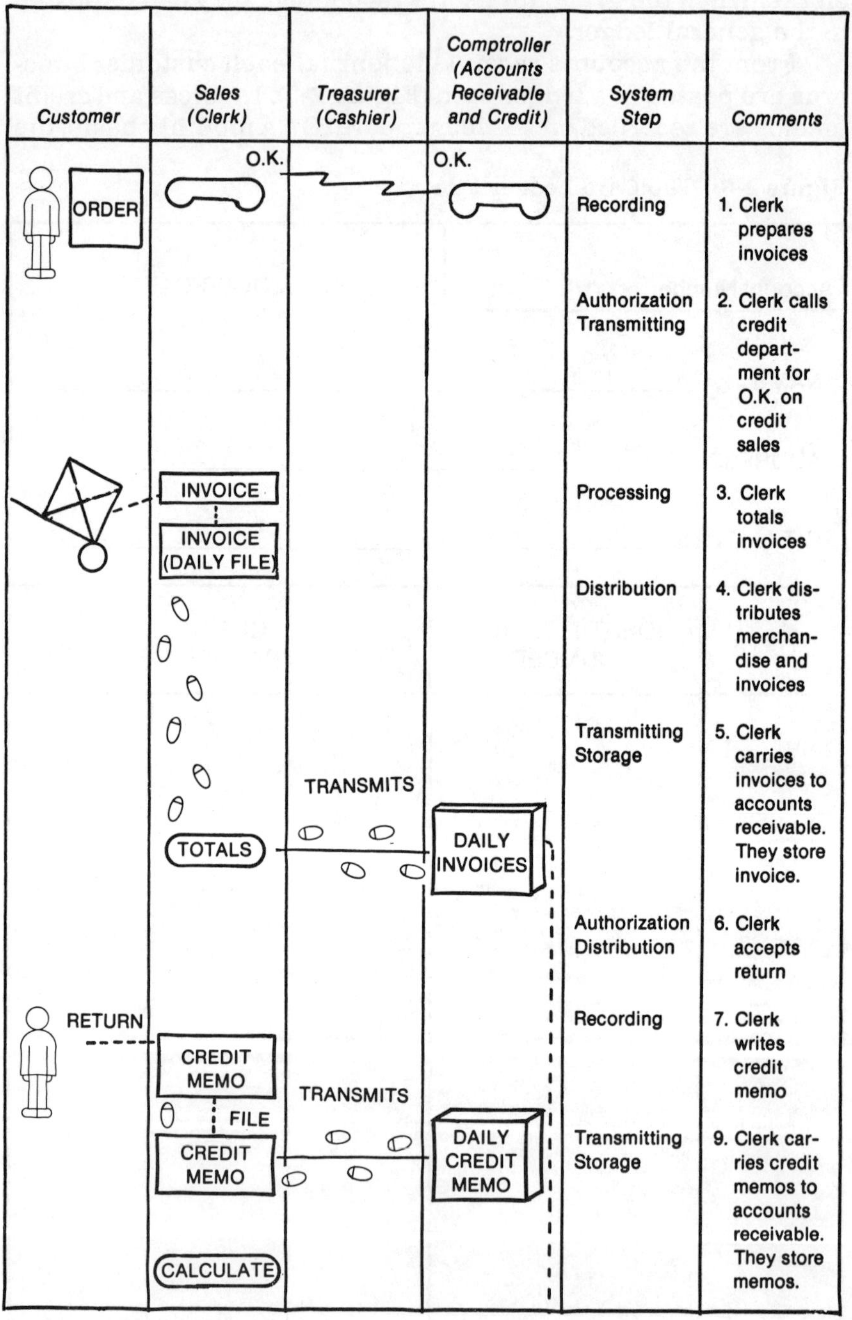

Figure 2-4. *(continued)*

Customer	*Sales (Clerk)*	*Treasurer (Cashier)*	*Comptroller (Accounts Receivable and Credit)*	*System Step*	*Comments*
			POST ACCOUNTS RECEIVABLE REGISTER CALCULATE	Processing	10. Invoices and credits are recorded on accounts receivable register
	TOTAL	COMPARE	TOTAL	Processing Transmitting	11. Register balanced to clerk's totals
			POST Ledger Card	Processing	12. Post balance to general ledger
				Processing	13. Customer's record posted to individual customer ledger card
			TOTAL	Processing	14. Customer's detail balanced to general ledger control
			POST CALCULATE MONTHLY STATEMENT	Processing	15. Customer's monthly statement prepared from customer's ledger card

Figure 2-4. *(continued)*

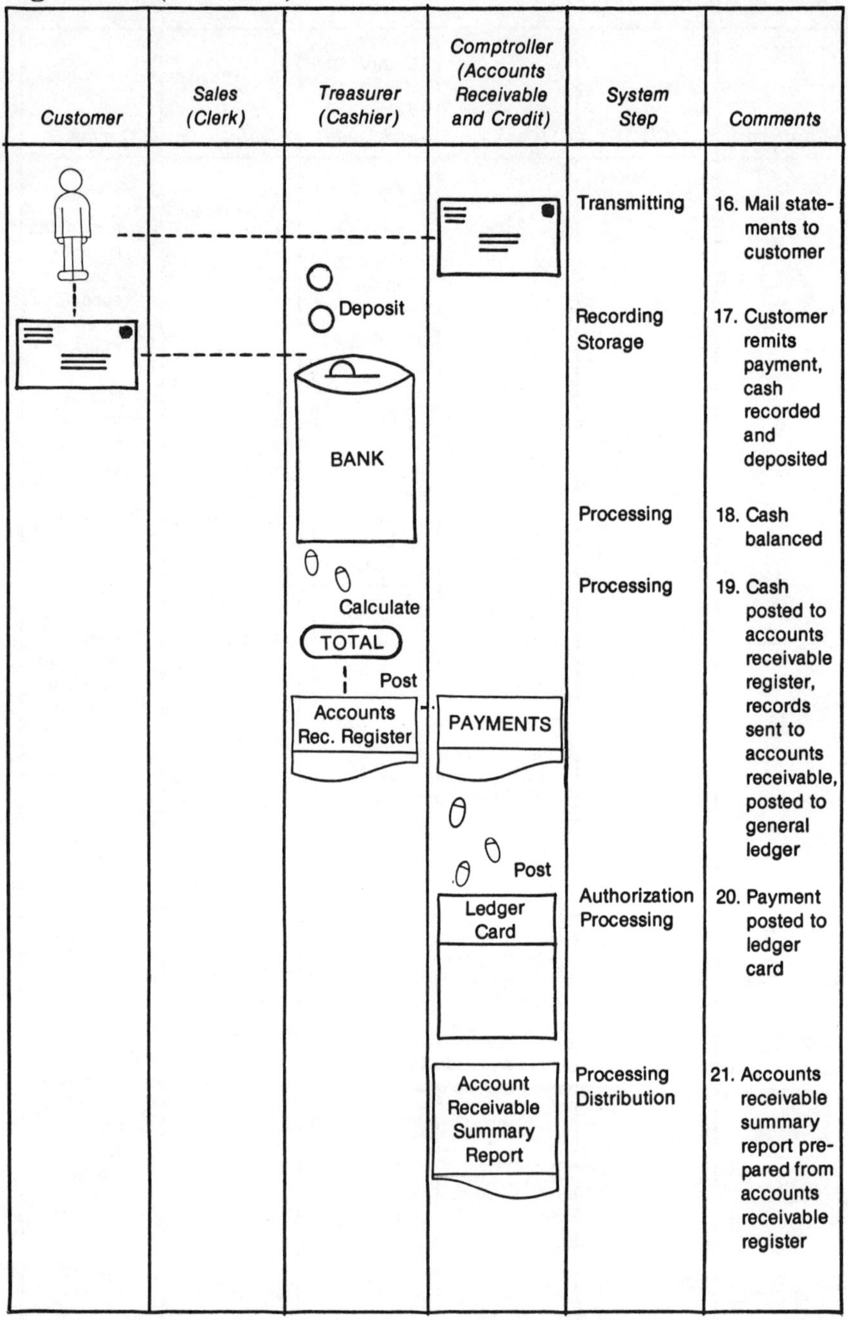

Figure 2-4. *(continued)*

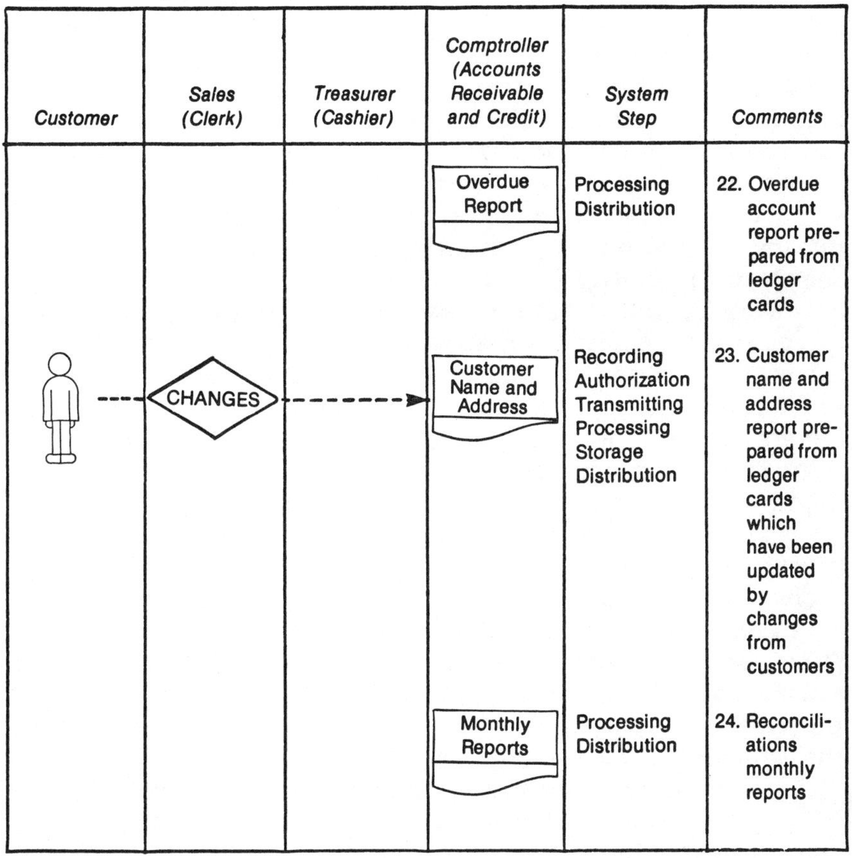

detailed ledger cards are accumulated and balanced to the general ledger accounts receivable account. After this process, monthly statements are prepared from the customer's ledger card. The monthly statement is a list of each invoice, credit memo, and cash payment. Included with the monthly statement are a copy of the invoice and the credit memo. The monthly statement, together with the enclosures, is then mailed to the customer.

If all goes as planned, the customer will remit the amount due together with the upper half of the statement, which enables the store to identify the customer by number. The mail room sends the funds to the cashier and the top half of the statement to the accounts receivable department. The cashier deposits the incoming funds in the bank. The cashier calculates the total amount of incoming cash and records the cash receipts in the general ledger. The top half of the monthly statements are transmitted to the accounts receivable section so that the customer's payment can be posted to the ledger card.

At the end of each month, the accounts receivable department prepares a series of accounting reports. Typically, these include the accounts receivable summary report, overdue account balance report, and customers' name and address report. Other monthly reports are prepared as required. These reports are used by the comptroller and others in the store (e.g., marketing, purchasing, and customer relations personnel) who need the information for operating purposes.

A customers' name and address file is maintained, though usually with great difficulty. Customers are continually being added or deleted, and information is constantly changing. These changes may include name (e.g., in case of marriage), address, credit limits, number of cards issued, and so on. This record is particularly difficult to maintain in a manual system. The updating of this file may be several weeks behind the date an account is opened, closed, or modified.

Automated processing

Let us revisit 2M two years later. The company has added substantially to the amount of data processing equipment it uses. Point-of-sale cash registers are available to the sales clerks. These cash registers are connected to the computer and transmit information immediately between the computer and the cash register so that the sales clerk can access information stored in

Figure 2-5. Automated Processing of Accounts Receivable

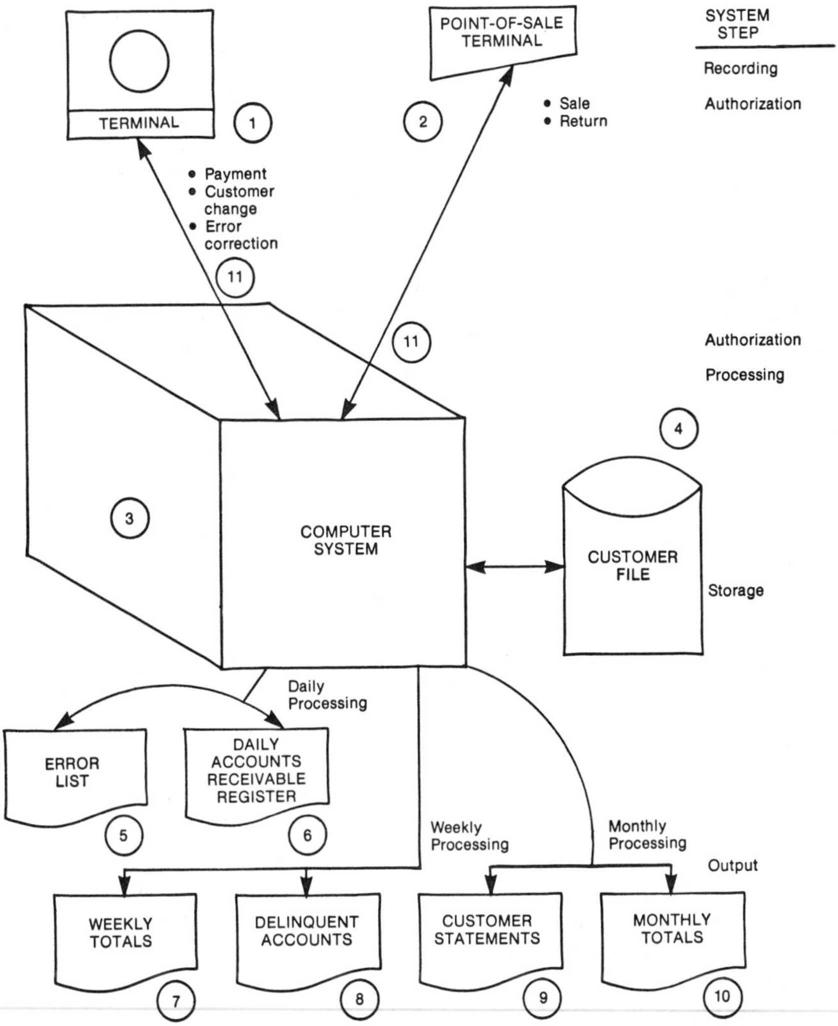

the computer. Figure 2-5 illustrates how automated processing of accounts receivable works.

The accounting personnel now have access to terminals that help them to process accounting information. The tub card files and adding machines that you saw during the days of manual processing have been replaced by on-line terminals and the computer. The records that were stored in the tub files are now stored on a device that can be accessed by the computer. (We will discuss these information storage devices in later chapters.)

As we walk into the customer shopping area of the store, we observe a customer making a purchase. The sales clerk inserts a blank invoice into the point-of-sale cash register terminal and then, by pushing the appropriate keys, enters the customer number and the product number of the item into the terminal. If the computer system is unable to authorize the sale, a special light flashes on the point-of-sale cash register terminal, signaling the clerk to call the credit department for additional information. On completion of the invoice at the point-of-sale terminal, the computer program updates all the customer's records to reflect that sale. The point-of-sale terminal then automatically prints the invoice. The computer has taken the price from its storage device, has extended price times quantity purchased, calculated tax, and totaled the invoice—a relatively simple procedure for the sales clerk. The procedure to return merchandise is similar to that for a sale.

The processing that is done in the manual system at the end of each day is accomplished in the computer system as soon as the transaction is recorded. Whenever reports from the automated accounts receivable system are needed, they can be produced within a matter of minutes. The computer operator commands the computer to produce the desired report. The reports contain basically the same information as those in the manual system. The primary difference is that, with the computer, the reports can be prepared with much greater ease and speed. However, because of the computer's ability to manipulate data, additional reports can be prepared that would be uneconomical in a manual system. For example, data can be resequenced to show in what part of the city their active customers are located. Having access to these reports enables management to control their operations better.

Customer records are maintained on a file accessible by computer programs. The cashier separates the cash from the statement stubs. The payment memo goes to a clerk in the accounts receivable department. Using an on-line terminal, the clerk calls for the customer information. The information that was on the ledger card in the manual system is displayed on the terminal screen. The clerk enters the payment into the customer account. If there are any discrepancies or problems, the clerk can handle them while "conversing" with the computer. Changes of customers' address, for example, as well as new accounts or accounts being closed, can be handled by the same clerk.

With the 2M example in mind, let's examine each of the six steps in a system and analyze some of the differences between the manual and computerized accounts receivable systems:

Recording

In the manual system, recording is done on paper by people. In the automated system, people use the computer to record the transaction. In our example, the latter is done by a sales clerk on a point-of-sale terminal. The other accounting transactions, such as posting cash to the accounts receivable customer account, are performed on an on-line terminal. The terminal operator can "converse" with the computer to process a transaction. Such conversing permits the operator to make decisions during processing, such as accepting a payment that is less than the amount due. A point worthy of note is that, in an automated system, errors can be corrected as the transaction is being recorded. In a manual system, errors in a transaction are not subjected to the same rigorous review as in computer systems; thus, they may not be found until later, if at all.

Authorization

In this step, the computer assumes some of the responsibility that previously was reserved for people. In the manual system authorization was entirely manual; people decided whether or not to authorize a transaction. In the automated system, the same thought processes that people use to determine whether to authorize a transaction are coded into computer programs and handled automatically.

Transmitting

The difference between the manual and automated system is dramatic in this step. Whereas in manual systems all transmitting is performed by people, in the computerized system the step is automatic. In automated systems, transmitting is done through telecommunications lines. Although this reduces transmitting time substantially, the big change is the ability to get answers back from the computer in time to use the answer in the performance of a task.

Processing

As we discussed previously, the large number of procedures in the manual system is an indication of why manual processing is so time consuming. Processing occurs at many different points in a manual system. In automated systems, people use computer programs to do the processing. For example, whereas the sales clerk using the manual system has to determine the price and extend price times quantity to obtain sales amount, the computerized system handles this automatically. The clerk enters the product number and units sold into the point-of-sale equipment, and all further processing is performed by the computer.

Storage

In the manual system, people store paper documents in file cabinets or other storage facilities. In an automated system, the data is maintained on computer-readable media (i.e., punched cards, tapes, disks, and so on). Many of the input source documents need not be filed unless there is a legal reason to do so. For example, there is no reason to save invoices or credit memos for billing purposes, since those data are stored already in the computer. This is why most computerized accounts receivable systems do not return invoices with monthly statements. Most organizations save input only until they are assured that processing has occurred, ranging from one day to several weeks. At 2M, input documents are retained until a reasonable time has passed for customers to pay charge account balances. The input documents are stored by day of purchase and not by customer.

Output

There is little difference between the manual system and the automated system in dealing with a customer in the store. In manual systems, reports are produced manually by the comptroller's department, whereas in automated systems, reports are processed by computer programs. In order to get reports in automated systems, a computer operator need only direct the computer as to what report is needed; the computer then produces the report in a matter of minutes. In a manual system, preparation of reports is time consuming and often frustrating to the people involved.

Effects of automated systems

By reviewing the accounts receivable system, we have seen some of the changes that occur when a manual system is automated. The methods of processing change, as does the equipment on which the processing occurs. The people involved in the execution of the system perform different functions than they did when the system was manual. These changes can bring both desirable and undesirable results to the area that has been automated.

Now we need to step back and ask, "How has this automated system affected the organization?" The answer to that question involves people, organizations, cost, and control. We must look at each of these factors individually to appreciate the impact an automated system has on an organization.

Effects of automated systems on people

Automated systems affect all aspects of work. The advent of such systems has been called the dominant advance of the twentieth century, and for good reason. People have strong feelings about computers, some very positive and others very negative. Let us examine how the mysterious black box has affected people.

- *New professions created.* New professions have been created to support the computer. These include program and systems personnel, operators, and input-entry clerks, as well as people involved in the manufacture, service, and support of automated systems.
- *Machines assume people's tasks.* Many decision-making processes previously reserved for people have been automated by computers. We saw in our accounts receivable system that, in most cases, the computer could decide whether credit could be extended on a sale.
- *Massive training is needed.* The computer affects most jobs. Literally millions of people must be trained in basic concepts of data processing. People who work more closely with computers require even more training. It is not unusual for individuals to have six months of training before they perform the first useful task for their organization.

- *Importance of people is underestimated.* Once computers are installed, there is a tendency to downplay the role of input personnel and users of systems. In reality, it is these people who either make or break the automated system.
- *People are dehumanized.* The computer has done for many organizations what the assembly line did for the factory. People perform small aspects of the total operation, but they do not see how their repetitive job fits into the overall system.
- *Computer is a scapegoat.* Failure to recognize the role of people in automated systems makes it easy to say, "The computer goofed," or "I can't make the correction because the computer won't accept it." These are fallacies, because it is people who design and operate automated systems.
- *Precise input is required.* The computer system demands perfection. Anything less results in errors.

Effects of automated systems on organizations

Organizations must be restructured to complement the characteristics of automated systems. Just as systems change people's jobs, they also change the structure of organizations in some of the following ways:

- *Create new EDP department.* There is a need to create a new department or division in an organization. This department then interacts with other departments in the processing of information. Both the creation of the new department and the close interaction with other departments necessitates restructuring of other departments.
- *Integrate functions.* More than one function (e.g., accounts receivable, inventory) can be combined in one automated system.
- *Require reorganization.* New methods of doing work require reorganization of the groups that do that work.
- *Require methodical operations.* Organizations must reflect the methodical way in which automated systems function.
- *Reduce planning cycle.* Because of the greater speed with which computers do processing, more current information can be obtained more quickly. This feature enables management to make decisions on a shorter planning cycle.

Effects of automated systems on cost

When procedures are performed in new ways, the cost of their performance changes. We often hear how expensive automated equipment is. However, we should reflect a bit on how use of automated equipment affects the cost of doing a job.

- *Systems must be built before they can be used.* There is an initial cost to build a system before any return can be expected.
- *Initial increase in cost may occur when a new system begins operation.* There can be an initial surge in cost in a new system. For example, an inventory control system designed to minimize inventories actually increases inventory costs initially.
- *Performs repetitive jobs more cheaply than people.* What the computer does best is perform the same task repeatedly with accuracy. It is in this volume of repetitive tasks that the computer saves money.
- *Increase or decrease in volume has minimal effect on cost.* In manual systems, an increase in volume requires an increase in personnel, whereas in computer systems, volume has only a minimal effect on processing costs. After the first transaction, the incremental cost for the second is extremely low.

Effects of automated systems on control

As organizations must be restructured to complement the characteristics of automated systems, so must control. As systems change, so must control mechanisms. Factors that affect control are:

- *Less hard copy.* What was depended upon for control in a manual system may not even exist in a computerized environment. For example, information entered through terminals is not recorded on traditional hard copy.
- *More, but different, transaction documentation.* While traditional hard copy does not exist, documentation of transactions is considerably more extensive. It has been stated many times that the computer can produce more data than people can read.
- *Control is programmed into machines.* The controls that were exercised by people in manual systems have been automated in computerized applications. The rules that govern the controls have been documented and built into computer programs. The programs then execute the controls automatically.
- *Concentration of control.* A key element of control in manual systems is division of responsibility. Automated sys-

tems centralize the responsibility that is divided so carefully in manual systems.

- *Security is more important.* Because of the concentration of processing and control in the data processing operation, the security of that operation becomes more important than when the operation was spread out over several floors or buildings and under the control of many individuals.
- *Privacy is more important.* Because all the data related to individuals are concentrated in the computer area, they are more vulnerable. Also, the data can be manipulated or transferred more easily than in a manual environment.

Characteristics of a computer system

Many machines have warning lights to indicate when the equipment is malfunctioning. If your automobile begins to overheat, a red warning light appears on the dashboard to indicate a potential malfunction. The driver then can take the necessary action to preserve the machine from self-destruction. Unfortunately, computer systems frequently do not possess these needed warning lights.

Understanding the characteristics of computer systems enables you to anticipate problem areas. For example, knowing that an automobile has to dissipate heat alerts you to the fact that an automobile engine could overheat. With this knowledge, you are prepared to monitor the automobile in order to determine whether the engine is experiencing a problem. Although the characteristics of a computer are more subtle, they still exist.

The example of 2M showed you how systems change when they are computerized. Now we are going to organize and categorize those differences so that you can measure the pulse of potential problems.

Although most of us can deal with the characteristics of manual systems, we find the characteristics of computers more confusing. These characteristics are the differences that can cause problems. Table 2-1 lists these characteristics, which are described below individually, together with the concerns that people should have about them.

Single input

In most computer systems, data are entered only once. We saw in the manual example at 2M that data were recorded, rerecorded,

Table 2-1. Computer System Characteristics and Their Associated Concerns

Computer Characteristic	*Concern*
Single input	Input will be wrong
Structured input	Input in wrong input area
Machine-readable data	Loss of people-readable documents
Consistent processing	Processing rules will be wrong
Complex processing	Not understandable to people
All-inclusive processing	Something missing
Structured processing	Cannot be changed
Authoritative output	People will not question reasonableness
Limited output	Needed information will not be printed
Coded data	Wrong codes will be used
Reusable storage	Needed data will be destroyed
Rapid processing	Loss of reaction time
Reliance on system	Loss of control/integrity

and rerecorded again. At each recording stage, there was both an opportunity to make an error and to correct an error. For example, each time a price was obtained for a product, the price could be verified. However, in a computer system the item is entered only once, and if it is wrong it will be wrong every time it is used.

This characteristic raises concern over the accuracy of data entered into a computer system, and people who design or use computer systems should take this into account. You should verify the type of procedures that ensures the data entered are correct.

Computer Survival Rule #8

Verify that appropriate steps are taken to ensure the accuracy and completeness of input data.

Structured input

Computers cannot see data. Therefore, they interpret the meaning of the data by where the data are located. If data are not in the normal location, the computer probably will misinterpret the meaning. Even free-form input, which is a characteristic of some computer systems, still is structured so that it is recognizable.

People need to be concerned that input data will be placed in the wrong input area. For example, if you were ordering a product and put the price in the quantity area, the quantity you would receive would be the numeric value of the price. For example, if the price is $.99, the computer would send you 99 of those items.

Computer Survival Rule #9

Verify that procedures are adequate to ensure that input data will be placed in the proper location.

Machine-readable data

Most computer input devices are structured to read data that are in machine-readable format. For example, with punched cards the data are coded in holes punched into the card. Optically read documents require special lines, bars, or type fonts and frequently require a special step to convert data from people-readable data to machine-readable data.

The concern that this raises is loss of people-readable documents. Associated with that may be a loss of control. For example, a customer credit memo must be approved with a supervisor's signature; however, the signature cannot be transcribed intact into machine-readable format. It is difficult to pick up a punched card and know that the holes in those cards have been properly authorized.

Computer Survival Rule #10

The same attention to control of people-readable documents should be extended to machine-readable data.

Consistent processing

A dominant characteristic of the computer is consistency. Whatever the computer does, it does it the same way every time it performs the task. Manual systems, on the other hand, are noted for inconsistency. Industrial psychologists tell us that the times for greatest inconsistency among people are Monday mornings and Friday afternoons. Consistency means being either consistently correct or consistently incorrect.

The prime concern of people is that a computer system will consistently produce erroneous results. Occasionally we read about hundreds of errors that occur within seconds. This is an ever-present concern and should be dealt with according to the magnitude of the risk involved.

Computer Suvival Rule #11

Evaluate the risk of inconsistent processing in a computer application, and develop controls that are commensurate with the risk.

Complex processing

Computer systems can perform processing logic that can boggle the mind. The computer is able to execute millions of instructions in a very short time and thus can coordinate complex relationships. For example, product pricing structures can offer complex discount structures on the basis of combinations of products ordered that would be difficult for people to price manually.

The concern over this complex processing is that it is not understandable to people. In other words, computer systems can be so large and complex that only a handful of people in a very large corporation understand how the system functions. This raises concerns about explaining to employees why the system performs certain processing steps, as well as how to change one area of the system without affecting other areas adversely:

Computer Survival Rule #12

Don't permit processing to become more complex than people can understand.

All-inclusive processing

The computer cannot reason or think. Therefore, everything the computer system does must be determined before the condition occurs. The computer system must be prepared to handle every possible condition, both expected and unexpected. For example, if the computer were an automobile going down a road leading to where a bridge was out, the computer would wait for the bridge to be rebuilt if it had not been instructed otherwise. That is, if the instructions say go across the bridge, the computer will wait forever until the bridge is ready to be crossed.

The concern people have is the occurrence of unanticipated conditions. When this happens, there is no easy way of telling what the computer will do. However, it will do something and that something may be erratic and damaging to the organization. For example, if entering of alphabetic data in the field of payroll hours worked is not expected, the calculation of very unusual payment amounts may result.

Computer Survival Rule #13

Spend the time necessary to anticipate all the unusual conditions that might occur in an application system. Then include the system instructions on what to do if those conditions occur.

Structured processing

Everything in a computer system is predetermined. Nothing happens unless it is preplanned. Knowledge of the structure of an application system can allow us to determine what would happen in any possible condition, even if what happens is erratic.

The concern about structured processing is the ease with which modifications can be made in the structure. In many ways the computer system is like a house. Some changes, such as painting a room, are relatively inexpensive and easy. On the other hand, the cost of changes such as extending a room by two feet may be prohibitive. The analogy holds true for computer systems.

Computer Survival Rule #14

Build a computer system a little larger than necessary in order to accommodate future needs. Installation of extra capabilities during construction usually is nominal in cost.

Authoritative output

Output from a computer system intimidates many people. It has an authoritative image in that it is computer produced, and its printed format makes it look official. It is difficult for a person to question the integrity of the computer. It is tough to fight the system.

The concern this raises is that people will accept the results of computer processing even if the results appear unreasonable. It is easier to accept the results of computer processing as accurate and complete than to question the computer. This tendency can lead to erroneous decisions and false processing.

Computer Survival Rule #15

The integrity of output from computer systems should always be questioned.

Limited output

For years data-processing personnel have encouraged exception processing reporting. In other words, rather than print extremely large reports, people should print only the items that require attention. This approach accomplishes two goals: first, it substantially reduces the amount of paper to be handled; and, second, it identifies the items that require attention.

The problem with exception reporting is that information may be needed that is not included on the reports. This can result from a misinterpretation of the type of data needed, or data may be excluded because someone deemed them unimportant. This situation can lead to overlooking of problem areas and to poor management decisions.

Computer Survival Rule #16

Know what information is contained in the computer system but is not routinely printed.

Coded data

Computers process numbers, not words. Computer systems attempt to change everything from names to numbers. People's names are unimportant and product names are unimportant;

only numbers are important. Unless you know the secret number, processing data through a computer system is difficult.

The concern people have is twofold. The first is fear of dehumanization. Fortunately, people are getting used to the characteristic of computers that changes names to numbers. Second is the problem of inserting wrong numbers. For example, the product number for a needle and a sewing machine might be one digit apart. By entering the wrong number, the customer might get a gross of sewing machines rather than a gross of needles.

Computer Survival Rule #17

Verify that procedures are adequate to ensure that codes can be verified properly.

Reusable storage

Magnetic storage media can be used again and again. The most common reusable storage media are tapes and disks. Information is stored until its useful life is ended; then the media can be reallocated for new information.

The reusability of computer media raises two concerns: first, that the data will not be retained as long as they are needed; and, second, in the event of computer problems, data on reusable storage media may be destroyed. For example, a power failure or computer failure may render the information on computer media unreadable. Most data-processing departments establish procedures to safeguard against these two possible problems.

Computer Survival Rule #18

Determine whether the data-processing department has adequate procedures to protect information on reusable magnetic storage media.

Rapid processing

Computers are noted for their speed of processing. Computer speeds are referred to in microseconds and nanoseconds (one-millionth and one-billionth of a second, respectively). Millions of instructions can be executed in a matter of minutes. The concern this capacity raises is the limited reaction time of people. With manual processing, people have some time to think about any unusual transaction characteristics of a given task. When decisions are made in nanoseconds, however, people are disregarded and processing occurs instantaneously. For example, when credit is approved electronically in a department store, the sale is made and the customer leaves the store with the merchandise. In electronic funds transfer systems, large amounts of money are moved almost instantaneously. These decisions are made by a machine based on predetermined rules, not by people weighing the characteristics of the situation.

Computer Survival Rule #19

Recognize the risks of making instantaneous decisions.

Reliance on system

Systems that make instantaneous decisions, systems that remove people from the decision-making process, are systems run by machines. Organizations must rely solely on the integrity of processing by those machines. Thus, procedures must be established to ensure that processing is truly reliable.

The obvious concern is that people rely on machines that may be unreliable. A $1 million study conducted by Stanford Research Institute for the International Business Machines (IBM) Corporation concluded that, in one computer environment, too little attention had been paid to controls.

The concern that people should have about computer systems is that controls are inadequate and that erroneous processing thus will not be detected so that corrective action can be taken. The cost of controls should be recouped by the occurrence of fewer systems problems.

Computer Survival Rule #20

Pennies spent on controls usually reap dollar savings through fewer systems problems.

Survival guide self-assessment document

A computer survival kit is like a canteen of water to the desert traveler. The size of the canteen should be related to the size of the desert. If it takes three days to cross the desert, the traveler should have at least a three-day supply of water.

The following self-assessment checklist provides a guide to the magnitude of the survival kit you need for computer systems. The questionnaire only provides an indication of the severity of your computer survival problem. The questions are designed to be answered "yes" or "no." "Yes" indicates a survival problem. On completion of the questionnaire, total the "yes" answers. The number of "yes" answers can be interpreted as follows:

No. of "Yes" Answers	*Interpretation*
7–10	You have a serious survival problem. Read this book immediately. Don't sleep or take any other action until you have finished the book.
4–6	You could be in trouble, but it doesn't look serious. You needn't finish the book today, but finish it.
0–3	Your computer problems appear to be minimal; read the book at your leisure and enjoy it. Take pleasure in knowing that you're not one of the people who has serious problems.

Checklist 2-1. Survival Guide Self-Assessment Checklist

	Response			
Question	*Yes*	*No*	*N/A*	*Other*
1. Does your organization process more transactions by computer than manually?	____	____	____	________
2. Are your organization's data-processing systems developed by a data-processing department?	____	____	____	________

Checklist 2-1. Survival Guide Self-Assessment Checklist (continued)

Question	*Response* Yes	No	N/A	Other
3. Are your data-processing managers usually excluded from serious consideration in the top management selection process in your organization?	____	____	____	________
4. Does each function in your organization control the data used for that function; for example, does the payroll department control payroll data?	____	____	____	________
5. Does your organization use data-base and telecommunication technology?	____	____	____	________
6. Do you personally use results of computer processing in your daily work?	____	____	____	________
7. Do you personally rely on computer-produced information for decisions you make in the course of your daily work?	____	____	____	________
8. Do you have concerns about the accuracy, completeness, and authorization of computer-produced data?	____	____	____	________
9. Do you have problems communicating your needs and questions to data-processing personnel?	____	____	____	________
10. Are the methods by which computers process data confusing to you?	____	____	____	________

Conclusion

The computer has done for information processing what automated equipment did for the factory. The information revolution has occurred in our lifetime. The first systems to be automated were those that involved many repetitive tasks. These were not complex systems, but they took advantage of the power of the computer either to reduce or to stabilize processing costs. With improved technology, we truly are beginning to use the power of the computer in resystematizing the way business operates. More and more of the decision-making process is being built into computers. Computers are being connected in networks that can pass information from one organization to another.

The conversion of processing from manual to automated has enabled organizations to get more current information more quickly and in the desired format. However, this change is not without its effects on the organizations. The computer has affected people, organizational structure, cost of processing, and methods of control.

Electronic data processing has created a new profession. In addition, it has affected most people's jobs and lives. As people change their manner of working, so organizational structure also changes. Not only have data-processing departments been created, but other parts of organization also have been restructured to complement the characteristics of computerized applications. The installation of a computer tends to stabilize the cost of its application. Once the system is installed, increased volumes can be processed with nominal increases in cost. However, controls that were effective in manual systems must be restructured for use in automated systems. With the advent of computer terminals, traditional hard copy is disappearing rapidly. Privacy and security are becoming more important with the concentration of processing within the computer. The need for increased control is receiving heavy support from the federal government.

The computer offers boundless opportunities for organizations to become more effective and efficient. However, it requires that all business personnel become familiar with the computer and realize its advantages and limitations. In addition, people must develop a better understanding of how the introduction of computerized applications affects their organization and its employees. People need to survive computer systems.

3/ Why everything must fit into boxes

Introduction

You walk into a department store to apply for a credit card. The clerk smiles and hands you a form to fill out. Your eyes glance at the form and observe that it is a maze of boxes. You feel like you are in kindergarten and the teacher is instructing you how to print.

You apply for a job, join a mail-order book club, or order merchandise from a catalog, and it's all the same. Boxes, boxes, and more boxes. What's the matter with this thing called a computer that makes me print everything I want to say to it in little boxes? Maybe it's true what they say: a computer has only the mentality of a two-year-old!

Putting information in boxes for the computer to read may raise the following questions in your mind: What if I have more letters or numbers than there are boxes? What happens if I don't put my information into the boxes? What happens if I use the wrong boxes? If some of the information doesn't go into the boxes, does it mean that nobody cares about it?

Data processing is two words

The concept of data processing seems like a single entity to many people. We talk of electronic data processing, automatic data processing, advanced data processing, manual data processing, and so on. We may qualify the term *data processing,* but we rarely segregate the term into its component parts.

Surprisingly enough, data processing is comprised of two separate words: *data* and *processing.* The *data* part refers to the information entered into, manipulated, and output from the computer system; the *processing* part refers to the rules that are applied to the entered data.

Let's look at a simplified example that differentiates the data concept from the processing concept. Joe is an employee of the

Orlando Corporation. This week Joe works forty-five hours at a rate of $10 per hour. We now know three pieces of data about Joe. First, we know that his name is Joe. We also know the number of hours he has worked and the hourly rate. All of these data must be entered into the computer system. The data are needed before processing can commence.

The Orlando Corporation must determine the processing rules for payroll. Some of this may be legislated by the government, but most of the rules are determined by the corporation. In later chapters, we will explain how these rules are defined, entered into the computer, and executed by the computer.

In this simplified example, let's consider just the rule that deals with calculation of gross pay. The rule states that gross pay is equal to the number of hours worked times the hourly rate plus the number of hours over forty worked times one-half the hourly rate. In executing this rule, the computer needs to know both the number of hours Joe worked plus his hourly rate. These factors are considered to be data. First they are multiplied to give a regular pay amount of $450 (45 × $10). Then overtime is calculated at $25 [(45 − 40) × $5]. The two amounts are added to produce a gross pay of $475. When this amount has been computed, the processing part of data processing is complete. Note, however, that the processing has yielded new data: Joe's gross pay. These data can then be manipulated by additional processing rules.

In order to understand the functioning of computer systems, we need to differentiate between data and processing. Each has its own attributes and idiosyncracies. If we are going to survive in the computer era, we need this basic computer understanding. In the data-processing aspect of organizations, we are even beginning to find that people specialize in either data or processing.

What is data?

Everybody knows what data are. Data are represented by the numbers, letters, or special characters used to transmit information. So what's the big deal?

The big deal is that data in the context that people read and understand it are not the same type of data that are fed to and used by computers. In other words, the means of communication used by people is far too complex for today's computer to comprehend. For example, we put decimal points in our numbers to differentiate between whole and partial numbers. Isn't this something you would think the computer would do? The answer is yes, but the computer doesn't do it. There are no decimal points in computer systems until data are printed for people to read. How, then, does the computer know whether we are talking about, say, dollars and cents? Read on, and this aspect of the computer will be demystified.

In a computer system, we need to reorient our thinking about data. We need to understand why and how data are constructed and what the attributes of data are in order to use data successfully. It's not overly complex, but is different from our usual orientation toward data. Computer systems are designed to achieve specific results, which may include compensating employees for their work, billing customers for products they ordered, or keeping track of an organization's inventory. This is what computer systems are all about. Both data and processing are important elements in the accomplishment of these objectives.

The people who work to satisfy the needs of organizations through computer systems define the data needed to accomplish objectives. Thus, for practical purposes, computer data can be defined in the way that best achieves the desired systems results. The definition of data in computer systems usually is very specific in order to eliminate ambiguities in meaning, a typical characteristic of most information.

Computer people define data to meet specific needs. For this reason, two people who define data to meet the same need may define that data differently. If a third person is added to the team, that person may define the data differently than the first two. Let's look at an example.

Assume we are working with a payroll system. We have been given the responsibility of designing the system, and we must decide on some method for identifying our employees, such as Joe in our previous example. If I were to design the system, I might say, "Let's give every employee a five-digit number that will be used to identify an employee uniquely." For example, I might give Joe the employee number 12345. If you were to design the system, you might say, "Each employee already has a unique number, so let's use the nine-digit social security number to identify each employee." Joe's social security number might be 123-45-6789, in which case the number 123456789 would be assigned as Joe's employee number. A third systems designer may be a word person instead of a number person and thus may decide to use the employee's name for identification. Thus, JOE is the employee identifier for Joe.

We now have seen that the same system need—data that uniquely identify an employee—can be defined in three different ways. We can identify our employee Joe equally well with any of the following three identifiers: 12345, 123456789, or JOE.

One method is not necessarily better than the other methods, and each has advantages and disadvantages. We need to understand the importance and the attributes of data before we can make the proper decisions about defining data and about using and understanding data in computer systems.

The importance of data

Try to visualize a network of railroad tracks over a large geographic area. The tracks provide options for going to all of the major cities in that geographic area. Let's assume there are five cities, called A, B, C, D, and E. The cities are illustrated in Figure 3-1. The illustration shows direct paths from each city to the other cities. Thus, when a train leaves one city it goes on a direct path to another city, and, unless the train breaks down, it will arrive at its designated location if it leaves on the correct track.

In Figure 3-2, we see the same five cities but with a different network of tracks. In this example, you must go through city E in order to go between any two cities. Thus, if you want to go from city A to city B, you must take the path from A to E to B.

Most computer systems are constructed like the railroad track configuration in Figure 3-2. It is obvious that this arrangement minimizes the amount of track and provides the most flexibility for adding rail service to another city, such as city F. In this example, it is important for the train to know where it is going. For example, when the train leaves city A and is heading for city B, someone must know where the train is headed when it reaches city E, because many options are available for that train at that location. Should the train be misrouted to city D, there would be many unhappy passengers aboard.

Computer systems work approximately in the same manner as this railroad switching network. The data entering the system have attributes that predetermine the paths that the data will take through the computer system, just as the train leaving city A had attributes that would route it through city E to city B. In our payroll example, Joe worked forty-five hours. These data

Figure 3-1. Direct Routing Between Cities

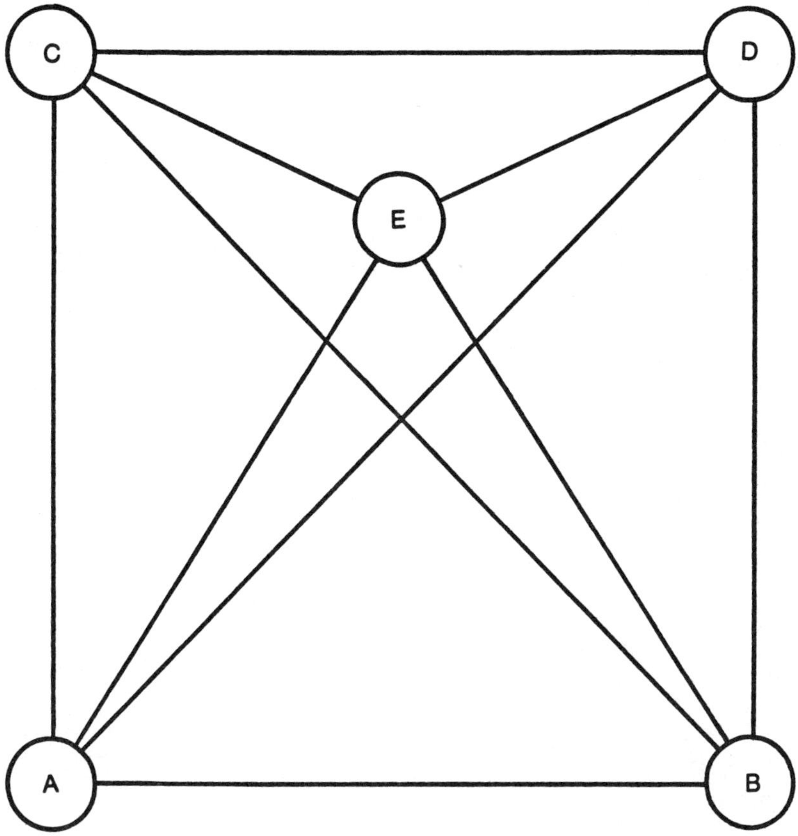

attributes cause the data to be routed through the path in the system that is designed to calculate overtime pay.

Computer systems are data-directed systems. The attributes of the data direct the data through the appropriate processing path in the computer system so that the proper processing occurs and the system objectives are met. As the data attributes change, the computer system directs the data through different processing paths in order to produce different results. As in our train example, if a train left city A destined for city B, it would take a different path than a train leaving city A for city D.

The accuracy, completeness, and proper authorization of input data are essential if the desired processing results are to

Figure 3-2. Switched Routing Between Cities

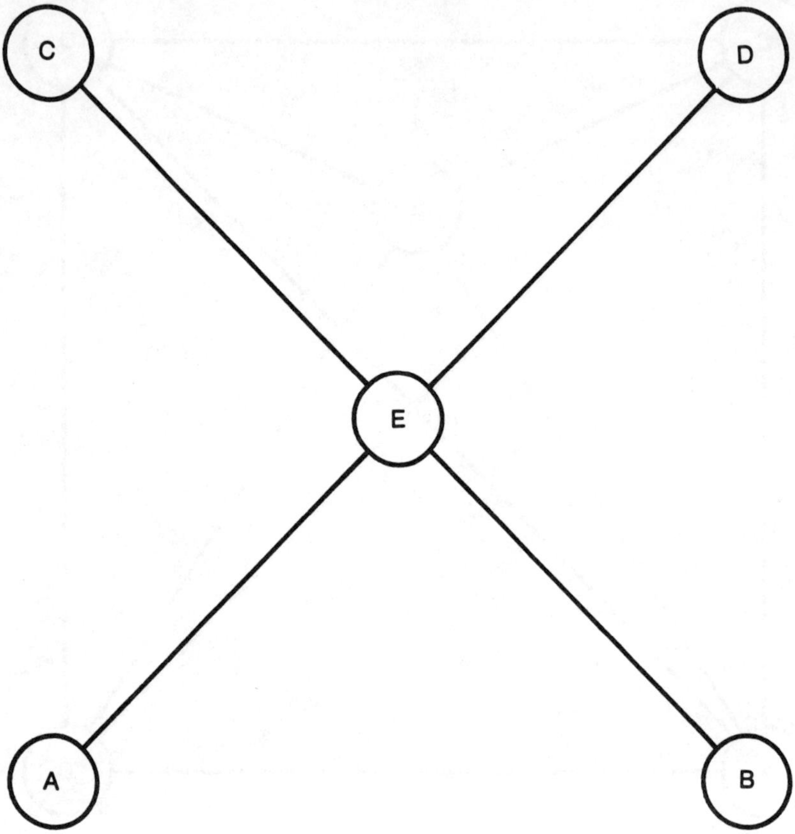

be achieved. If the train were marked for city B but should have been marked for city D, it will go to city B if it is routed by a computer system. Likewise, if Joe's pay had been recorded as fifty-four hours instead of forty-five hours, Joe would have been paid for fifty-four hours.

Most of the problems in computer systems are due to improperly entered data. Thus, perhaps the single most important thing a person using a computer system can do is to help ensure the accuracy, completeness, and proper authorization of data going into the computer system. Frequently this requires only a little extra effort. For example, if you are flying to a distant city and want to be assured that your baggage will arrive with you,

you can expend a little extra effort by checking that the baggage clerk marks your bag for the proper city.

> **Computer Survival Rule #21**
>
> *A crucial check in computer systems is verification of the accuracy, completeness, and proper authorization of data that are to be entered into the computer system.*

How a computer reads data

Why should you care how a computer reads data? The answer is that the computer is very explicit in how it reads data, and, if you don't follow the rules, it may misread your data. The more you know about the computer, the higher the probability of getting the desired results from the computer system.

Visualize a blind person attempting to remove from a set of encyclopedias the volume containing information about items beginning with the letter M. All of the volumes are of equal size and thickness, and there are no physical distinctions in the markings on the volumes that can be detected other than visually. If the volumes of the encyclopedia are unstructured, the task is impossible. In other words, if the volumes are in random order, the blind person cannot pick out the right volume. On the other hand, if the volumes are in a predetermined order, such as alphabetical, the task is quite simple for the blind person. He or she merely locates the first volume and counts to the thirteenth volume, which is the thirteenth letter (M). The task may take a little longer for a blind person than for a sighted person, but it can be accomplished with equal accuracy. In fact, if the blind person is fast in arm movement, he or she might find the volume more quickly than the sighted person.

The computer reads data in the same manner that the blind person removes a book from a shelf. The computer must know exactly where the data are located in order to find them. In addition, after the computer finds the data, its only assurance that it has found the correct data is that the data came from the right location. In other words, if the R volume of the encyclopedia had been placed erroneously where the M volume should have been, the blind person would pull the R volume and state emphatically that it was the M volume.

The computer operates the same way. When it reads a piece of information, it is convinced that it has the right information whether or not the information actually is correct. This situation leads to both erroneous and illogical processing by the computer system.

Computer Survival Rule #22

Don't err in the placement of data in a computer system.

Let's examine how the misplacement of data in a computer system can cause erroneous results. Suppose there is a field of data called order quantity. This field represents the quantity of a certain product you might need. For example, if the product is books and you want a quantity of five, you enter the number five in the quantity field. This indicates to the computer the quantity you want. Let's assume further that, in the system we are working with, the quantity field has been designated as a three-digit field. In other words, the system will accept a quantity of one through 999. Thus, the field requires the use of three boxes.

Figure 3-3 shows three ways in which the number five can be entered in the three boxes and the three possible interpretations the computer can make according to the box in which the five is placed. We see that, if the five is entered correctly (i.e., in accordance with the rules of the system), the computer will recognize that five books are wanted. This is because it assumes the number five is in what we identify as box number three. To the computer, a number in box three indicates a single digit. However, when the five is placed in box two, it carries the significance of a tens digit, and the computer interprets the number as fifty. Similarly, if the five is placed in box one, the computer recognizes it as the hundreds digit and places an order for 500 books. Remember that the computer is reaching on the shelf for a book and can identify it only by the book's location.

So that's what boxes are all about

Any data that the computer works with can be assumed to be contained in a box. For purposes of recognition, data must be considered as an alphabetic letter, a numeric digit, or a special character. Although in actual practice the computer is a little

Figure 3-3. Significance of Data Placement

SITUATION

A three-digit order entry field

Case 1

#1	#2	#3
		5

Means 5 to the computer

Case 2

#1	#2	#3
	5	

Means 50 to the computer

Case 3

#1	#2	#3
5		

Means 500 to the computer

more complex, conceptually we need only visualize a series of boxes, each of which contains a letter, number, or special character.

Each box must be identified uniquely so that the computer and the individual instructing the computer can talk from a common base of understanding. In Figure 3-3 we had three boxes that we put together and called a three-digit order quantity field. We identified each box uniquely by calling it box number one, number two, and number three. We told the computer that the units position would be put in box three, the tens position in box two, and the hundreds position in box one. The computer believed us. However, in case two the number five was placed erroneously in box two and the computer interpreted this as fifty. The reason for the computer's error is that previously we had instructed the computer to look for the tens digit in box two. Since nothing was placed in box three, the computer assumed that meant zero and concluded that you wanted fifty books. In case three, misplacement of the five in box one created an even greater error, resulting in an order for 500 books.

Perhaps now you can understand why the computer can issue a payroll check for $1 million. It's not the computer's error, but the error of the person who entered the number in the wrong box.

No matter how many boxes the computer works with, each box must be identified uniquely. Even when the computer has the capability of storing millions of pieces of information, each piece is placed in a uniquely identified box. Fortunately, the computer can remember exactly what is in each box and process it according to predetermined criteria.

Explaining data to computers and people

If you design or work with computer systems, data are your friends. We said that data drive the system and produce the desired results. Therefore, if we want to establish a friendship with data, we need to become familiar with and understand it. The more we know about data, the more comfortable we'll feel about our friendship. On the other hand, if we don't have a close friendship with data, we might be suspicious about this relationship.

Let's look at another example of an order quantity field to see how friendly or unfriendly data may be to us. In this example, we are the merchants of a store and we see that 475 of item X have been ordered. We look at our inventory of item X and find we have only 200. On the basis of this information, we may go out and order 500 more of item X. However, if we knew our data better, we might not make that decision. For example, some of the characteristics of those 475 items on order might include:

- 200 items have been shipped already, but the quantity on order has not been reduced because the shipping paperwork has not yet been processed. It takes 24 to 48 hours after actual shipment before the shipment is reflected in the on-hand inventory.
- 200 items have been ordered, but shipment is not wanted for six months.
- 75 items are wanted for immediate shipment.

If we were friendlier with our data, we would know that the quantity of 475 on order really requires only a reduction in inventory of seventy-five; thus, it may not be necessary to order more of the product at this time.

There are certain attributes of computer data that we should know about so that we can be friendly with our data. Frequently, users of computer data do not understand these attributes and create needless problems for themselves. The following list of data attributes illustrates what you should know about data. The list is not meant to be comprehensive; rather, it includes the most common attributes of computer data (see Table 3-1).

Name

The name of the data serves to identify the data uniquely. For example, in a payroll system the amount of dollars that an employee receives is frequently called by the name "Net Pay."

Alternative name

Often a single piece of data is known by different names. For example, people with the name William frequently are called Bill. Likewise, in a computer system the data called "Net Pay" may be known also as "Compensation." This frequently occurs when different units of an organization have called the same piece of data different names before the two parts of the organization are incorporated into the same computer system. At that point, both parts still want to call the data by the name that is familiar to them.

Description

It is important to explain what the item of data is. Description usually is a narrative explanation that tells people specifically about the data. For example, we could describe "Net Pay" as the amount of funds given to an employee at the end of a pay period. In actual practice, the description might be quite extensive.

Owner

Somebody should own data. Many problems occur because nobody believes they own a particular piece of data. For example, in the conversion of the zip code from five digits to nine, it is important to know who owns those data so that we know who

Table 3-1. Attributes of Computer Data

Attribute	*Description*	*Example*
Name	Identifier of data	Net pay
Alternative name	Nickname	Compensation
Description	Narrative explanation of data	The amount of funds given to an employee at the end of a pay period
Owner	Who is responsible for the data	Manager, payroll department
User	The people and/or computer system who can have the data	Payroll computer system
Type of use	Purpose for which the user of data is authorized	Read only
Custodian	Who is responsible for storing the data	Payroll computer system project leader
Origin	Where data originate	From the calculation of net pay
Length	The number of boxes needed to hold the data	Six
Decimal places	Number of decimal positions in the data	Two (i.e., 0000.00)
Type	Numeric, alphabetic, special characters, alphanumeric	Numeric
Sign	How to know whether the data are positive or negative	Negative field will include a negative sign
Validation characteristics	How to determine whether the data are accurate	All data must be positive numeric characters and in the range of 000001 through 199999
Save	How long data are to be saved	Three years
Output format	Picture of how people want to see the data printed	$0,000.00

is responsible for making the change. The "Net Pay" data may be owned by the manager of the payroll department, and that individual would be responsible for the accuracy and completeness of the calculated net pay.

User

Although there can be only one owner of an item of data, there may be many users. Each user should be identified so that it is known who has authorized access to the data. Users can be defined either as people, such as the manager of the payroll department, or as computer systems, such as the payroll computer system.

Type of use

People use data for different purposes. The more precisely that use is defined, the better the data can be controlled. For example, one criterion for determining net pay is the employee's hourly rate. The system that calculates net pay should read only the pay rate. Other computer systems may need to initiate, change, or delete the net pay amount, but the payroll system does not have to have those capabilities. The payroll system should be authorized only to read net pay, not to change it. This feature helps to control the accuracy of the data.

Custodian

The owner may not be the custodian of the data. For example, many of us keep important information in a safe deposit box in a bank. Thus, although you are the owner of those documents, you are not the custodian—the bank is. In our payroll example, the project leader of the payroll computer system may be the custodian of the "Net Pay" data.

Origin

It is important to know where data originate so that you can go back to the source of data, if necessary. For example, in a previous payroll illustration we said that our employee Joe might have reported fifty-four hours work, when forty-five is the correct number. If people rarely work more than ten hours overtime, the system should question the validity of fourteen hours reported as overtime. If it is known where the data originate, control personnel can go to the source and question the validity of the data. In our example, the hours of overtime should originate from the employee's department manager.

Length

The computer must know precisely how many boxes are designated to contain specific computer data. In order to define data length we need only define the number of boxes, which is the total amount of space allocated for describing the computer data. In our payroll example, we might specify that six boxes be allocated to contain the net pay amount. This would allow for a net pay amount of up to $9,999.99. Remember, the computer does not put decimals or commas in numeric data.

Decimal places

If fields are numeric, we need to know the number of decimal places in that field. We indicated earlier that the decimal point does not exist in numeric fields in the computer system. Therefore, in defining the data, we need to indicate where the decimal point should be. In the computer, it is possible for the decimal point to exist either within the data or outside the data. For example, you probably have read financial reports that say "000" is omitted. In such an instance, a one really means one thousand. It is possible to enter a one in a computer system and mean one thousand, in which case the definition of that data must define that there are three additional decimal places not indicated by the data. We can assume that our "Net Pay" data field is a normal dollar-and-cents field and thus that there are two decimal places included within the field to represent cents.

Type

The computer needs to be told as much about the data as possible. One of the characteristics that has meaning to the computer is whether a field is entirely numeric, entirely alphabetic, whether it contains some or all special characters, or whether it is alphanumeric. In our "Net Pay" example, the field would be numeric.

Sign

Numeric data can be either positive or negative. For example, in an accounts receivable balance, it is possible either for a customer to owe money to the store or for the store to owe money to the customer. Computers are designed to differentiate between positive and negative numbers. This distinction usually is determined by placement of a positive or negative indicator somewhere in the numeric field. The definition of the data must indicate how negative and positive fields are indicated.

Validation characteristics

The more we know about computer data, the more we can do to validate the accuracy and completeness of the data. Data definition systems should specify the validation characteristics for an item of data that describes in either narrative or quantitative format what is considered to be accurate and complete data. For example, the "Net Pay" amount, if valid, can be described as entirely numeric; that is, there should be no alphabetic or special characters in the field. In addition, the field must be positive, because the organization does not want to issue checks for a negative amount. The data might be defined as being in the range of 000001 through 199999; that is, the company does not want to issue a payroll check for more than $1,999.99. Definition of these validation characteristics enables data-processing personnel to ascertain whether the actual data entered or produced fall within those characteristics. If they do not, the owner of the data can be informed and manual checking can be performed.

Save

The custodian of computer data needs to know how long the data should be saved. Usually, one of the responsibilities of the custodian is to get rid of unwanted data. In our payroll example, it might be decided that the information should be saved for three years. This tells the custodian how long the "Net Pay" data should be saved. At the end of three years, the data will be destroyed, so that users wanting to access "Net Pay" data that originated three years earlier will not be able to retrieve it.

Output format

The data entered into and held by computer systems may not be in a format that is readily understandable. For example, we said that our net pay field would be a six-digit numeric field with a positive or negative sign contained somewhere in the data. If people saw this, they might not understand what it meant. Therefore, people need to specify how they want to see that data when it is printed out. In some computer languages, this is called a PICTURE of the data. The output PICTURE of our net pay field would probably be $0,000.00.

Computer Survival Rule #23

Don't work with computer data unless you are friendly with that data.

Who specifies data attributes?

If you want to play the computer game, you need to know who decides how the game is played. Maybe you don't like the way the game is structured and would like to make some changes. Maybe you have a right to change the way the game is played and maybe you don't; you may not know your rights until you know who the players are and who makes the rules.

Each organization decides who they will allow to play the data definition game. However, with the increasing importance of computer systems in the day-to-day operation of organizations, the definition of data takes on greater importance. Remember that data drive the system and that data can be defined any way people want to define them. If you have a specific data need, you should be involved in the data definition process.

Computer Survival Rule #24

The definition of data should be delimited by the people whose needs must be satisfied by those data.

Let's look at the players who can get involved in data definition by continuing with our example of the "Net Pay" data field. The players are described below and are illustrated in Figure 3-4.

Senior management

As data are shared by multiple users, the reliability, consistency, and timing of data increase in importance. For example, there may be disputes between the accounting and marketing departments regarding when a sale should be recorded. The

Figure 3-4. Who Specifies Computer Data

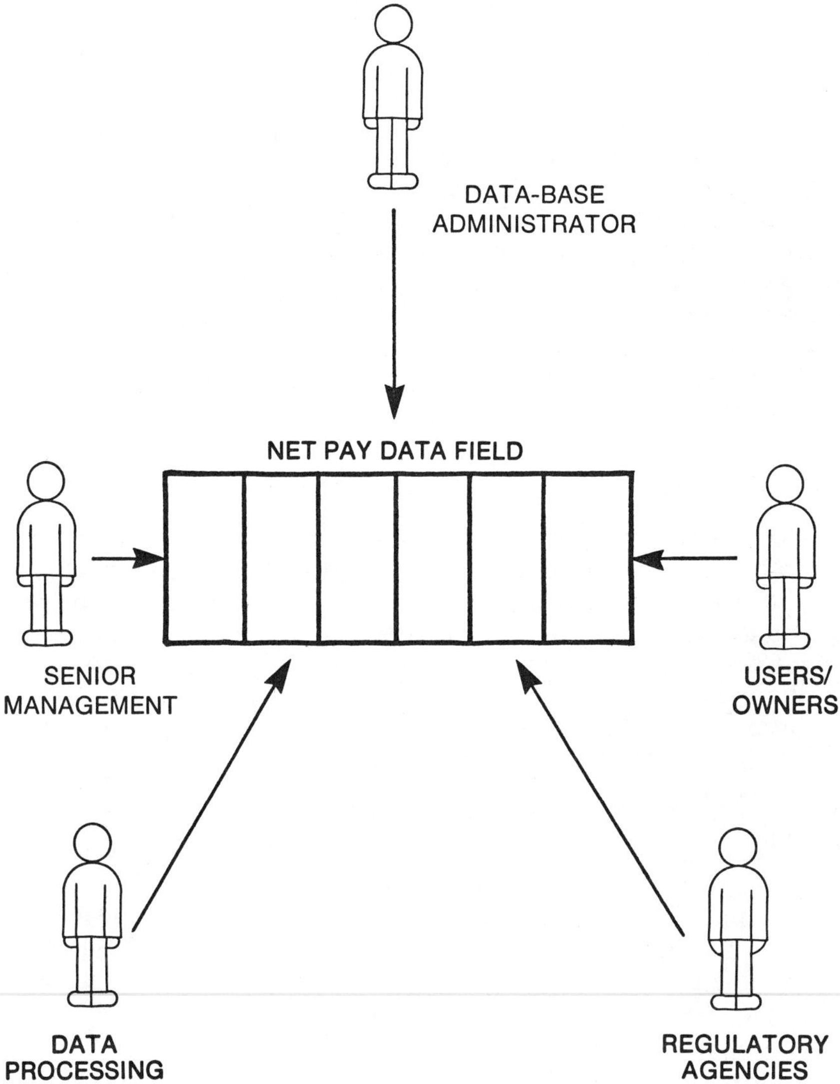

former is concerned with accounting purposes and the latter with commission purposes. The purpose of involving senior management in data definition is to provide policy decisions regarding data attributes. In some organizations this responsibility is fulfilled by an individual called a data administrator.

The data administrator usually is a member of senior management who may not be technically knowledgeable about data processing but is knowledgeable about the data needs and requirements of the organization.

Data-base administrator

The data administrator establishes data policy while the database administrator implements that policy. Part of the implementing process involves recording the attributes of the data. Recording of data attributes may be more complex technically than it appears. Organizations that use the services of a database administrator usually use an automated system to manage and/or document data. The data-base administrator may also be the custodian of the data.

Users/owners

Both the person responsible for the data and the users of the data usually are the major contributors to data attributes. These people define the data attributes that were described earlier. While there is only one data owner, there may be many users involved in this process. Disputes among individuals in this group may need to be arbitrated either by the data-base administrator or by a member of senior management.

Data processing

The data-processing people design and operate computer systems. Their function is to satisfy the needs of the user and, at the same time, optimize the use of the hardware and the software. Fulfillment of these responsibilities usually contributes to the definition, and, in some instances, trade-offs between data definition and performance will be necessary.

Regulatory agencies

Government requirements and regulations may specify some data attributes. For example, the U.S. Internal Revenue Service states that data used for tax purposes must be saved for three full calendar years after the year in which the data originated.

Computer Survival Rule #25

Verify that all parties involved have contributed their requirements to the data definition process.

What happens if data do not meet requirements?

Murphy's law states that anything that can go wrong will go wrong. A corollary, sometimes known as Mrs. Murphy's law, states that, if a cake falls to the ground, it will fall icing side down. Stated in data-processing terminology, Mrs. Murphy says that the probability of something going wrong in data processing is directly proportional to the severity of the problem. The more serious the consequence, the more probable that the computer results will be wrong.

You would tire of reading an exhaustive list of the types of problems that can occur with computer data. Therefore, I will present only a partial list of problem-related situations (see the cases in Figure 3-5). These are examples of the most common causes of what can go wrong when data are entered into a computer system.

We have already reviewed what can happen when data are entered into the wrong box (case 1, Figure 3-5). You probably can visualize the face of a customer who receives ten or one hundred times the quantity he or she ordered. It has happened and will continue to happen.

Having either too many or too few data to enter into the boxes is known as the never-right syndrome (cases 2 through 4). The customer's name never seems to fit exactly into the number of boxes allocated. The never-right syndrome continually plagues data-processing personnel in their efforts to define the proper data attributes.

Picture yourself as the designer of a computer system that includes people's names and addresses. The decision you must make is how much space to allot for a person's name, street address, city, and state. Let's look at some of the dilemmas that can arise with personal names. If you allot too much space for a person's name and you have thousands of customers, you literally waste hundreds of thousands of potential computer storage

Figure 3-5. Examples of What Can Go Wrong with Computer Data

Case 1 Wrong box

	#1	#2	#3	
Meant "5"		5		Means "50" to computer

Case 2 Too much data (left justified)

	#1	#2	#3	#4	
Wanted "COVER"	C	O	V	E	Got "cove" / "R" is lost

Case 3 Too much data (right justified)

	#1	#2	#3	#4	
Wanted "COVER"	O	V	E	R	Got "over" / "C" is lost

Case 4 Too few data (right justified)

	#1	#2	#3	#4	
Wanted "34"	9	7	3	4	Got 9734

Case 5 Sign not specified

	#1	#2	
Wanted − 16	1	6	Got + 16

Case 6 Wrong data entered

	#1	
Wanted "female" entered "M"	M	Got "male"

Case 7 Wrong attributed entered

	#1	#2	
Wanted 1 dozen entered "12"	1	2	Got 12 dozen (144 items) Computer read data as dozens

positions. On the other hand, if you allow too few spaces, you won't be able to record people's names properly. How, then, do most systems designers decide how many boxes to allot?

Some of their approaches include WG: wild guess; 95%: allow enough space to permit the full spelling of 95% of your customers' names; and SA: perform a statistical analysis on the file to determine the mean, median, and mode of name length.

No matter what you do, Murphy wins. If you allot fifteen spaces for last names, at least one of your customers will have a sixteen-letter name; if you allot twenty-five positions, at least one of your customers will have a twenty-six-letter name; and so on. If you allot fifty positions, you waste money.

The real question deals with justification of the name or number, since you must plan to be at least one position short. Justification refers to which end of the name or number will lose characters. Unfortunately, you can't "write small" with computers. Only one letter goes into one box. Case 2 is an example of too many data that are justified on the left (Figure 3-5). In other words, the word to be entered begins from the left, one letter at a time. In this instance, the letter R is lost. In case 3, the data are entered from the right, one character at a time, and the leftmost character is lost. The general rule in data processing is to left-justify alphabetic data (i.e., to lose the rightmost characters) and to right-justify numeric data (i.e., to lose the leftmost characters).

Too few data can pose other problems. Unless special steps are taken, computer storage will be filled with meaningless numbers or letters. An analogy would be a tape recorder on which the tape has been used previously. Wherever you rerecord over tape, the most recent recording replaces the information that is already on the tape. However, if you don't record over a previous recording, the latter will remain intact. The same situation is true with computers. Case 4 shows an example of a two-digit number that is entered into four boxes. The four boxes in our example contained the characters 97XX. When thirty-four was entered in a right-justified manner, it overlaid the XX but left the ninety-seven, resulting in the number 9734. In this case, if a customer had ordered 34 books, 9,734 books would have been received. What a surprise!

Let's examine the case of the missing-sign syndrome (case 5). Unless you instruct the computer specifically that you are dealing with a positive or negative number, it will treat everything as positive or everything as negative. Case 5 is an example of a user wanting to enter a negative sixteen but failing to instruct the computer properly. The result was a positive sixteen.

The most prevalent of all mistakes is the wrong-data-entered syndrome. This is a mistake to which we are all susceptible, and there is no known cure. The incidence of the syndrome can be reduced, but it can't be eradicated. The example in case 6 shows that the code for female should have been entered, but an M (i.e., male) was entered mistakenly. The dumb computer sees M and thinks that male is wanted. That's the best the computer can do.

Our last example is the wrong-attribute syndrome. This is a variation of the wrong-data syndrome but actually is more a problem of miscommunication. Case 7 illustrates our previous example of entering twelve, (i.e., twelve items wanted), while to the computer twelve means a dozen, and twelve dozen means that 144 are shipped. This syndrome also has no known cure.

Computer Survival Rule #26

If you want to be sure data are accurate and complete, check, recheck, cross-check, and back-check. Even then, things may go wrong.

Data definition checklist

You should question each piece of data before you enter it into the computer or rely on it. The data-processing community has coined the term *user-friendly* to mean an easy-to-use system. You need to make sure that any system you use is data-friendly to you.

You can't be friendly with data until you know something about the data. Checklist 3-1 is designed to help you get to know your data better. "Yes" indicates friendly attributes of data, and "no" indicates potentially unfriendly data. If you encounter too many "no" responses, you or your function may run into problems associated with data.

Conclusion

Alice dropped through a hole and fell into Wonderland. As you begin to work with computers and drop data into that vast hole known as data processing, you hope you can travel the friendly yellow brick road of Computerland. Some people can, some can't.

Checklist 3-1. Understanding Data Attributes Checklist

Question	*Response* Yes	No	N/A	Other
1. Do users understand that much of the success of any computer system is related to the accuracy and completeness of input data?	____	____	____	__________
2. Do users understand the significance of the requirement to enter data in boxes on input forms?	____	____	____	__________
3. Does each item of data have a unique name identifier?	____	____	____	__________
4. Is each item of data described in sufficient detail to avoid misunderstandings of the content of that item?	____	____	____	__________
5. Is one individual assigned as the owner of each item of data?	____	____	____	__________
6. Are users of data identified?	____	____	____	__________
7. Is the use that each user can make of data specified?	____	____	____	__________
8. Is someone appointed as custodian of data if the owner is not the custodian?	____	____	____	__________
9. Is the origin of the data documented?	____	____	____	__________
10. Is the length of the data documented?	____	____	____	__________
11. Is the type of data documented?	____	____	____	__________
12. If the data field is numeric, are the number of decimal points documented?	____	____	____	__________

Checklist 3-1. Understanding Data Attributes Checklist (continued)

Question	*Response* Yes	No	N/A	Other
13. If the field is numeric, is the method of recording the sign of the field documented?	____	____	____	____________
14. Has it been determined how long the data should be saved?	____	____	____	____________
15. Has the output format of the data been documented?	____	____	____	____________
16. Have the security and privacy criteria for the data been identified and documented?	____	____	____	____________
17. Have appropriate validation steps been taken to ensure that the data characteristics are achieved?	____	____	____	____________
18. Have all the involved parties provided input into the data definition process?	____	____	____	____________
19. Has one individual been designated responsible for documenting data?	____	____	____	____________
20. Have regulatory agency requirements been identified, documented, and incorporated into the data attributes?	____	____	____	____________
21. Have the most common data errors been identified so that people can be trained in the prevention, detection, and correction of those errors?	____	____	____	____________

Checklist 3-1. Understanding Data Attributes Checklist (continued)

Question	Response			
	Yes	*No*	*N/A*	*Other*
22. Has a member of senior management been appointed to coordinate and arbitrate data differences in the organization?	___	___	___	___
23. Does someone have the responsibility to explain to users of data the attributes and types of data available to them?	___	___	___	___
24. Is data retained in accordance with the data retention schedules of the organization?	___	___	___	___

One of the keys to survival in the data-processing field is understanding data. This is one of the most important survival tools when the computer stands between you and success. Although it is not practical for many users of data processing to master the technical facets of the computer, all users can reach an understanding of data attributes. Data drive systems, but, unfortunately, they can drive systems either correctly or incorrectly. Knowledge of data attributes can significantly improve your probability of success in obtaining the desired results from computer systems.

4/ Information is a resource of an organization

Introduction

Organizations have four major resources: people, machines, money, and information. Money and machines are recorded in the books of the organization and are quantified, controlled, and safeguarded. Usually, people and information are not recorded as assets in the books of the organization. One can speculate that the reason is either they are not worth anything or they are too valuable to quantify. As a person, I like to believe the latter is true.

Computer data are part of the information systems of an organization. The information resource coordinates the uses of machines, money, and people. The proper management of information can be crucial to the success of the organization.

This chapter provides the tools for surviving information. Information is not a loose configuration of data; rather, more often it is a highly structured network of data. The relationships and structure of data must be understood before users can capitalize on the multiple capabilities of their organization's information systems.

The use of data gives it meaning

You pick up a piece of paper and see the numbers "45" written on it. The paper and the numbers are meaningless, so you discard it quickly. Data are there, but they haven't conveyed any information to you.

Look again, but now you are holding Joe's timecard. It is the end of the first week in January, which is indicated on the timecard, and it shows that Joe has worked forty-five hours. Now "45" means something. It means that Joe has worked that number of hours, and his organization is obligated to compensate Joe for those hours at an agreed-on hourly rate. In addition, because Joe is on the payroll, you know that the U.S. Federal Wage and

Hour Law dictates that Joe must be compensated for five hours of overtime.

When we saw simply "45" on a piece of paper, we had only data; however, when the same number appeared on Joe's timecard, we had information. Thus, we can define information as data whose significance we understand. We have to know precisely what data mean, because "45" could just as easily have meant the number of products ordered, or the gross profit percent on the sale of product X, or even the number of days until a payment is due.

One of the dilemmas in data processing is to ensure that all the parties involved have a common understanding of the meaning of the data. Unless they all view the data from the same perspective, they may draw entirely different conclusions from the same piece of data. Thus, common information is not conveyed by common values of data.

A disaster story

A large manufacturing organization decided to automate job scheduling in their job shop operation. Complex machinery was being assembled, and, under the manual system, it was difficult to determine the status of the various subassemblies. Frequently, entire machines would fall behind schedule when a seemingly insignificant subassembly was not finished on time.

The automated approach which the organization selected used data-collection equipment to collect job status. All machinists were given magnetically encoded cards to identify themselves, and each part and subassembly was accompanied by a punched card for identification. When each part reached a new work station, the machinist was to enter his or her card into the data-collection equipment, together with the punched card that accompanied the part. This process would immediately signal the status of any part or subassembly to the computer.

To gain maximal benefit from the system, the machinists' pay also was calculated by having the machinists report their daily starting and stopping time. Since the machinists worked on the basis of incentive, incentive pay could be calculated from their job-status information. When the computer system began operation, the plant became embroiled in chaos. The job status reported by the machinists did not reflect production in the plant. Some work reported as complete was not complete, and some work that was finished was not reported as such. On analysis, the reason was quite simple.

The machinists had always reported the production of parts in order to optimize their incentive pay. If it was not advantageous for pay purposes, parts were not recorded as complete, while in other instances it was beneficial for the machinist to report work not done as being complete. Over a period, machinists would do all of the work they reported for pay purposes. They had been reporting work in this manner for years and found no reason to change their practices because a computer system was installed.

A problem is associated with using one piece of data for two purposes, each of which has different reliability standards. The organization could accept some errors introduced into data used for payroll purposes. Unfortunately, however, the information entered by the machinists for job scheduling required a high degree of accuracy. The organization solved the data problem at considerable cost by putting expeditors on the factory floor to record job status independently of what the machinists reported for pay purposes. This situation is not good information-system practice; rather, it illustrates the realities of not defining information.

Many options are available for structuring data for information systems. We will examine these in an effort to alleviate this type of disaster.

Uses of information

All information is not equal. Some information is more valuable than other information. In addition, information can be used in different ways.

Information can be classified into the following five categories which readily explain how the information is used (see Figure 4-1).

Transaction

When we say that data drive computer systems, we usually refer to transaction-driven systems. Transactions instigate action in most computer systems. For example, a completed timecard drives the payroll system. An order transaction from a customer drives an order entry/product distribution system. A check re-

Figure 4-1. Categories of Information

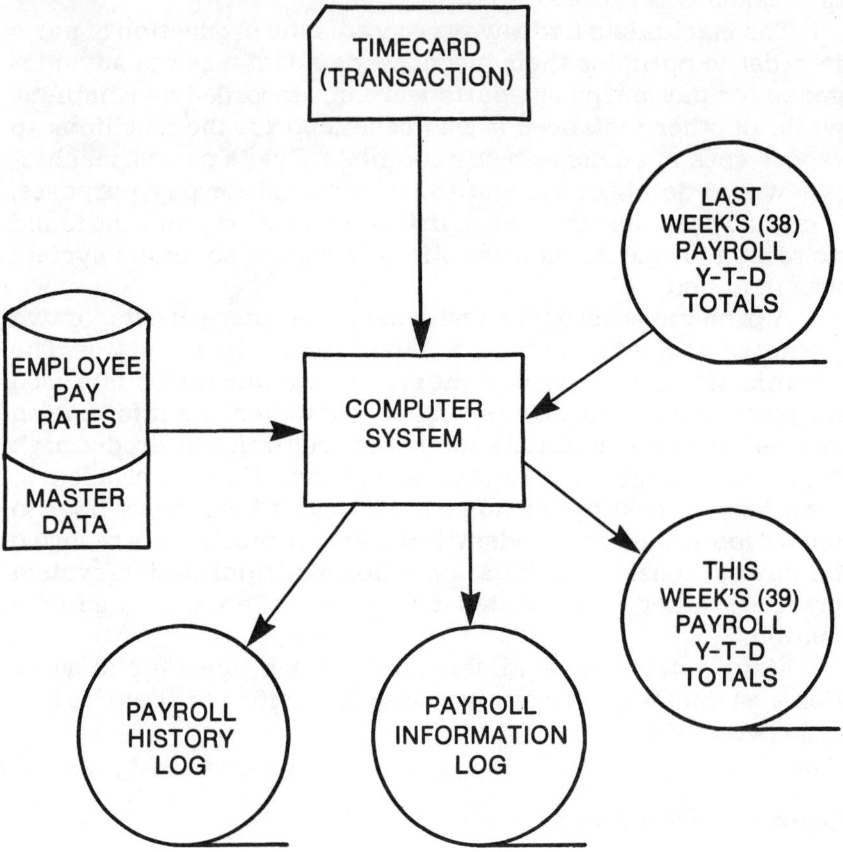

ceived by an organization is a transaction that drives a cash receipt/accounts receivable system. Thus, a transaction can be defined as the documentation of an event that will instigate computer processing. This type of information usually is recorded and entered into the computer system only once. After it has been entered and processed, the transaction serves no additional useful purpose other than retention to maintain a chain of events.

Recirculation

Much of the information in computer systems circulates through the system. As the information circulates, it may be extended, modified, or deleted. In accounting jargon, this category of information would be referred to as ledgers. The information in circulating files reflects the results of processing. Examples of recirculating files include year-to-date payroll files, accounts receivable files, inventory files, accounts payable files, and demand deposit accounts. For example, in demand deposit accounts, transactions are added to or subtracted from the totals in the recirculating files. Each deposit, withdrawal, interest, or service charge is reflected in the customer's deposit balances.

Master files

Each organization has groups of semipermanent information. The type and quantity of this category of information vary from organization to organization. Examples of master information include files of pay rates, merchandise prices, lists of customers' names and addresses, and lists of employees' job skills. Naturally, this information changes, but usually it does not change during any processing cycle. For example, employees' pay rates may change, but they would be fixed at the time payroll is run for any given pay period; hence, the connotation of master or semipermanent information.

History

Organizations retain much of their information for historical purposes. Some information is required by legislation, while other data are retained for reconstruction or analysis. The type of information and the length of time it is retained vary from organization to organization. Many organizations have elaborate record retention programs that specify what is to be saved and for how long. Historical information is rarely used for production purposes, except when a problem occurs and the information is needed in order to reconstruct current processing.

Information logs

Many manual systems retain information logs that are used to verify the status of transactions and, frequently, to reconstruct processing steps. Advanced computer technology has created the need for the same category of information. Communications systems maintain logs of messages that are sent and received over communications lines should questions arise regarding a message that has been lost. Also, many users maintain logs of transactions that are rejected from computer systems so they may be sure the transactions are not lost before reentry into the system. Although the useful life of a log is relatively short, it can be an important piece of the information network in the event that problems occur.

The five categories of information are illustrated in Figure 4-1 in a hypothetical computer system. This is a payroll system that shows the timecard being entered as a transaction file. Should the information be rejected, an information log records the rejected data and maintains records of those data so that they may be reentered properly. A recirculating file is represented by a file of each employee's year-to-date totals as of pay week 38; the year-to-date file is updated after pay week 39 has been completed. The pay rates and deduction schedules for each employee are based on the payroll master file, which contains information about each employee's hourly rate, the type of deductions the employee has authorized, and information about that employee that may not be on the transaction file, such as the employee's full name and address. Finally, the figure shows a history file, which provides a history of how each employee's gross and net pay was calculated. Should any question be raised about the accuracy of pay calculations, the history information will substantiate how payroll information was calculated.

Computer Survival Rule #27

The category of information will give you the same insight into the information as does the table of contents in a book.

Computer information hierarchy

An old song explains how the ankle bone is connected to the shin bone, which is connected to the knee bone, which is connected to the thigh bone, and so on. In a rather amusing fashion, the song tells how the human skeleton is structured. Information in computer systems has its own hierarchical structure.

We have already used much of the terminology that describes the information hierarchy. These words were slipped in with minimal explanation, not to confuse you, but to prepare you for enlightenment about this hierarchy. We have used the words digit, character, field, record, and file, all of which have specific definitions in data processing. These terms describe most of the hierarchy, so that we need only introduce one more word—data base—in order for you to know the terminology of computer data structure.

The song we referred to begins with the toe bone, so let us begin with the smallest piece of information and work our way up to the highest. Unlike the bones in the body, the pieces of information in the hierarchy are not separate. The data in the lower levels of the hierarchy are part of the higher levels. Let's look at the pieces individually (see Figure 4-2).

Figure 4-2. Hierarchy of Computer Data

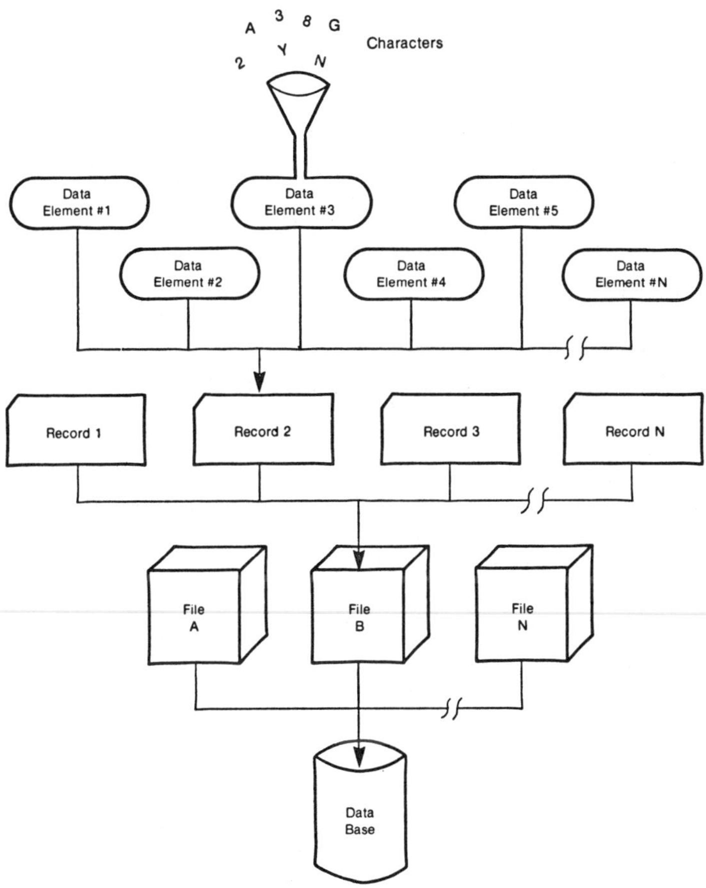

Characte,

In defining the attributes of data, we discussed how individual items of data may have alternative names or nicknames. What is referred to in one place as a character may be called a digit or a byte elsewhere. Let us define a character as one piece of data, such as a number, character, or special symbol. This broad definition is made because the term *digit* usually refers only to a number, and the word byte refers more to a box that a computer can recognize than to what is contained in the box. The same is true for computers that refer to a box as a word. In these computers, a "word" may contain the equivalent of many numeric or alphabetic pieces of information. The character is recognizable but usually meaningless. Until it is given definition, it is only a number, letter, or special character.

Field

A field is the smallest piece of meaningful information. It can be of any length (or number of boxes), including one. We have discussed several fields, although we have not always called them fields. For example, the "Net Pay" piece of information is more properly called a field. It may be made up of any number of characters or digits, all of which are meaningless until they are put together as a field. Examples of fields include employee number, product name, day of the week, and amount due. However, although fields have meaning, their meaning often is limited until the field is associated with other fields.

Record

A record is a group of fields held together by a common bond. The common bond gives meaning to the information contained in the field. For example, $4.75 may be the value in a field called "Pay Rate." However, while it is recognizable that it is a pay rate, it has only limited value until it is associated with an individual, such as Joe. Then it becomes Joe's pay rate. When we begin to put together several fields, all held together by a common bond such as Joe, we have Joe's payroll record. This record contains all the fields that relate to Joe's pay.

File

A file is a group of records held together by a common bond. In our payroll example, all of the records for all of the employees of a given corporation would be considered that organization's payroll file. We are familiar with this type of hierarchy in our own personal files. Let's look at a file of checks that we might keep in our desk at home. Each number and letter on that check is a character. By themselves they have little meaning. As we begin to put the characters together, we get fields. The fields on our checks include the date, the payee, the amount, and the account number. The sum of all the information on the check comprises the check record, and the total of all the checks we have in our possession is our file of checks.

This example is simplistic as compared with the complexity of the information hierarchy of most computer systems. Fields are a common denominator to organizations and thus provide the significance for describing data properly.

The particular composition of records and files is created at the convenience of the designer of a computer system. Two people who satisfy the same organizational need may develop computer systems with completely different records and files. The users of computer systems should not look for commonality in the makeup of different computer systems that cover similar types of applications. For example, if one organization has two divisions, and each division has its own payroll system, the divisions may have entirely different records and files, although most likely they would have basically the same data fields. As we discussed earlier, fields can be of different lengths and characteristics.

Why do we need a data base?

If data are tied together in an effective structure, why would we want to change that structure? Why not stick with what works instead of introducing something new, such as a data base? Besides, what *is* a data base?

The golden rule of data processing says, "Thou shalt satisfy thy users' needs." As we have indicated, this goal usually is accomplished by data-driven systems. In other words, if the needs of the payroll department must be satisfied, the data-processing department and the payroll department jointly create whatever data are needed to drive the system and thus satisfy the need. Similarly, if the personnel department has a need, the data-processing department helps them to create data to drive their system to help satisfy their need. The same is true for the pension department, and so on.

The satisfaction of one need at a time provides us with three systems (i.e., payroll, personnel, and pension). All these systems are data driven and all satisfy user needs. Everybody's happy, you say. Why change things?

The reasons are numerous. Among them are lower cost, greater reliability, greater consistency, and better documentation. If this is possible, you may ask, why didn't organizations switch to data base years ago? The answer is that there is a tremendous amount of internal overhead involved in the administration of a data base. Until the cost of the hardware to store data can be reduced substantially, the concept of the data base is not practical. The cost of increased advantages must be offset by the benefits.

The concept of the data base introduces another rule for successful data processing: it is best to enter data only once and then devote extra time and effort to ensure the accuracy and completeness of the data. If we enter data numerous times, as in our personnel system, for example (i.e., once for payroll, once for personnel, once for pensions), we may enter it twice correctly and once incorrectly. In contrast, if we enter the data correctly into our data base, then it will be correct for all three systems. On the other hand, if we enter it incorrectly, it would be incorrect for all three systems.

Computer Survival Rule #28

A piece of data should be entered into an organization's computer system only once. Then it should be checked sufficiently to ensure its accuracy and completeness.

How does a data base work?

A data base is a central repository for an organization's data. It functions much like a bank vault. People enter data into a data base as they would deposit their valuables in a bank vault. The information is then secured in a data base and made available only to people who can prove that they have authority to access the data (i.e., the combination to the vault). The difference between the bank vault and the data base is that, with the data base, multiple users share the same data, whereas with the bank vault, a safe deposit box usually belongs to a single individual.

In a data oase, data are owned by a single individual but may be used by many individuals. It is both the way data are used and the fact of their use that add to the administrative overhead of data-base technology. Data-base management routines must ensure that two users do not perform conflicting functions concurrently. For example, if two people were to remove the same element of data and then change it, neither would be aware of what the other was doing. Fortunately, data-base management systems have controls to handle this situation adequately.

One misconception about data-base technology is that all the organization's data are deposited into a single data base. Not true. Organizations have multiple data bases. For example, one data base might be for employee records, another for customer records, another for production records, and so on. The concept of multiple data bases increases the problem of consistency of common data elements in multiple data bases.

Data-base technology is becoming the rule, not the exception, and the advantages to its use are great if it is implemented properly. Proper implementation usually requires intervention and coordination by senior management of the organization.

Computer Survival Rule #29

If your organization chooses data-base technology, it also should choose a member of senior management to administer the data.

Data organization

Computers can remember where they put things. We have discussed the concept of boxes and how each box is uniquely identified. This sounds too simple, doesn't it? It is. There is more to it than just remembering the number of the box. The computer needs some other identifier to find a specific employee's record, customer's record, or status of an inventory item.

We establish a structure for most of our personal possessions. We put our clothes in the dresser, our food in the pantry and refrigerator, and our paperwork in the desk. If we are looking for food, we don't go to the bureau or desk; likewise, we don't look for our bank records in the refrigerator. Unfortunately, while our system sounds simple, it would be too complex for a computer. Computers need a more methodical process for finding data.

Two types of access methods are used in computer systems: sequential and direct. Sequential file organization is associated with sequential access. The method requires that you locate a record from the file by looking at the first item in the file; if that's not it, you look at the second item; and so on throughout the file until you find the item you want. The direct method permits you to access more or less directly the data item(s) you want.

Why would anybody use the sequential method when they can find something directly? After all, if I want to get a shirt out of my bureau, it doesn't make sense to open the top drawer and look at everything in the top drawer, then open the second drawer and look at everything in the second drawer, and so on until I find my shirt. I know it's in the bottom drawer and I go there directly and get it. It's an efficient method. Why don't computers work that way? Again, the answer is administrative overhead. It's a matter of economics. If the computer is going to permit you to access something directly, it must keep extensive indexes on how to find a particular piece of data.

Let's look at how a telephone book can be used both sequentially and directly. Suppose you wanted to find Bill Perry in the telephone book. With the sequential method, you open the book to the first page, look at the first name, and see if it is Bill Perry; if it is not, you look at the second name, and so on until you find it. With the direct method, you would use the telephone book index. Many telephone books have two indexes. One is alphabetic, which permits you to open it directly to section "P," thereby eliminating in one step all of the previous sections (i.e., letters A through O). The second index is located at the top of the page. You begin skimming the pages quickly until you come to "Per," at which point you know you are getting close. Then you can begin to look at that page until you find the name Perry, and then look for a Perry with a first name of Bill.

Use of the telephone book by starting with the first name on the first page and going through it name by name is sequential approach. The use of indexes is called index sequential. In this method, the data are still organized sequentially, but indexes help you find the item you want quickly. There are variations of the index sequential file, but they all work according to the same direct concept. In some instances, indexes are called pointers, or they will show the relations among data; however, the index sequential concept remains the same.

The sequential file usually is a more economical structure if a large percentage of the records in the file need to be accessed each time the file is processed. For example, in a payroll file it is normal to use almost every record in the file when payroll is processed. Thus, the administrative overhead for accessing data directly is unwarranted because there is no need for that type of processing. On the other hand, an airline reservation system requires that the airline reservation clerk be able to find out immediately whether or not a specific flight is filled. In this type of processing it would be impractical to look at every record in the file to find the record of the particular flight. An airline reservation system is an ideal candidate for an index sequential access method.

Is accessing of data bases different?

Data base is a complex version of an index sequential file. In fact, a data base usually is many index sequential files combined into a single file. Confusing? Yes, data-base technology is confusing, but the concept is easily explained.

The only rule that you must remember in understanding technology is that everything must be predetermined. Nothing happens by chance, and nothing happens that has not been predetermined. Thus, if data base permits you to operate as though several files are combined into one file (which it does), that is determined before processing occurs.

The telephone book example can be converted into a data base that contains many different files. Remember that a file is a group of records held together by a common bond. Some of the files included in the telephone book are a file of doctors, a file of hotels, a file of lawyers, and so on. When we use the telephone book, we often use the yellow pages—which duplicate the white pages but in different sequences—to find special information. However, if the telephone book were a data base, it would be stored on computer media, not on paper. In a data base it is not necessary to repeat Dr. Jones' name, address, and telephone number in both the white and yellow pages. Rather, the data base permits several different paths to access Dr. Jones' telephone information.

In a telephone directory data base, Dr. Jones' data appear only once. However, there are multiple indexes that help us find Dr. Jones. One is an alphabetic index, which lets us find the name alphabetically; another is a medical index, which lets us find Dr. Jones according to profession. This concept is illustrated in Figure 4-3. The illustration shows two indexes and a listing of many names. One index is the familiar alphabetic index, which first tells us what pages include the letter J, and then on what page we can find Dr. Jones. The other index is an index of doctors, which also leads us to Dr. Jones.

Figure 4-3. Finding Data Using Multiple Indexes

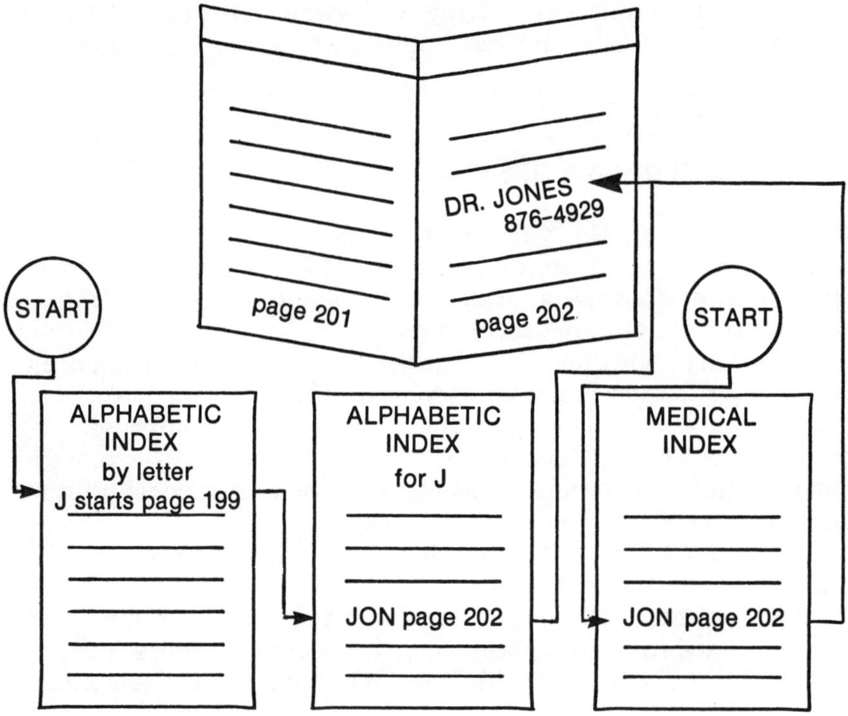

Computer Survival Rule #30

Determine how you want to use data, and then determine the best method to organize data to achieve your objective.

How are data processed?

The computer does everything step by step (see Figure 4-4). It's very methodical, precise, and organized. Again, things don't happen unless they are predetermined and performed methodically.

Visualize an individual getting dressed in the morning. They don't go from undressed to dressed in a single step. It's underwear first, then pants, then shirt, then socks, then shoes, and so on. The processing of data occurs in the same methodical type of order.

First, someone must decide to do something, just as we first have to make the decision to get dressed in the morning. Making a decision to do something in computer systems is called transaction origination. That is, someone has a need that must be satisfied; taking action on this need results in a transaction, such as issuing a purchase order.

After a decision has been made to do something, the decision must be entered into the computer system. Perhaps there is no equivalent human step for this. The entry of data into a computer system may be a unique, automated step in data processing, but it has to happen. This can be accomplished by entering the data on punched cards, into a terminal, or electronically reading a check by a machine.

The entered data then goes through processing. Processing is associated with storage. As we get dressed, processing consists of the placement of clothes on our body. During the process of getting dressed, we may have to refer to storage frequently. Our storage is the bureau and closet in which our clothes are stored. The computer has a different type of storage where data are located (e.g., prices, inventory status).

It is difficult to specify processing for a computer. It is not necessary to understand how a computer processes data any more than it is necessary to learn how an automobile produces power in order to drive it. However, it is helpful to raise the hood and see how complex the engine is. Let's do a small exercise to help understand some of the complexities of describing processing to a computer.

Figure 4-5 provides space to write a series of instructions. The worksheet has two columns, one for the instruction number, the other for the instruction itself. Using this form, take a few moments to write the instructions for tying shoelaces. The starting point has the two shoelaces fully extended at the top of the

Figure 4-4. Steps in the Processing of Data

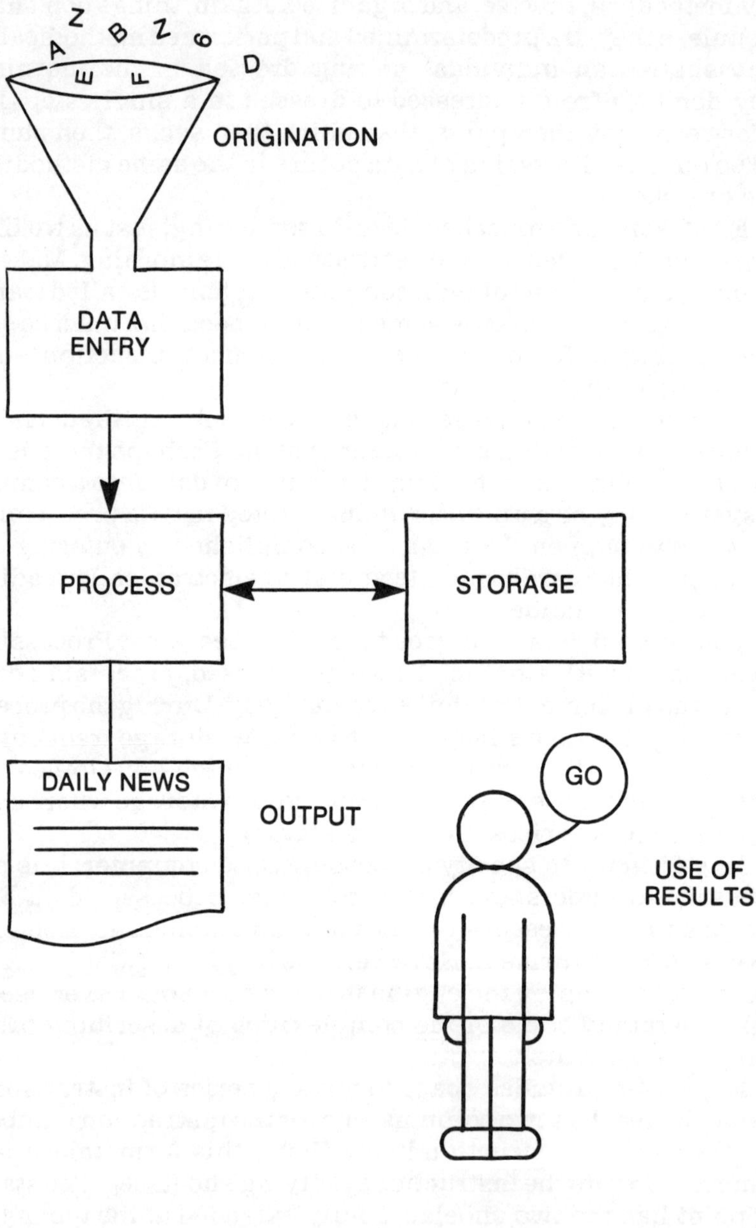

Figure 4-5. Writing Processing Instructions for Tying Shoes

START: Laces fully extended

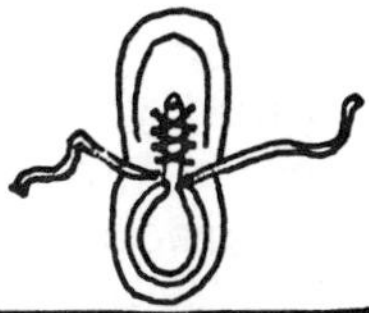

NUMBER	INSTRUCTION
1.	

lacing, ready to be tied. Now write the instructions on how to do it in as few or as many details as you feel necessary.

When you have completed the exercise, find a reasonably intelligent person. Ask him or her to follow the instructions explicitly: not to do anything because they know it should be done, but to follow your instructions precisely. In most cases, the person will not be able to tie the shoelaces. Try it. It is certainly a much simpler task than sending a rocket to the moon, but it gives you an appreciation of the difficulty of breaking down relatively simple tasks into component parts and then explaining them specifically enough so that there can be no misunderstanding.

After data have been processed, they are ready for use. Output is the step between processing and use. Output transcribes data from computer storage to a medium, such as paper, so that it can be understood by people.

Now comes what computer systems are all about: using the results in the day-to-day operation of an organization. As they say in the tire industry, this is when the rubber hits the road.

The effectiveness of the whole processing segment is dependent upon the timeliness, integrity, accuracy, completeness, and consistency of the output data. If the data going in is inaccurate or incomplete, the data coming out will be equally erroneous. Too frequently the computer gets blamed for people's mistakes.

Computer Survival Rule #31

GIGO: Garbage In, Garbage Out. This means that, if the data going into the computer are no good, then the data coming out also will be no good.

What happens if the data fail to meet the need?

Suppose the system is operating and you find that it doesn't meet your requirements because something has happened to the data. For example, the U.S. Post Office operated with a five-digit zip code for years before it decided that a nine-digit zip code would be more efficient. In a matter of moments, all the zip code data that had an attribute of five digits in length became obsolete.

This phenomenon happens continuously. Let's look at some of the conditions that can cause an organization to change its data attributes:

- Inflation pushes the numeric field to a larger size.
- A new product or service is added.
- A new plant or sales unit is added that requires new codes.
- A new company benefit is added.

Data is a continually changing aspect of data processing. Data are fluid, not fixed. Many organizations have a full-time staff that documents and implements new data fields and new data attributes for current fields. There is little likelihood that this aspect of data processing will change. In fact, as more aspects of organizations are computerized, the prospect of accelerating change in data attributes becomes more likely.

Computer Survival Rule #32

Organizations need an individual who is responsible for overseeing the currentness and usability of data in the organization. (This individual frequently is called the data administrator or data-base administrator.)

The change process for data varies from simple to near-crisis proportions. The costs many organizations face in going from a five-digit to a nine-digit zip code are large. To estimate the consequence and complexity of such a change, one need only count the number of systems that have zip codes and the number of people, forms, and so on that use zip codes. It's not uncommon in large organizations for a data change of that type to cost several hundred thousand dollars. Fortunately, such major changes occur only infrequently.

The process for changing data should be orderly. It is important to touch all bases before implementing a change in data attributes. The steps include:

1. Document the new data element or the change in a data attribute.
2. Gain agreement from all the parties affected that the documented change is desired. Many organizations require the

affected users to "sign-off" that the documented changes are in fact the ones desired. The reason for this is to force users to be responsible for their actions.

3. Document all the uses of that data element in the organization.
4. Develop a coordinated plan that will permit all departments using the data element to implement the changes at the same time.
5. Prepare work orders covering the type of changes or the impact caused by the change for all the areas affected.
6. Conduct whatever testing is needed to ensure that all the changes are made properly.
7. Issue the necessary action to ensure that all the changes go into a production status at the same time.
8. Change data documentation wherever necessary to reflect the new attributes.

Building data capability checklist

Many individuals find that they are either directly or indirectly responsible for the accuracy, completeness, consistency, and reliability of computer data. Without extensive knowledge of the organization and data processing, this may appear to be an overwhelming task. However, in reality it is more a matter of common sense than of heavy technical analysis. Data are what people use, while processing reflects how data are manipulated and implemented through computer processing.

A non-data processor may have difficulty understanding the reason for some of the technical attributes of computer data. Such an individual must question and challenge data-processing personnel in their definition of data. This can be a major step in the process of ensuring data integrity. Checklist 4-1 is provided as a tool to surviving bad computer data. The checklist is designed to evaluate the use of data in solving problems rather than the completeness of the technical attributes of data. A "no" answer indicates a potential data problem. The checklist should be addressed to data-processing personnel. If they are unable to assure you that the items on the checklist have been handled adequately, you may need to conduct additional investigation to determine the impact of not addressing that aspect of data definition and usage.

Conclusion

Information is the lifeblood of an organization. Without the proper information, organizations may lose their competitive advantage. With this information, organizations can avoid many errors and poor management decisions.

The data produced by computer systems are no better than the data that go into those systems. In addition, the type of data available to users of computer systems may be restricted by the structure of the data in the organization. This chapter has provided an overview of how data are structured, how they flow through systems, and how they are maintained. This information on information is designed to help you survive inadequately structured data by providing advice on challenging, questioning, and specifying your data needs so they can be incorporated into computer systems.

Checklist 4-1. Building Data Capability Checklist

	Response			
Question	*Yes*	*No*	*N/A*	*Other*
1. Is someone in your organization responsible for the accuracy, completeness, consistency, and reliability of data?	____	____	____	________
2. Is the use of information documented so that you can determine how and where each data field is used?	____	____	____	________
3. Is sufficient data saved so that transactions can be reconstructed?	____	____	____	________
4. Is an audit trail available that enables you to trace transactions from the source documents to summarized company records?	____	____	____	________

Checklist 4-1. Building Data Capability Checklist (continued)

Question	Response: Yes	No	N/A	Other
5. Is an audit trail available that enables you to trace data from the summarized company records back to all of the source documents comprising that summary?	____	____	____	____________
6. Has your organization documented its data hierarchy?	____	____	____	____________
7. Has your organization evaluated the advantages and disadvantages of using data-base technology to meet your data needs?	____	____	____	____________
8. Is the hierarchy of your data structure responsive to your organization's data needs?	____	____	____	____________
9. Can data be retrieved from your files or data base in the required time?	____	____	____	____________
10. Has your organization established a formal procedure to modify data attributes?	____	____	____	____________
11. When data attributes are modified, is the user required to "sign-off" those changes?	____	____	____	____________
12. Are the attributes of data formally documented?	____	____	____	____________
13. When the attributes change, is the data documentation updated promptly?	____	____	____	____________

5/ Communication with computer people

The data-processing image

The image of a data-processing professional manifests itself in a wide spectrum of people and varies by organization. Some organizations visualize people wearing sandals, dirty jeans, and wild T-shirts, walking up and down the walls as they attempt to master technology. Other organizations view the data-processing professional as a prima donna who lives outside traditional organizational norms. Other organizations view data processors as highly specialized technicians whose careers are limited to data-processing technology. Others are awed by the ability of data-processing people to change the way organizations function—usually for the better. The spectrum ranges from weirdo to savior.

Whatever your image, it probably is wrong. Data-processing professionals are people like you and me. Even though they practice a different trade and can do things with computers that you and I can't do, there are things that you and I can do that the computer professional can't. Therefore, we would do better to dwell more on the commonalities between data processors and non-data processors than on the differences.

We need to recognize that we all work for the same organization or are attempting to achieve the same goal. As with any other relationship, it won't be good until we start talking. A rule of thumb says that the more data-processing professionals and users converse, the better the computer systems and the more data-processing personnel will be able to satisfy users' needs. When communication breaks down, systems often crash shortly thereafter.

This chapter is designed to explain both how to talk to computer people and what you should talk about. Once you begin to understand the world of data processing, communicating with its specialists will be easier. You don't have to be a doctor to talk about your health; nor do you have to be a data-processing professional to talk about computer systems. All you must do is talk.

What should you talk about?

When you go to a doctor, you usually talk about your health. When you go to an accountant, you talk about your financial records. Therefore, when you go to a data-processing person, you are going to talk about the computer systems that affect your jobs and your needs. To do this, you need to understand the components of a computer system and how those components conflict.

It is the resolution of the conflict among the components of computer systems that will encompass most of your time and your conversation. The fewer the problems, the less you have to talk about. The same analogy holds true for your health. If all the components of your body are functioning properly, you have little to talk about with the doctor. You should have regular medical checkups to discuss what to do to ensure good health, but that's usually just a friendly discussion. Similarly, when the conflicts among system components have been resolved, your discussions with data-processing people will center around keeping your systems healthy and on target.

Complications in understanding systems

Conceptually, it is quite easy to comprehend a system; however, analysis of a system may seem very complex. The easiest way to explain this dilemma is to look at an application. For example, take the registration system for most professional education courses. In order to register, the student must go through a series of steps, each of which accomplishes bits and pieces of the registration process.

Let's assume you are registering for a three-day course at a local college and you look at the registration procedure to see how the system will be used. Meeting the needs of the users of the system makes that system successful. First, let's see who needs data from the system and what data are needed. The main users and their requirements are shown in Table 5-1.

At some colleges and universities, there may be more users of registration data than the table indicates. Any of the users can use data for purposes not considered when the system was built. For example, the college may decide to hold postgraduate seminars and may want to reach alumni who hold degrees in special areas.

Table 5-1. College Registration System Users and Needs

User of System	*Data Needed by This User*
Student	Class schedule, invoice.
Teacher	List of students for each class.
Continuing education department	Lists of courses which have been filled, and lists showing which courses cannot be held because too few students have registered.
Cashier	Invoices and payments for registration.
Controller	Lists of registrations against payments showing amounts collected and to be collected.
Deans of schools	Data to plan for future seminars.
Admissions office	Students who have registered and students who have not registered.
Bookstore	Information on the titles and quantities of books needed, based on registration.
College officers	Reports showing the registration and financial status for the coming semester.
Registration office	Most registration data.
Data processing department	Information for updating all records dealing with registration.
Support functions, such as cafeterias, etc.	Registration data to plan the support needed.
Parking and security	Size of the student population.

We have said that there are three components of a system: data, rules, and people. Because the registration system has so many users, it will have many different needs placed on it. The registration system will include many records and many files, since several college departments are involved and each has its rules and procedures that must be followed.

The complexity of a system increases in proportion to the number of users and how many different needs each has. This can lead to disharmony among the components of an information system. Figure 5-1 illustrates this disharmony. The dis-

Figure 5-1. Disharmony of Components of a Large Information System

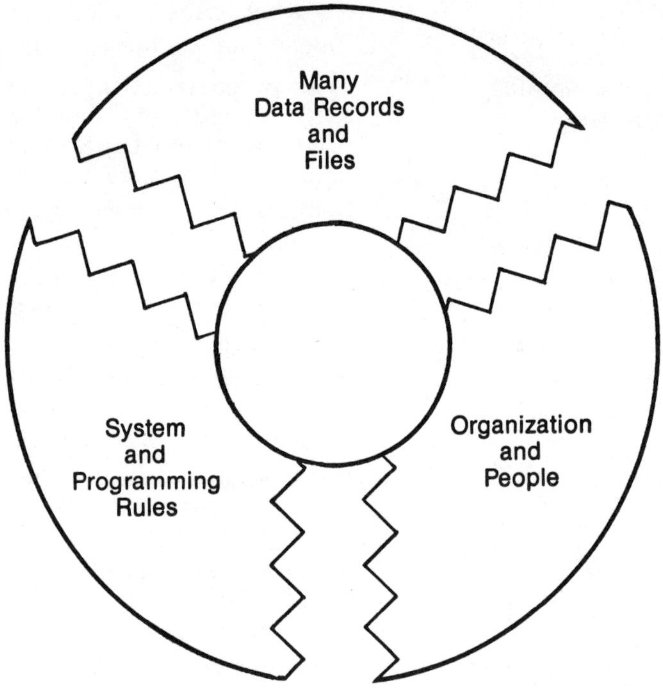

harmony occurs for three reasons. First, data are comprised, not of a single record, but of many records and files, as illustrated in the registration system. Second, the people involved come from different communities (e.g., students, faculty, administration) and from different departments in the organization; each has different requirements at different times. Third, the rules and procedures must be broken down so that users of the system can execute one step at a time. However, the system appears to be more complicated when the rules are broken down into small pieces. When you look at these small pieces, it is often difficult to visualize the entire system.

Systems in conflict

It is difficult for the three components of a system to work in harmony, since each component has certain needs that put it in conflict with the other two components.

Real-world requirements prevent the resolution of conflict among the components. These requirements are (1) processing of transactions on a timely basis, and (2) segregation of accounting information by accounting periods. It would be nice to wait until all the information on an event is collected before processing, but this is impractical when thousands of such events (e.g., orders) occur each day. Therefore, for example, we must process an order even if we cannot ship all the products requested. It also would be nice to process without having to segregate by accounting period, but we cannot run businesses without financial data.

The three systems components are all event oriented, but the accounting cycle is time oriented. Also, while data are event oriented, the entry of that data by transactions is time oriented. For example, data may be maintained by the event of a customer placing the order. However, many transactions, such as the order, the shipping notice, product back order, invoice, payment, and so on, are involved in this event.

The conflicts that occur in systems are illustrated in Figure 5-2. These conflicts are the cause of many systems problems and will be explained individually. By understanding these conflicts, you will understand the logic behind systems structure. Without an appreciation of these conflicts, the systems structure may appear illogical.

Conflict between people and data

A primary obstacle to understanding systems in organizations is the conflict between people and data. Figure 5-3 illustrates this conflict. People are organized into hierarchies that flow from the president at the top to the lowest clerk at the bottom. This is a vertical flow of authority that flows downward through delegation. In large organizations many such levels may exist. For example, the hierarchy of a controller's division might include the controller, assistant controller, department heads, supervisors, assistant supervisor, head clerk, and clerk. Reports, information, work, and directions all flow vertically, both up and down the chain of command.

Figure 5-2. Systems in Conflict

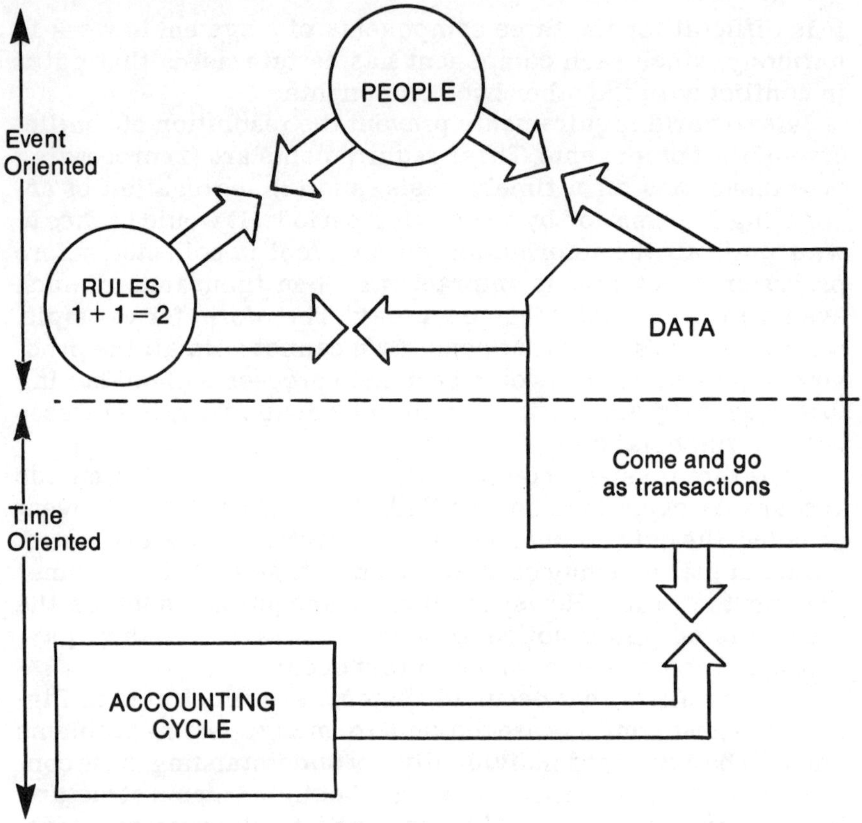

Data processed by the system flow horizontally. For example, take the order entry process. The order first goes to a sales representative, then to a marketing group for order entry, to a distribution function for shipping the merchandise, to an accounting function for billing, and so on. In the day-to-day working of a system, people must interact with individuals horizontal to them in the organization. Complicating matters is the fact that people in one department often have different priorities from those in another department. In addition, the data may be subject to different handling procedures as they flow from department to department. In addition, people in one department may not understand what people in another department do. The more departments that are involved in a particular system, the less any one department knows about the total system. Thus, our

Figure 5-3. Conflict Between People and Data

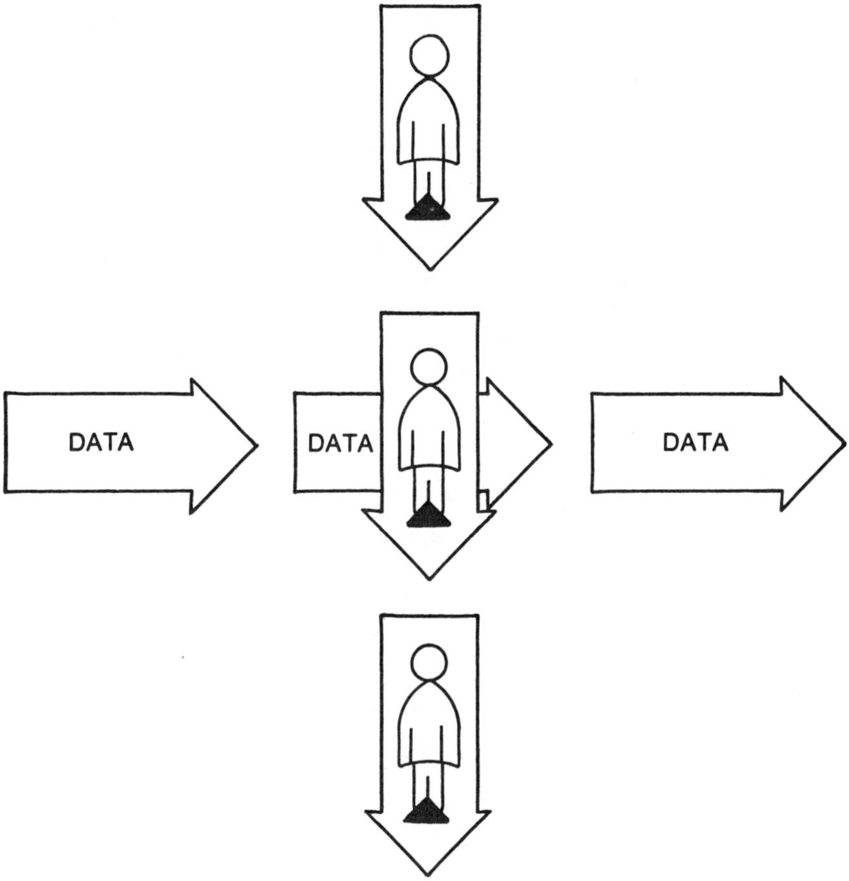

day-to-day work with data is horizontal among our peers, but our orders and directions come vertically from our superiors.

Conflict between rules and data

When policies and procedures are translated into rules, they apply to specific events, such as how to process an order. Rules remain constant. The time or day that data are entered into the system can affect how they are processed. We can say that data are time dependent and rules are not time dependent. In the example of the registration system for colleges and universities, the rules relate to the entire registration process. When a student goes to register, the same registration rules are in effect regardless of when the registration occurs. However, universities may offer preregistration for several weeks before classes start, have open registration for two or three days before classes, and have late registration after classes begin.

The day a student registers, data on that registration are entered into the system. Whether registration takes place four weeks before classes start, the day before classes begin, or after classes start, the data are prepared on that day. One of the conflicts that can occur is that there may be a discount for early registration and a fee for late registration. Figure 5-4 illustrates the conflict between rules and data.

Figure 5-4. Conflict Between Rules and Data

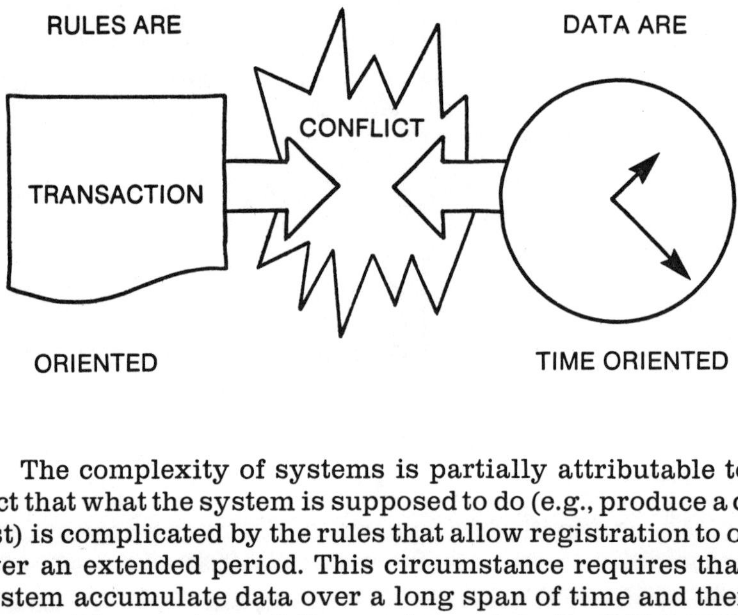

The complexity of systems is partially attributable to the fact that what the system is supposed to do (e.g., produce a class list) is complicated by the rules that allow registration to occur over an extended period. This circumstance requires that the system accumulate data over a long span of time and then sequence it by event (e.g., fall semester registration). For example, if registrations are to be accumulated according to class number, the process must continue over a period of weeks. This explains why class lists are produced at weekly intervals and why a teacher gets new class lists over a period of several weeks.

Conflict between people and rules

People handle problems and events as they occur. If an unusual request or situation arises, people react to it immediately and do what is necessary to solve the problem. Systems, on the other hand, do not have this flexibility. They follow rules precisely. To illustrate this, let's say that you are driving a car and you come to a point where the bridge is out. What will you do? Very likely you will seek an alternative route across the river. In contrast, if the system is driving the car, it would come to the point where the bridge was down, sit there and wait until a new one was built, and then proceed to the destination. Figure 5-5 illustrates this conflict. The system cannot handle situations for which rules have not been written. This can be extremely frustrating for users of the system. Once the system has processed data by its rules, the system's inflexibility may make corrections difficult. However, people in a manual environment have the flexibility that systems lack.

Now, to illustrate further how people operate in the present and react to situations as they occur, let's compare a manual

Figure 5-5. Conflict Between People and Rules

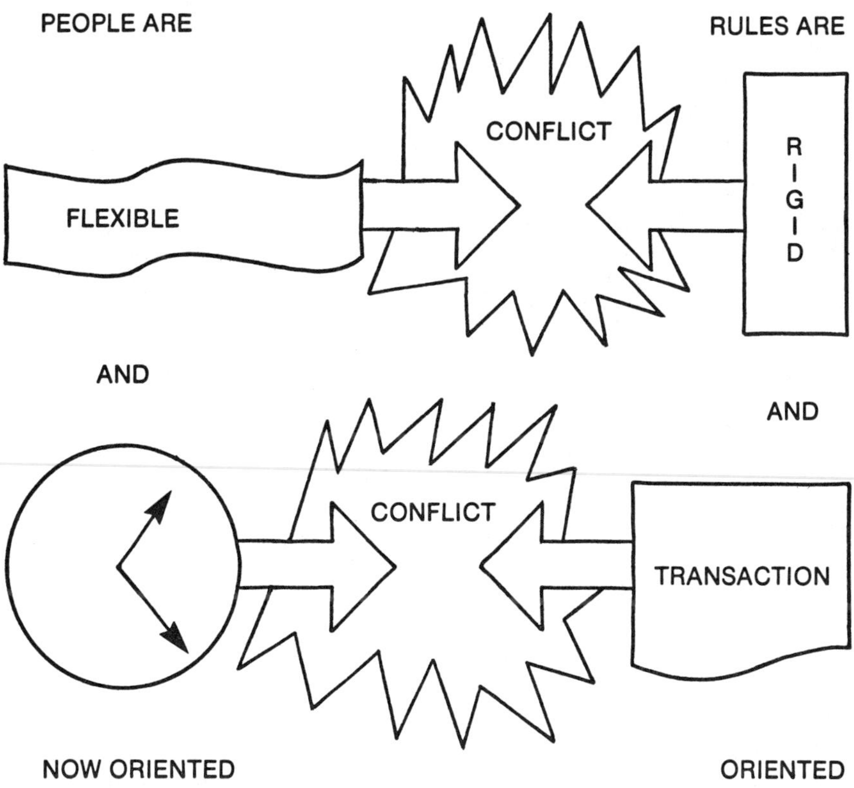

registration system with a computerized registration system. The human registrar handles each student who comes to the head of the line individually. If the student has a problem not directly related to registration, the person at the desk tries to handle that problem. The computerized registration system is transaction oriented. The system cannot process anything outside the scope of that transaction form. It must process transactions according to the rules, and it is difficult for the people who are entering the transaction data into the system to bend the rules. Thus, the computer can handle only the transactions for which it is programmed. What the computer can handle does not always correspond to people's immediate needs.

Conflict between transactions and accounting

The accounting function is oriented toward the preparation of financial statements at the end of a week, month, year, or other

Figure 5-6. Conflict Between Transactions and Accounting

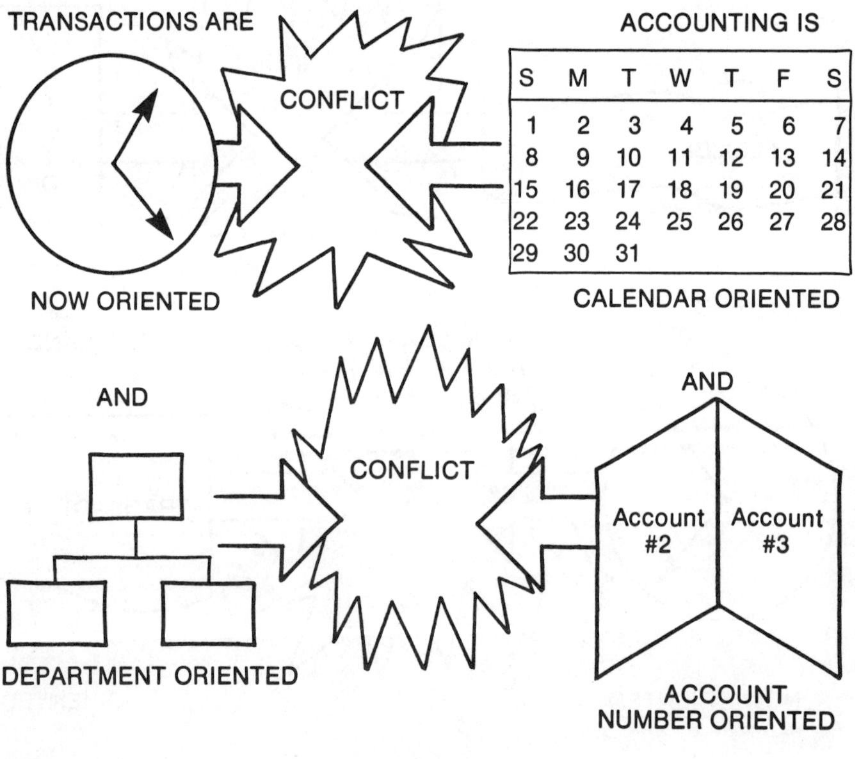

period. Accounting data are classified according to the chart of accounts. These two concepts generally are in conflict with the way transactions are entered. Figure 5-6 illustrates this conflict.

While accountants are trying to determine in which accounting period a transaction should be recorded, the people who process the transaction are more concerned with their immediate needs. Accounting cutoff procedures are one of the major causes of detail records being out of balance with control totals. In addition, accounting is account oriented, while transactions are department oriented. Accounts that encompass more than one department require some method of allocation among departments. This frequently is an area of discussion and conflict among departments.

Conclusions

The differences in viewpoint, time, and approach of the three components of an information system are the reasons for the conflicts described above. These conflicts add to the complexity of building and understanding information systems. To be able to step back and analyze systems for potential problems, you must learn to recognize and resolve these conflicts, because it is at this point that problems will arise. Computer systems that process data and immediately return the results to users eliminate many of the systems conflicts we have discussed. The new systems are especially helpful in reducing time conflicts. These are called on-line real-time systems and will be discussed later.

Communication is the key to building a successful system. First we need to understand how to improve communication; second, we need to start communicating.

Why is it difficult to talk to computer people?

Who says it's difficult to talk to computer people? The answer lies in the people who try to talk to them. The difficulty is due to both vocabulary and the environment in which data-processing people operate. Fortunately, both of these difficulties are solvable. Of the two problems, vocabulary is easier to solve. Either data-processing people have to learn to speak English, or the non-data-processing people need to learn "computerese." In actual practice, the marriage that will work the best is when each can speak some of the other's language. A few simple primers on vocabulary for the non-data-processing professional can help resolve the language dilemma.

The parts of a computer environment are easy to understand but sometimes make the process difficult to achieve. The computer environment is comprised of three parts: people, requirements, and methods. These three parts may restrict the data-processing professional's ability to function (see Figure 5-7). Understanding this work cocoon helps to build a good working relationship between data processors and users.

All three parts affect the ability of data-processing people to react to your needs. We need to look at these parts individually to see how they influence communication.

Methods

Data processing is a very structured and methodical discipline. Things don't just happen; they are planned, detailed, taken apart, reassembled, replanned, built, tested, and so on. The amount of

Figure 5-7. Parts of the Computer Environment

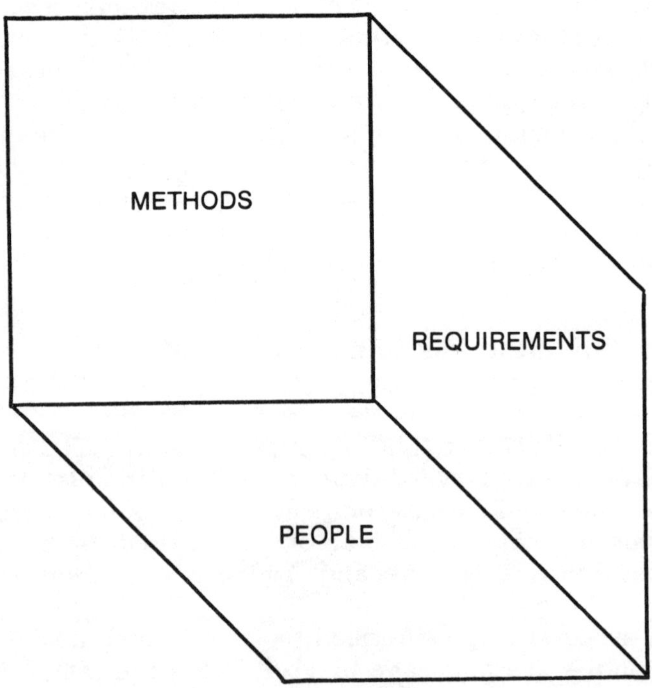

detail required to bring a large system into production is almost incomprehensible to the non-data-processing person.

Most data-processing departments have policies, procedures, and standards to define the methods that determine how data-processing people must operate. Each phase of the implementation of an automated system requires considerable documentation, much of it on prespecified forms, with each piece defined in great detail.

When data-processing people appear to be probing beyond what looks reasonable, they may do so because their methodology dictates it. In our discussion of data, we talked about the multiple attributes of data. Each of these attributes must be specified before systems or enhancements to systems can be undertaken. The methods stipulate the steps to be performed in crossing the t's and dotting the i's throughout the systems development process.

Requirements

In a previous exercise, you were asked to write out the instructions for tying shoelaces. This is the dilemma that data-processing personnel face as they attempt to satisfy your needs. Understanding people's meanings is so difficult that the data-processing person must go into great detail to ensure full and complete communication. Even then, we know from experience that, when two people talk about the same thing, they often visualize it in an entirely different manner.

People

People are the problem and the solution. The problem is lack of or poor communication. The solution is extensive and good communication. The first part of the chapter has described the problem. The remainder of the chapter enunciates the solution.

To whom should you talk?

If you walk into the computer room, you may find that most of the people are busy. In fact, they might not want to talk to you. If you have a question to ask or a need to satisfy, to whom should you talk?

One of the lessons I have learned the hard way is never argue with a clerk. Too frequently I have put my blood pressure gauge to the test by explaining to a clerk why I should be able to return a broken product, or explaining to a policeman why it was necessary to do something beyond the letter of the law but within the intent of the law, or explaining to a receptionist why I needed to see someone quickly. You don't discuss with a clerk business that exceeds their authority.

Computer Survival Rule #33

If the rules states that employees are not allowed access to a certain part of a building, a clerk would rather let them be cremated in a burning building than allow deviation from a rule over which that clerk has enforcement authority. In other words, argue your case in the right court.

The key to action in data processing, as in any other area, is finding the appropriate king or queen in whose domain you need action. This requires an understanding of both the data-processing department and the organizational structure. The process also works in reverse when the data-processing person attempts to get information and action from the user.

Many years ago, I worked as a systems analyst on the design and sale of a new system. I made several presentations to user-area management but with no results. Things seemed to be going well at first, but shortly after every presentation I got a negative response. I finally learned that the department manager was not the king over the area in which I was involved. As soon as I found out who the king was, I could pay my tribute to that king and honor him accordingly. The system then was accepted, installed, and operated without a hitch. However, had I not paid appropriate homage to the proper king, that system would have been sabotaged just like many other installed data-processing systems.

Data processing has its kings and queens, and when you learn who they are and pay them appropriate homage, you too will get good results. Remember that there is both a formal and an informal organization to every department. The two may or may not be the same. When I was in the army, I learned that the master sergeants ran the army, although the officers had the rank. It was only when I forgot this lesson in industry that I ran into serious communications problems. Not that we didn't talk; it's just that no action or results occurred.

The data-processing area in most organizations is divided into different armies of technicians. Each army guards a certain piece of the data-processing kingdom. You need to identify the army, find its leader, and talk to that individual. Let's look at some of the different specialties in data processing to identify who you need to talk to:

Systems analysts

These are the people who translate your needs and requirements into technical specifications. If you want to request a change in what is being done or add a new requirement, talk to the systems analyst. In most instances, this is your primary contact area for most of your data-processing needs.

Programmer

This is the individual who translates the technical requirements prepared by the systems analyst into computer language—that is, into a language that the computer can understand. If you appear to be getting erroneous results from your computer system or you have a question about the validity of computer-produced results, you may want to talk to the programmer. The systems analyst knows what should happen, but the programmer knows how it happens. The difference between talking to the systems analyst and talking to the programmer is equivalent to the difference between talking to a supervisor and a clerk. If you ask a supervisor what the procedures are, the supervisor will tell you what they should be. However, the clerk will tell you what they actually are.

Systems programmer

This is the person with the highest level of technical competence in most data-processing departments. This is the individual who puts all the pieces together and makes them work on the computer. We haven't discussed the pieces, but suffice it to say that there are a lot of them. You probably never want to talk to this individual, but if you do it will be about the intricacies of the computer.

Data-base administrator

Have data definition problems? Want to know what data are available for your use? Need to make some changes in data? This is the individual to talk to. The data-base administrator administers the definition, consistency, reliability, and use of data in an organization.

Operations

These are the people responsible for making your system work on the computer. Among the tasks performed by this group are assembling all the pieces in order to produce your needed results. If your reports aren't ready on time, if you want changes in the time of operation or number of copies of a report, or if you are going to be late in getting data to the computer, talk to the operations people.

Control group

Many data-processing organizations establish a control group to verify that what is supposed to work does work. This group verifies that your system is run at the scheduled time, that all the inputs have arrived and are complete, and that the output appears reasonable and is delivered to you. While they often are not a primary contact, if you find an unbalanced condition, don't understand error messages, or the like, you may want to talk to this group.

Data-processing management

These are the people who are supposed to run the shop. Usually they don't know anything that will be of direct interest to you, but you may find it interesting to talk to them; besides, they might be lonely. However, if you are not getting the answers you want from the other people, talk to management. If you are told your schedules can't be met, talk to management. If you don't like the estimates you have been given for a job, talk to management. In other words, if you can accomplish everything you need successfully by working with the workers, do it; however, if you are frustrated and not getting what you want, talk to management.

Data-processing management's management

This individual is often referred to as a vice president of information systems or an equivalent title. This is someone who absolutely can't help you solve your day-to-day problems but who can allocate resources toward finding a solution. In most organizations, this individual is the last resort. Don't go there often, but go when necessary.

Knowing who to go to is often as important as knowing what to say. The who-to-go-to decision is a simple two-step process: (1) outline in your mind the action that is necessary to achieve your goal; and (2) decide who is the individual who can instigate that action. This is the individual to talk to.

When should you talk?

When you have something to say, shouldn't you say it? The answer is yes, but the question is: What should you say? Too many people talk before they think. In terms of data-processing dollars, failure to preplan can be expensive.

Data-processing departments in large organizations frequently charge for their services. It's not uncommon to charge users $50 or $60 per hour for the services of data-processing personnel. Even if they don't charge, time is money.

Get your facts in order before your mouth runneth over. Ask yourself: Is it worth $50 an hour to have somebody listen to what I am going to say? If the answer is no, then it is not time to talk.

When you prepare for discussions with data-processing personnel, you need to answer the following questions:

1. What type of information or action do I want from the data-processing personnel?
2. What am I willing to pay to get that action or information?
3. When do I want that action or information?
4. What type of assistance am I willing to give the data-processing personnel to help them perform their function?
5. Do I care how the job is done, or am I willing to let them decide the best way to do it?

6. Can I tell them the names of people in my area to contact about doing their work?
7. Do I have all the supporting information available and ready to give to data-processing people in order for them to do their job?
8. Have I completed forms or other procedures necessary to instigate action in the data-processing department?

If you were able to answer all of the above questions affirmatively, then you are ready to talk to the data-processing people. You know who you should talk to, you know the story that you want to tell them, and you know the results that you would like. All that remains is knowing how to talk in a language that data-processing personnel can understand.

Computer Survival Rule #34

If you wouldn't pay $50 an hour to hear yourself talk, do some additional preparatory work before you begin discussions with data-processing personnel.

How do you talk computerese?

There is a story told about a group of people who used to tell jokes to one another continuously. Over time, they developed a core of jokes that they would tell repeatedly. The stories got funnier the more they were repeated. As time went on, they found it wasn't necessary to repeat the story, but only to tell the punch line in order to evoke rounds of laughter. Eventually, they shortened even the punch line so that it was necessary to say only, "Remember joke number 17," and everyone would start to laugh and laugh.

The analogy holds true for the computer field, even though people don't laugh at all the jargon. The computer field is filled with long, technical phrases, such as job control language, basic access telecommunications method, and index access sequential method. Since these items have become too cumbersome and wordy to repeat constantly, data-processing personnel have shortened them to JCL, BTAM, and ISAM. This, in turn, reduces the amount of time needed to communicate the terms but still conveys the same meaning. Unfortunately, non-computer people don't know what computer people are saying when the latter ask, "Have you written the JCL for your BTAM and ISAM systems?"

Enter the uninitiated user. "What's taking so long?" he or she asks. The data-processing professional responds, "I'm having trouble with my BTAM JCL." "Your what?" asks the user. "My BTAM JCL," responds the data-processing professional. The user exits, shaking his or her head, and the data-processing professional can't understand what's wrong with the user.

This scenario illustrates the two major communication problems in data processing. First, the data-processing professional speaks in very technical jargon that is incomprehensible to the non-data processor. Second, and equally responsible for the miscommunication, is the failure of the user to ask to have the jargon explained.

What is data-processing jargon?

Data-processing jargon, or computerese, can be divided into three different dialects: professional, technical, and organizational. Let's explain the dialects first and then review the need for learning them.

Professional dialect

The data-processing profession is associated with a body of terms that define the business of the profession. We have already discussed many of these terms, such as data base, file, record, and so on. This is the language of data-processing professionals, and it describes the tools that they use, the methods by which they work (e.g., systems development life cycle), and the jobs and tasks within the profession (e.g., systems analysts). Members of the profession must know these terms, and the people who talk to these professionals also need to know some of their language.

When you go to a doctor, you don't need to know all of the medical terms in order to discuss your problem; however, the more you know, the better. Terms like electrocardiogram, blood pressure, temperature, and hardening of the arteries should have meaning to the non-medical person. If you do not know any of these terms, you can still communicate with the doctor, but not nearly as well.

Technical dialect

The vendors who produce the computers and the operating systems that make the computer work describe their product in technical terms, such as BTAM. This tells the data-processing professional some valuable information about what the vendor is offering and how the product works. However, this information may be of minimal value to the non-data-processing professional.

A suitable analogy is a doctor who uses medicine or diagnostic techniques to cure the patient. This type of information has to do with cure rather than diagnosis. The language that is of most interest to the user, however, is related to diagnosis rather than to the structure of the solution.

Company dialect

In an organization, and in a data-processing department, a whole language evolves that describes how the organization functions. Each organization has its own language that may have evolved over a period of years. Much of this language is known throughout the organization, but some of it is unique to specific departments in the organization. The data-processing department is no exception. This is the type of language that users must understand in order to survive computer systems.

In our medical example, the language would relate to such things as the name of our medical insurance policy (e.g., Blue Cross), the form numbers that we have to fill out (e.g., form T), our policy number (e.g., policy number N376285), and so on. We would find it difficult to survive an illness without being able to speak this language.

How does communication occur?

A good working relationship between data-processing professionals and users requires effort by both parties. It's like a marriage. Each party must feel that they are giving 75% or the relationship doesn't work.

Unfortunately, few users take the time and effort that is necessary to develop a good working relationship with data-processing personnel, even though the expenditure of that effort usually is rewarded. As with any other aspect of data processing, the communication process can be broken down into its component steps. The steps for the user are different than those for the data processor.

How users talk to data-processing personnel

In order to develop good communication with data-processing personnel, it is necessary for the user to:

1. Understand the basic data-processing terminology (professional dialect). Most of the terms you will need are included in the glossary at the end of this book.
2. Recognize that it will take time and effort to develop a good dialogue.
3. Make the data-processing professional explain every word or phrase that you do not understand. Write them down and learn them so that the explanation need not be repeated. However, be sure you understand it.
4. Take your data-processing colleague to lunch. It's important to know your colleagues both professionally and socially. One of the major ingredients for improving communication is to know the person you are talking to on a first-name basis. This means more than just knowing their first name; it means knowing a little bit about how the person lives, what they like, and who they are.
5. Appreciate the time and effort that the data-processing professional must expend in order to explain data-processing concepts and terminology to you.
6. Know what you want as a user and be willing to spend the same time and effort in explaining your needs, requirements, and jargon to the data-processing person.

How data processing people talk to users

In most organizations, data processing is a service: data processors sell and the users buy. Therefore, data processors have the added obligation of explaining their role to the user in order to satisfy the latter's needs, as well as improving the image and professionalism of data processing and its personnel.

The data-processing professional should take the following steps when talking to the user:

1. Try to minimize the amount of jargon.
2. When using jargon, regardless of the dialect, make sure that the user understands the meaning of the terms and the impact of the concepts on the fulfillment of their needs.
3. Take the time and effort to learn user jargon and needs. If the

Checklist 5-1. Communication Self-Assessment Guide

Question	*Response* Yes	No	N/A	Other
1. Do you understand the types of problems (i.e., conflicts) that occur in data-processing systems that need to be resolved?	____	____	____	____________
2. Do you have a directory of data-processing people with whom you need to interact?	____	____	____	____________
3. Have you made an effort to meet the data-processing people with whom you will interact personally (e.g., go to lunch with them)?	____	____	____	____________
4. Do you understand basic data-processing concepts and terminology (i.e., professional dialects)?	____	____	____	____________
5. Do you document your needs before you talk to the data-processing person, in order not to waste their time?	____	____	____	____________
6. Do you ask data-processing personnel to clarify terms you don't understand?	____	____	____	____________
7. Do you always attempt to satisfy your problems at the lowest level possible in the data-processing organization?	____	____	____	____________
8. If you don't get the results you need from talking to your usual contact, do you go to higher levels of management?	____	____	____	____________

user uses terminology that is unfamiliar to the data processor, the latter should find out what the term means and write it down so that the explanation need not be repeated.

4. Take a user to lunch. It's just as important for a data-processing person to get to know the user as it is for the user to get to know the data-processing person; besides that's two lunches out!
5. Spend whatever time is necessary to understand fully what the user wants. This may be an involved interaction, but it is essential in order to avoid implementation of unnecessary or incorrect requirements.

Communication checklist

Checklist 5-1 is a self-checklist for people who wish to communicate with data-processing people. It is designed to quiz you on both your preparation for such discussions and your ability to discuss your needs with these professionals. Items to which you answer "no" should spur you to do some additional study so that you will be better prepared for effective communication with data-processing personnel.

Conclusion

It is easier to talk than it is to say something worthwhile. This chapter simply has said to think before you talk and be prepared to talk in a language that is understandable to the person with whom you are talking. It also suggests that you speak to the person who can perform the action that will give you the desired results. Try spending that extra time and effort preparing and talking; you will like it. It has been known to provide amazing results.

6/ How to talk to the computer

Introduction

A leading expert in computer systems recently characterized the past twenty years in systems development as a "great rip-off."[1] In essence, the author cited the major disappointments that practically all organizations involved in the development of computerized systems experience. These disappointments include:

The wrong system. The system did not do what it was supposed to do. This occurred because either (1) no one knew exactly what the new system was supposed to do, or (2) the system proposed simply was not technologically feasible.

Cost was too high. The history of systems development indicates that costs that exceed budget is the rule rather than the exception. It is not at all uncommon for projects to be completed at three to four times the cost originally projected.

Delivery is delayed. The general rule has been that many projects are not completed in a timely manner. Systems may be a year or more late when they are finally delivered, and then they may not accomplish what the user desires.

Obviously, such a track record is of concern to the systems manager. If an organization can manage the development of new construction projects or marketing plans effectively, why can't it do the same for the development of information systems? Fortunately, the state of the art in systems development is now reaching a point where development projects can be controlled better. This chapter will discuss some of the methodologies an organization can use to survive the systems development process and to achieve systems that are controlled, auditable, and cost beneficial and that meet user needs.

[1]Harry T. Larson, "EDP: A 20 Year Ripoff," *Infosystems*, November 1974.

Most systems failures result from lack of planning before, during, and after the systems development process. The systems development process presented in this chapter emphasizes the organizational planning necessary for a successful process.

New systems development versus systems maintenance

What is a new system? When does a major modification of an existing system evolve from a maintenance project and become a new systems development? Should the same methodology for project control be applied to new systems developments and maintenance projects? It has been estimated that 75 percent of major systems efforts in the next few years might be classified as systems maintenance rather than systems development.

The distinction between new systems developments and systems maintenance is important because of the differences in the amount of time involved, length of the project, and the appropriate control methodologies. We will define new systems development as follows:

> A new systems development is a project that requires a significant development effort (i.e., three months or longer) in which the systems analysts and the user explore alternatives to satisfy user needs better. The system to be developed is not encumbered by a predisposed specification of how items are to be handled or processed.

We will define a systems maintenance project as follows:

> A systems maintenance project is one that requires a modification to an existing system (in particular, the program component of the system) to (1) correct errors, (2) improve processing efficiency, (3) improve the quality of user output (reports or documents), or (4) adapt the system to new government regulations or environmental changes. A systems maintenance project usually should take three months or less to complete.

Other approaches have been used to distinguish systems development from systems maintenance. One large company distinguishes between development and maintenance on the basis of cost. For example, all projects that cost more than $25,000 are considered to be development projects, while those

Table 6-1. Comparison of New Systems Developments with Systems Maintenance

Comparison Base	*New Systems Developments*	*Systems Maintenance*
Length of time to complete	Long (usually > 3 months)	Short (< 3 months, or as little as 1-2 hours).
Cost	Large	Generally small.
User participation	Active	Generally only a request for modification.
Scope	Can be large, affecting multiple users or processes.	Narrow, focusing on improvement in existing system.
New analysis required	Yes. Not constrained by current method of data processing.	No. Usually a correction, improvement, modification, or enhancement of current system.
Susceptibility to formal controls	High	Partial. Degree of controls likely will vary with type of maintenance.
Examples	Develop a comprehensive system to coordinate and centralize information that pertain to all aspects of employee fringe benefit programs and associated federal and state regulations.	Change the existing payroll program to incorporate new wage schedules and new state and federal tax withholding schedules.
	Develop a management information simulation system to aid in making decisions regarding new store locations.	Change the format of a management report to include a more detailed breakdown of product expense (data already are gathered and processed by the system).

Table 6-1. Comparison of New Systems Developments with Systems Maintenance (continued)

Comparison Base	*New Systems Developments*	*Systems Maintenance*
Examples *(cont.)*	Develop a system to implement better reporting and inventory control using point-of-sale equipment.	Fix an error in an existing program that has just caused the system to "crash."

that cost less than $25,000 are considered to be maintenance and are subject to different controls. The major point is the difference in methodology. Table 6-1 presents some examples of new systems developments and maintenance projects. The methods that are effective in building good new systems are also effective in maintaining existing systems.

Surviving systems development

The data-processing function exists to provide service to other parts of the organization. Thus, it is important that control of new systems or of the data-processing function is not left solely in the hands of the data-processing staff. Rather, control should begin with the organization and include at least the following:

- An EDP steering committee (or its equivalent).
- A coordinated philosophy regarding the systems effort (long-range systems plan).
- A trained, participatory user group (user role).
- A systematic approach or framework for developing new systems (system development life cycle) including (1) company standards regarding new system developments and control requirements; (2) a well-trained, organized data-processing function; and (3) an internal audit staff trained in EDP.

Computer Survival Rule #35

Data processing is too important a function to be left entirely in the hands of data-processing personnel.

EDP steering committee

The existence of an active EDP steering committee exhibits a strong management commitment to the data-processing function. As it generally is conceived, an EDP steering committee is composed of members at the vice-presidential level in the organization. This assures the committee of a corporatewide view of data-processing issues that affect the organization. By establishing an EDP steering committee, management recognizes that a well-managed data-processing function is a corporate resource.

The EDP steering committee generally is responsible for reviewing requests for new developments, resolving problems posed by conflicting requests, and monitoring the development and implementation of new systems. An analogy can be made between the EDP steering committee and a capital budgeting committee. Both are concerned with optimal allocation of resources and successful completion of budgeted projects.

An EDP steering committee is effective in insulating the data-processing manager from conflicting pressures that might arise among various user groups. If such a committee did not exist, there might be a tendency to give greatest priority to projects whose proponents were the most vocal rather than to projects offering the greatest long-term benefits.

Long-range systems plan

Successful information systems begin with a sound long-range plan. The existence of a master systems plan recognizes that resources are scarce and that the organization must plan future systems developments carefully. The plan should consider both information needs and data-processing needs and usually should include organizational goals and objectives; an inventory and assessment of current processing capabilities; an analysis of proposed systems and their priorities; a forecast of developments that affect the plan; and an implementation schedule.

The components of the master systems plan are shown in more detail in Figure 6-1. The plan provides a structure for new developments in the EDP area. However, the master plan should not be regarded as absolute. Rather, it should change along with changes in both organizational environment and technology. The plan should be reviewed and revised as necessary on an annual basis.

Figure 6-1. Components of a Master Systems Plan

I. Organizational Goals and Objectives

- A. Competive goals that affect data-processing or information systems
- B. Forecasts of management information needs
- C. Forecasts of environmental/regulatory changes
- D. Organizational constraints, such as management philosophy or organization structure
- E. Objectives and role of information systems
- F. Organizational structure of information systems

II. Assessment of Current Capabilities

- A. Inventory and assessment of current and approved systems
  - 1. Status of systems
    - a developed
      - 1. working well
      - 2. require maintenance
      - 3. require substantial maintenance or new development
    - b. in progress
  - 2. Summary of significant deficiencies
- B. Inventory and assessment of current equipment
  - 1. Equipment and capabilities
    - a. main processing unit
    - b. peripheral equipment
    - c. operating system
  - 2. Current utilization
    - a. capacity utilization by component
    - b. analysis of expense
- C. Inventory and assessment of current generalized software
  - 1. Systems software
  - 2. Data-base management system
  - 3. Audit and security software
  - 4. Other
- D. Inventory and assessment of current personnel and associated skills
- E. Assessment of current strengths and weakness
- F. Identification of priorities

III. Analysis of Proposed Systems and Their Priorities

- A. Systems approved
- B. Proposals under consideration
- C. Assessment of information needs to meet organizational goals (part I)

Figure 6-1. Components of a Master Systems Plan (continued)

IV. Forecast of Future Developments Affecting Plan

A. Technological developments (computers and processing alternatives made available by technological advances)
B. Competitive developments
C. Audit and control requirements
D Government or other external user needs

V. Current Implementation Schedule

A. Projects in progress (e.g., analysis of time, personnel required, and processing requirements)
B. Projects committed
C. Flex time (i.e., time built in to accommodate unexpected developments)

User role in new developments

The organization's approach to analysis of and response to user needs and requests also may affect the types of controls, such as chargeout schemes, that might be implemented to control systems developments. The three major approaches to new systems developments are data analysis (often referred to as bottom-up), decision analysis (referred to as top-down), and data base.

Data analysis and decision analysis focus on user functions or decisions; as such, they should include user participation in the design (and in the request for design and responsibility for costs) of the system. The data base may take many forms. One form that is discussed most often views data as a resource marketed by the data-processing department.

Data analysis

The data analysis approach, sometimes referred to as the bottom-up approach, focuses on data that are received currently by a manager in order to determine (1) what data a manager receives currently, and (2) what data the manager needs but does not receive currently. This approach relies heavily on analysis of existing documents and manager-analyst interaction. The basic approach is as follows:

1. Examine all reports, files, and other information sources drawn on by the manager.
2. Discuss with the manager the use of each piece of information examined.
3. Eliminate unnecessary information.
4. Determine unfulfilled information needs through interaction with the manager.

In summary, the data analysis approach involves analysis of the manager's existing information flow to determine what information is no longer required, what information should be retained, and what new information is needed. Information that no longer is required is eliminated; information that is still required is provided by the information system applications where appropriate. The user department can pursue either an active or a passive role in such an approach. The analyst must rely heavily on the user because the user is more intimately familiar with the complexities of their decisions. For budgeting and control purposes, the approach may be considered user oriented.

Decision analysis

The decision analysis approach is more free form than the data analysis approach. That is, the analyst is not influenced by the content of information that the manager receives currently. Rather, the focus is on the decisions made in the organization. The analyst's aim is to (1) determine the decisions to be made, and (2) develop a model of the decision process to ascertain what information is relevant to that decision. An outline of the decision approach is as follows:

1. Determine major decision responsibilities through discussions with managers.
2. Determine policy and organizational objectives relevant to the decision areas.
3. Determine specific steps required to complete each major decision.

4. Develop a model (flowchart) of each decision.
5. Examine flowchart to determine what information is required at each step in the decision.

With this approach, the analyst first must determine the major decision responsibilities that are consistent with organizational policies and objectives. The decision-making steps and information needs are then articulated into a decision flowchart, a decision table, or some other information-gathering device.

Data base

The data-base approach recognizes that the information needs of the organization and individual decision makers will change over time. The approach treats data as a separate, important organizational resource that should be subject to the same kind of competitive protection as other important resources. Data bases will exist for logically related data, such as sales, customers, and part numbers. Decision makers will interact with the data-base administrator and the data-base management system to obtain both regular and special decision reports.

The data-base approach differs from the first two approaches in that it focuses on data rather than on decisions or processing of data. Whereas the other approaches are application oriented, the data-base approach is data oriented. The following are some guidelines that have been proposed for the data-base approach:

1. The data base must be built for the whole company, not for individual managers.
2. Data-base development must follow a logical, well-orchestrated plan, not the path of least resistance.
3. Data processing must be intended to improve overall productivity by supplying accurate information based on management needs, not be justified through cost reductions based on personnel replacement.
4. Management must concentrate primarily on identification of the information it needs.
5. Data processing must control what is stored on the computer and how.
6. Company input responsibilities should be established and funded separately from output needs.
7. Data-processing departments must be given increased re-

sponsibility for input control and data integrity and, accordingly, authority for defining and obtaining required input.

8. Investments in hardware, software, and personnel must be based on the needs of the data-base control systems, not on requirements for specific applications.

Comparison of systems approaches

The data analysis approach is the approach used most widely, since it is both user oriented and data oriented. It is a tangible approach to building systems. The approach also has been criticized on the grounds that it can lead to (1) the generation of excess information, and (2) the omission of other data that are more relevant to a particular decision-making process.

The decision analysis approach has been offered as an alternative or a supplement to the data analysis approach. The advocates of the former claim that it is more forward looking and less constrained by existing organizational systems. Some of its critics complain that many decision makers do not fully understand their decision-making process and thus are not able to establish all the relevant factors. Other critics contend that the decision analysis approach leads to the development of models that managers cannot use and that fail to incorporate all aspects of important decisions.

The relative merits of the data analysis and decision analysis approaches are shown in Table 6-2. Neither approach is seen as the most appropriate approach to new systems developments. Some have argued that the data analysis approach is best, since it relies on situations that are well understood, such as routine, repetitive tasks. On the other hand, the decision analysis approach may be particularly beneficial in poorly understood, less routine, less repetitive situations. It is argued that the experience of attempting to construct a decision model for poorly understood situations is often beneficial for the participant.

From the user's standpoint, both approaches are oriented toward development of specific applications to meet user needs. Thus, both approaches will likely emerge from user department requests. It would be appropriate to charge users for the development of such systems and hold users responsible for the implementation and successful operation of the system.

The data-base approach is not application oriented. Rather, it is a logical construct that essentially involves storage of data, not information. It is up to the data-processing managers and

Table 6-2. Comparison of Data Analysis and Decision Analysis Approaches

Approach	*Advantages*	*Disadvantages*
Data analysis	Useful for structured decisions.	Requires managers to articulate information needs.
	Resultant information flow may provide greater flexibility.	Information needs not linked to decision and organizational objectives.
		No established procedures or standards.
Decision analysis	Explicitly links information needs to decisions and organizational objectives.	Information requirements may change if manager is replaced.
	Provides uniform results independent of analyst involved.	May be difficult to specify decision process in some situations.
	Useful for unstructured decisions.	
	Information tailored to personal decision-making style.	
	Improves decision process and information flow.	

the users to specify what data they need for a specific situation. This aspect may be very similar to the decision analysis approach. However, in the data-base environment, the data-processing manager must assume more responsibility for the completeness, integrity, and security of the data because the data are shared and are not the responsibility of individual user areas.

In the future, the three approaches to new systems developments will most likely exist in large organizations. The database approach is just emerging but should become much more commonplace with the continuing technological developments in the computer field. All three approaches will require the development of greater standardization and attention to such areas as data definitions, processing, and security.

Computer Survival Rule #36

Of all the systems development approaches, the best one is the one with heavy user involvement.

The systems development life cycle: a framework for planning and control

The development of new information systems in an organization ought to be planned and controlled as befits a major organizational expenditure on a competitive and necessary resource. The systems development life cycle (SDLC) presents such a framework for the development of new applications. Essentially, the SDLC recognizes that all new applications go through the same stages of development, and that these stages are identifiable and controllable. Further, the SDLC recognizes user's, data processer's, top management's, and auditor's responsibilities for the development of information systems that meet organizational needs and are well controlled and auditable.

The SDLC methodology is applicable to systems that have been approved and budgeted for development. The SDLC divides the systems development process into a small number of distinct phases with formal management control points between and during each phase. The objectives are to (1) provide a more structured management scheme for controlling costs and schedules, and (2) ensure proper and responsive communications channels among users, auditors, hardware, planning, personnel, top management, and data processors who are responsible for developing the application systems.

The number of phases in the SDLC vary according to how broadly or narrowly each phase is defined. Further, it should be recognized that the SDLC is project oriented. Systems will continue to change over time; there is no definite starting or ending point to a system's development. The SDLC provides a methodology for managing major new systems developments.

Table 6-3 presents a six-phase SDLC. The first four phases are referred to as the design phases, and the last two are referred to as postinstallation phases. Management risks associated with each phase are identified in column 3. The primary and secondary personnel requirements are shown in column 4. It should be noted that the methodology includes substantial analyst and user involvement, along with a defined role for the internal auditor.

A brief review of the SDLC presented in Table 6-3 indicates the following major issues:

Major Issues	*Primary Responsibility*
1. Allocating scarce resources to the best projects for the organization.	1. Steering committee determines the allocation. Users and systems analyst provide documentary support for alternatives.
2. Efficient project management.	2. Systems design team (analyst and users), with review and accountability to steering committee or its equivalent.
3. Development of systems that are controlled and auditable.	3. Systems design team (analyst and users), with review by internal auditors.

While many organizations devote considerable attention to the management of systems development projects, it is equally important that the organization have a mechanism to (1) allocate its resources efficiently to the right projects, and (2) ensure that the systems developed exhibit both integrity and control.

The actual number of phases will vary with each company. We will now look briefly at each phase and its major activities and control points.

Feasibility study

The feasibility study begins either when a user or management recognizes a need to improve a current system or to develop a

Table 6-3. Systems Development Life Cycle

Phases	Major Activities	Management Risks	Personnel Involvement: Primary	Personnel Involvement: Secondary
Design Phases				
1. Feasibility Assessment	Develop project proposal; prepare cost/benefit study; decide whether to proceed with the system; prepare time and cost budgets.	Risk of committing resources to an improperly formulated proposal (highest risk of applicable failure occurs at this point).	Users Systems Analyst	Steering Committee
2. Information Analysis and Systems Design	Determine information requirements for new system.	Risk of developing a system that is not suited to user needs; risk of conceptually developing a system that is physically inoperable (one of the two highest areas of cost incurrence).	Users Systems Analyst	Internal Audit Steering Committee
	Develop system and program specifications; determine equipment requirements; make equipment decision, if necessary; further define user needs; define security and audit needs.	Risk of ignoring needed processing controls; risk of poor design from operating standpoint.	Systems Analyst Users	Internal Audit

3. Procedure and Program Development	Code and debug programs; develop user manuals; develop processing manuals.	Risk of ignoring controls to be built into the programs and for processing outside the computer; risk of cost overrun.	Systems Analyst Users Programmers	Internal Audit
4. Testing and Conversion	Test the system; transfer processing to new system; educate users.	Risk of not testing controls fully; risk of implementing new system before all components are ready.	Systems Analyst Users Programmers EDP Quality Assurance	Internal Audit
Postinstallation Phases				
5. Operation and Maintenance	Modify as necessary; maintain ongoing operations.	Inadequate security provisions; improper, incomplete, or inadequate processing of data; inadequate liaison with users and input personnel; inefficient usage of data processing resource.	Users Data-Processing Quality Assurance Data-Processing Operations	Internal Audit
6. Postaudit	Critically review systems accomplishments in terms of time, cost/benefit, and user satisfaction. Recommend improvements for future developments.	System does not achieve objectives, and there is little chance for change.	Data-Processing Operations Users Data-Processing Maintenance personnel Internal Audit, Quality Assurance Function	

new way of handling processing needs or providing management information. In essence, the feasibility study is a ministudy of the current system and alternatives.

The major tasks associated with the feasibility study are (1) identification of systems alternatives, and (2) evaluation of the costs and benefits associated with systems alternatives. In many organizations, one system to be considered is the system already in use. An analysis of the present system, including its costs, limitations, and flexibility in handling future processing volumes, will serve as a base against which other alternatives can be compared.

Feasibility also implies practicality. Thus, the feasibility study should assess whether the proposed alternatives are compatible either with current facilities or with those proposed on the master systems development plan. The study also should contain an assessment of whether proposed system alternatives meet the minimum audit and security requirements.

On completion of these tasks, the proposed system is presented (along with other proposed systems) to the EDP steering committee, which is charged with making the first decision on whether or not to proceed with systems development. We say first decision here because the steering committee (or its equivalent) should reassess the project at key checkpoints to assess whether the organization should continue development of the project. If the decision is made to proceed, the project moves into the information analysis and systems design stage.

Information analysis and systems design

The information analysis and systems design phase consists of three major tasks: determination of the information requirements, development of the conceptual design to meet those requirements, and development of systems specifications to implement the system. Since this is the first major phase after approval of the project, the initial objective is the organization and planning of the systems development task. A project team must be structured and task responsibilities defined. Planning must occur to ensure the development process is controlled.

The design process proceeds from establishment of the information requirements within a logical design to the specifications for the actual systems design. At the end of the phase, the users evaluate the design and sign off if they are satisfied. Internal auditors should review the design for adequacy of controls and auditability. Finally, any significant changes in the estimates of costs and benefits associated with the system are reviewed by the EDP steering committee, and another decision will be made on the continuance of the project.

The total expenditures on a system through the information analysis and design stage generally will be about 40 percent of the total expected expenditures. It is important to note that, throughout this stage, (1) no programming has yet been performed, and (2) it is not too late to reassess the project's benefits or other features. In fact, it is essential at this point that the organization not only be convinced of the project's benefits, but also that it be convinced of the auditability and security that are built into the system.

Procedure and program development

The procedure and program development phase includes preparation and testing of computer programs, development of manual procedures and the attendant forms, and development of user manuals. As with the previous phases, some activities will be performed in parallel fashion.

During most of this phase, the programmer and systems analyst work on parallel projects. Since the key designs that are settled during this phase are crucial to the future success of the system, users should review the design for understandability and compatibility with the nature of operations. Internal auditors should review this phase to assess the adequacy of controls.

Testing and conversion

The testing and conversion phase consists of final testing of the developed system, and conversion from the previous system to the newly developed system. The first segment of this phase consists of a major test of the system and the training of all affected personnel in the operation of the system. The responsibility for testing should rest jointly with the users and data-processing personnel. One might wonder why users, who are not experts in either control or data processing, should be expected to be responsible for the adequacy of controls and the testing of the system. Actually, the answer is quite simple: *it is the user's system*. None of us are likely to buy a car without taking it out for a test run. The users know the types of transactions the system must handle and all the unusual fluctuations in processing that can be expected over time. Therefore, we argue that users ought to be involved integrally in testing the system before it is accepted for full-time use.

The need for involvement of users does not completely relieve data-processing personnel from responsibilities of testing. In fact, data processing needs to be involved because (1) the system is in part theirs, since they are part of the design team and thus should be part of the testing team; (2) they are knowledgeable about EDP and should be aware of tests that the user might not have considered; and (3) the responsibility for maintenance and control of the computerized aspects of the system falls within the area of data processing. Thus, data-processing personnel ensure that the system meets data-processing standards and is compatible with other systems. Along with involvement of data-processing personnel and users, some organizations may require additional testing by a quality assurance group that is a subsection of the data-processing department.

The final task in this phase is conversion from the old system to the new system. Considerable planning is required for successful completion of this phase. Users must be trained in all procedures. Generally there will be a time when both systems run concurrently to ensure that the new system is operating correctly.

Postinstallation phase: operations and maintenance

This phase recognizes that systems are continually evolving. Controls must be established both to ensure that necessary modifications are made to the system and to maintain the system's integrity.

Postaudit

The postaudit is a critical review of the system at some time between six months to a year after conversion. At least a six-month period should elapse to allow the system and its users to adapt to unanticipated operational factors. The postaudit generally is conducted by a task force composed of, for example, an internal auditor, a data-processing representative, and a user representative who is not involved in the project's design. This group should be as independent as possible from the design group in order to achieve an unbiased postaudit.

The postaudit is intended to provide feedback on the development process and should result in recommendations for improvements in future systems. This type of postaudit should not be confused with either the operational audit of an application by an internal auditor or with the normal type of audit made by the external auditor. The scope of the postaudit is much more limited and focuses on the particular system that has just been developed. In some organizations, the postaudit may be conducted by a quality assurance function, which is an independent group within the data-processing department.

Computer Survival Rule #37

Systems are not works of art; they require blueprints. The SDLC is the blueprint for a successful system.

How to prevent systems failure

Users' involvement has been cited as the key to systems success. Few systems fail when the user(s) take the time and effort to participate in each phase of the SDLC—that is, *real* participation by people who can make decisions. One data-processing department refused to develop systems unless the user guaranteed to invest sufficient time in the project, deemed by that organization to be 25 percent of the total systems development effort.

Users of data-processing services should ensure that adequate survival procedures are established in their organization to prevent systems failures. Some of the major survival procedures, those proved by practice, are listed in Table 6-4.

Computer Survival Rule #38

Computer system users should be prepared. Systems survival means installation of procedures during the SDLC that will minimize the probability of failure.

Table 6-4. Major Systems Development Survival Procedures

Procedure	*Description*
Sign-off Procedures	Checkpoints are built into various subphases of the development process. At the completion of each phase, the user, systems analyst, and internal auditor must sign off that the design meets users' and organizational needs, meets audit and integrity standards, and is worthy of further development.
Steering Committee	Consists of top organizational executives (e.g., vice presidents) who have the responsibility for allocating resources among competing projects and monitoring project developments.
Project Team Structure	Project teams are structured to include systems analysts, users, and programmers. Methodologies are adopted to promote active participation.
Internal Audit Review	The internal audit department participates in systems developments by reviewing development for the adequacy of application controls and/or reviewing the SDLC procedures for compliance with company policies.
Documentation Standards	The company (primarily data processing with internal audit review) develops documentation standards that communicate necessary information, enable the company to be programmer- or analyst-independent, and provide a sound basis for systems maintenance.
Development Standards	The organization develops standards (e.g., a defined SDLC) that specify the approach and involvement required in any new systems development.
Application Control Standards	The organization defines minimum security, integrity, and application controls standards (including minimum audit trail) that must be met in the development of any new system.
Programming Standards	Standards are developed that specify the way programming is to be done,

Table 6-4. Major Systems Development Survival Procedures (continued)

Procedure	*Description*
	including programming languages, methodology (e.g., structured programming), testing standards, and required program documentation.
Testing Standards	Specifies minimum testing requirements and testing responsibilities for all new systems.
Quality Assurance Review or Data-Processing Operations Review and Acceptance of Responsibility	A review is made of the system's compliance with data-processing standards. If performed by the operations section of data processing, the data-processing manager must consider acceptance of the responsibility for the operation of the system and thus must be willing to assert that (a) the system contains necessary documentation, (b) the system is operationally feasible in the current operating environment, (c) adequate operating manuals are included, and (d) the system is ready to use.

Talking-to-the-computer checklist

Users of data-processing services continually need to communicate with computer people about systems. The communication is concerned with new systems and with enhancements and corrections to existing systems. The right results only happen when needs and solutions can be communicated effectively.

The talking-to-the-computer checklist is designed to help you assess your ability to discuss systems development, enhancement, and error correction with data-processing personnel. If you can answer most of the questions affirmatively, you should feel confident in discussing your needs with data-processing personnel. However, if you are uncertain (i.e., give a "no" response), then you should read this section more carefully in an effort to grasp the communication concepts necessary to help you tell computer personnel what you want.

Checklist 6-1. Talking-to-the-Computer Checklist

Question	*Response* Yes	No	N/A	Other
1. Do you understand the major disappointments that organizations experience as they develop computerized systems?	____	____	____	____
2. Do you understand the differences between new systems development and systems maintenance?	____	____	____	____
3. Does your organization have different procedures for new systems development than for systems maintenance?	____	____	____	____
4. Does your organization have an EDP steering committee?	____	____	____	____
5. Has your organization established a long-range systems plan?	____	____	____	____
6. Are your users trained in how to interact with data-processing personnel during systems development?	____	____	____	____
7. Has your data-processing organization established a systematic approach or framework for development of new systems, such as an SDLC?	____	____	____	____
8. If your organization has an internal audit staff, is it trained to audit EDP systems?	____	____	____	____
9. Does your organization have standards for the development of new systems?	____	____	____	____

Checklist 6-1. Talking-to-the-Computer Checklist (continued)

Question	*Response*			
	Yes	*No*	*N/A*	*Other*
10. Does your organization have standards for maintenance of existing systems?	____	____	____	____________
11. Has your organization defined control requirements in the computer environment?	____	____	____	____________
12. Does each new system have an established development schedule?	____	____	____	____________
13. Does each new system have an established development budget?	____	____	____	____________
14. Is systems maintenance scheduled?	____	____	____	____________
15. Is a budget established for each systems change?	____	____	____	____________

Conclusion

This chapter has explored the reasons for failures in the development of new systems and has presented the elements of a control framework to minimize such failures. That framework is the SDLC and the attendant survival procedures that can be built into the structured development of new systems. The role of various participants also was explored. The principal participants in new systems developments are (1) the EDP steering committee, (2) representatives of user departments, (3) data-processing representatives (systems analysts and programmers), and (4) independent reviewers, such as auditors or quality assurance personnel.

7/ Designing systems that people can use

Introduction

The value of a data-processing system depends on whether people can use it effectively. People interface with systems at various points in the processing cycle. The main interface points are the preparation of input, the correction of errors, and the use of the results of processing. If the people who use the system understand fully how the system works and have enough information to act on situations that require their attention, the system will be valuable to the organization. On the other hand, if people have problems, either real or imagined, with the system, the probability of success is limited. Therefore, systems must be designed to meet the needs, capabilities, and desires of the people who use the system in the performance of their tasks.

The objectives of this chapter are to provide a perspective on the role people play in information processing systems; provide an understanding of how new systems affect people and their jobs; discuss what happens when people resist or resent systems; and explain how to design systems so that people's needs are satisfied.

The role of people in systems

People design, implement, operate, and use systems. The makeup of the people involved in these different aspects of the system differs in many ways. People have different educational and cultural backgrounds that cause them to view situations from different perspectives. Some people are content with clerical jobs, others are extremely ambitious and continually strive for promotion. Also, different people view the value of their work in the organization differently. Some feel it doesn't matter whether or not they do their job, while others see themselves as indispensable to the organization.

Figure 7-1. Interrelation of People, Rules, and Data

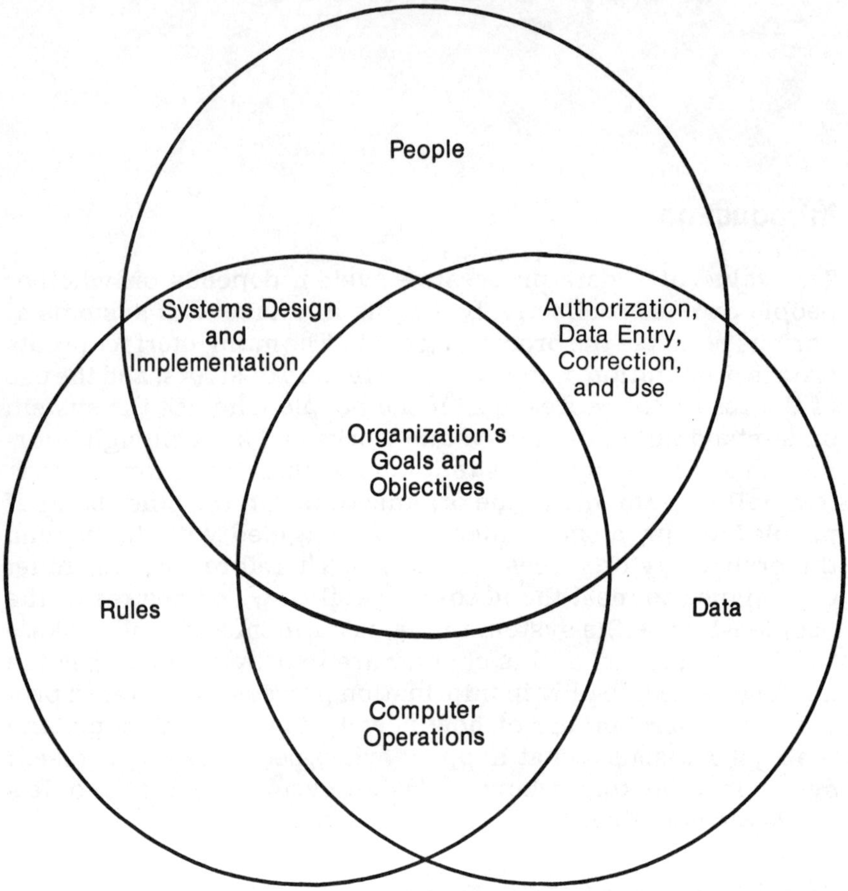

There is a natural tendency on the part of systems designers to build systems for people who are like themselves. Frequently, the result is a system that is too complicated for the user whose background and education differ from those of the designer. In addition, the user may receive the impression from the designer that the designer knows more about what is needed than the user knows. True, the designer knows more about designing systems than the user; however, the designer cannot design a successful system without considering the user's needs, qualifications, and support.

Interrelation of people, data, and rules

The three components of meeting an organization's goals and objectives are people, data, and rules. In studying systems, rules and data may tend to be overemphasized. But in reality, *people* make the system successful. When systems designers emphasize the role of people, the effectiveness of their systems improves greatly.

The center of Figure 7-1 shows that all three components are directed toward achievement of the organization's goals and objectives. People interface with systems in the design and implementation aspects. People and data interface in authorization of transactions, data entry, data correction, and data use. Data and systems interface in computer operations that pass the data through the system and when the rules built into the system are applied to the data.

The interrelation of people, rules, and data must be kept in harmony. Whenever disharmony appears in any one of the interface points, the organization's goals and objectives will not be met. Depending on the degree of disharmony, the results can range from annoying problems to bankruptcy.

Types of people involved in systems

Systems are complex processing networks that interface with most functions of an organization at various times. Certain functions of the organization interface with different parts of the system. For example, the accounts receivable function interfaces with the billing system for credit sales.

Figure 7-2 illustrates the seven groups of people who are involved with systems. It is important that people concerned with the control and integrity of systems understand the interrelation of these seven groups to the system. Here's how they interrelate:

1 *Executive management.* Individuals responsible for authorizing implementation of the system and for delegating authority to users of the system.

2. *Users.* Individual(s) responsible for providing specifications for the system, determining that the system works properly, and ascertaining whether the results are accurate and complete.

Figure 7-2. Categories of People Involved in Systems

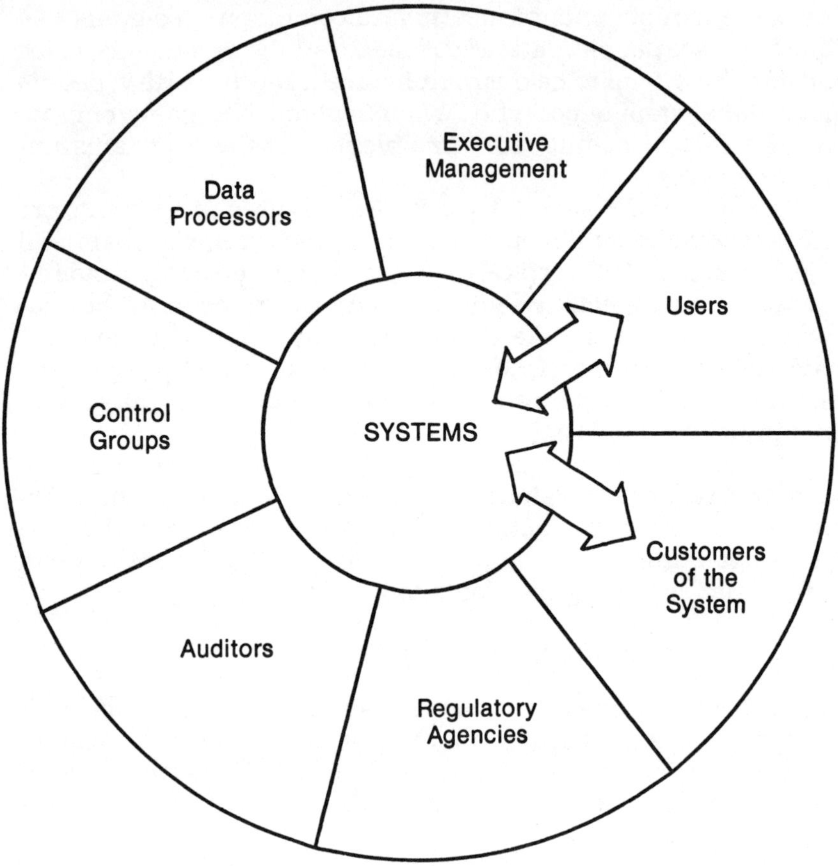

3. *Data processors.* Individuals who design, implement, and operate the systems in accordance with the user's specifications and the organization's policies and procedures.
4. *Customers of the system.* Third parties who either provide transactions (input) for the system or use data from the system. They have neither responsibility for nor authority over the system. However, they need the system in order to process their work.
5. *Regulatory agencies.* Government or other regulators that either specify some aspects of processing of a system or review the results of a system for conformance with govern-

ment regulations. For example, the IRS specifies how tax withholding is to be accomplished.

6. *Auditors.* Independent persons who are not involved directly in the design or use of the system. They may or may not be employees of the company. Auditors review the system to be sure that it is processing data in accordance with the organization's policies and procedures and that the results of processing are accurate and complete.
7. *Control groups.* Individuals charged with the responsibility of determining that the system is functioning properly on a day-to-day basis.

To illustrate these people's involvement with a system, let us use an example of a savings account system in a bank. Only *executive management* can authorize the development of a new savings account system. The *user,* or savings department, would specify what the system was supposed to do. From those specifications, the *data processors* would determine how the system should be implemented on computer hardware, write the necessary programs, and run the system in accordance with the needs of the user. Depositors of the bank who open savings accounts are *customers* of the system. *Control groups* would ascertain whether the cash received by the tellers balanced with the control totals and that other controls were functioning properly. *Regulatory agencies* specify the percentage of interest the bank can pay, bank reserve against deposits, and so forth. State banking agencies perform periodic reviews to determine the soundness of the bank. *Auditors* periodically check with the bank's customers to confirm that the customer's records agree with the bank's records.

Misuse of the system

The seven groups of people each become involved with systems in different ways. The general system/people relationships include building, maintenance, operation, and use. However, people also can misuse and destroy systems. Destruction of systems can be either intentional or unintentional, and it can happen in a number of different ways. The most common reason for unintentional destruction of systems results from failure to understand how the system operates or failure to follow instructions. Figure 7-3 illustrates the way people use systems, including the "destroy" possibility.

Figure 7-3. Relationships Between Systems and People

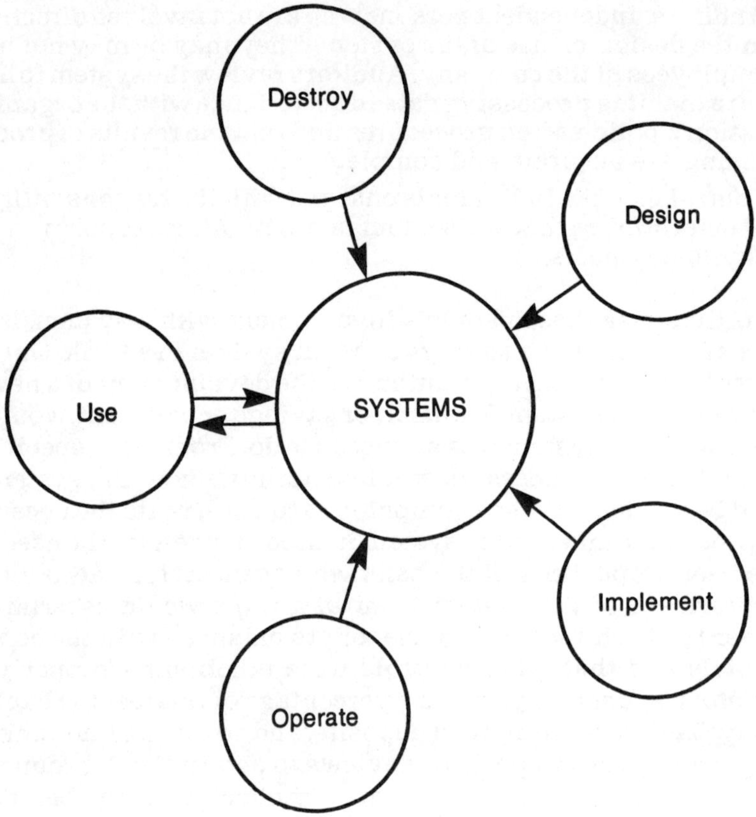

As systems become more complex, fewer and fewer people understand how the total system functions. Without this understanding, they cannot use the system properly. The total system can encompass several computer applications and numerous departments within the organization. In addition, many events are time-dependent activities. Some system events occur weekly, some monthly, some semiannually, and some annually.

Clerical employees who work with computer systems rarely understand how their job fits into the total system. Thus, they do not know how their mistakes affect the system. For example, if a keypunch operator enters a wrong code, an invalid transaction may be accepted or a transaction may be rejected. However, to the operator this signifies only a typing error, which can be corrected easily by punching another card at a later time.

Many clerks feel that large computer systems dehumanize their work, that authority and control are transferred to the computer programs, leaving only perfunctory jobs for people. On the other hand, systems managers recognize the vital importance of the proper preparation of data for computerized applications. This difference in viewpoint must be resolved. Clerical workers who use computer systems must understand the importance of their role in the system.

The single most effective technique for improving performance is education. Once people recognize how their function fits into the total systems concept, they can begin to appreciate the importance of their job. With this understanding, clerical workers react positively to new situations. When clerical workers respond well to unusual situations, the overall systems performance improves.

How people influence systems

Planning is a difficult task for most people, and it doesn't get easier simply because an individual is promoted to a management position. People are more comfortable working with today's problems today than planning for tomorrow's problems today. It should not come as a surprise, then, that management usually exerts its influence on a system just before implementation. Systems analysts usually have little contact with management during the feasibility and systems design phases, even though most major decisions are made during these phases. Once the system is virtually complete, management becomes concerned with the details. If management is to influence systems design, this trend must be reversed.

Figure 7-4 illustrates in what areas management can spend its time most effectively. The figure shows four points in the SDLC. We can see that management exerts only minimal influence during the early life cycle phases and very heavy influence just before implementation. Unfortunately, it is at the implementation phase of systems development that changes are the most difficult and costly. If a change costs $1 at feasibility time, it would cost $16 at implementation time. Thus, management spends its time at a point in the development cycle where it will have the least influence on the overall direction of the system.

Figure 7-4. Management's Influence on the System: Where Time Can Be Spent Most Effectively

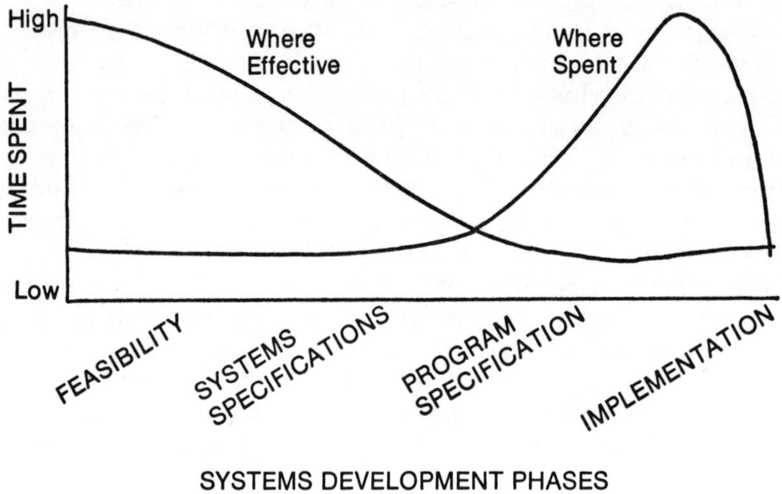

It is also the time when exerting influence is most costly. Management should get involved during the feasibility and systems specification phases, because then making any necessary, drastic changes is easy and economical.

Computer Survival Rule #39

Systems are built by people for people. If systems don't serve people, they are useless.

Systems bring unwanted changes

People like things the way they are. An old business proverb states, "Don't wish for a new king, the old one is bad enough." What this proverb implies is that, no matter how bad things are today, changing them can make them worse. Another way of putting it is that, once you have learned to live with the present system, you know you can survive. However, if a new king is appointed (or if a new system is installed), you may lose your position in the new kingdom.

Simply stated, the problem is that people do not like change, whether it is for the better or for the worse. This does not mean that you should avoid change; rather, it means you should recognize that people resist change. Once the change has been made and people come to accept it, they may be much happier. The systems analyst's job is to make change as painless as possible and to encourage people to accept and support the new system. Unfortunately, many systems analysts do not assume that responsibility. This results in the premature failure of many systems because people cannot or will not adapt to the changes a new system brings.

If individuals think that the changes in a system are threatening in some way, they might try to undermine the system. If they are successful in destroying the system, the threat is eliminated, resulting in peace of mind and greater security for those individuals. You must keep in mind that, whether the threat of the new or changed system is real or imagined, the resulting destruction is real.

Eliminating systems threats to people

People are threatened by systems for many reasons. Some reasons are very personal, such as wanting to work near a particular person. In order to understand the threats systems pose to people, we need to understand why people work. When one of these motivations is threatened, people become very resistant to change.

Many theories have been propounded about human motivation. Perhaps the most commonly accepted theories are those of Maslow. Maslow discusses the satisfaction of needs from the very basic ones, such as hunger, to the highly developed ones, such as self-gratification. From an employer's viewpoint, employees' needs can be summarized as money/benefits, job satisfaction, and human relations.

Figure 7-5 illustrates the three reasons why people work. Different individuals rank these three items differently. For example, many young people work almost exclusively for money. People who earn sufficient money to meet their needs work for either job satisfaction or the relations they build with fellow employees. Human relations include friendships with other people, responsibility as a team member, satisfaction in helping other people, and influence over other people (i.e., hold-

Figure 7-5. Work Triangle

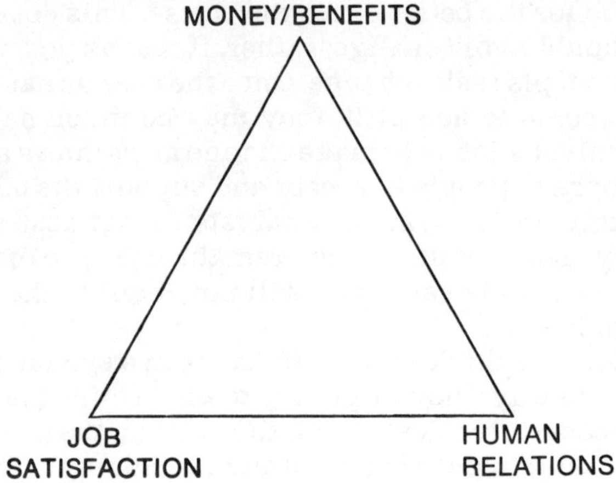

ing positions of power to which others must be subservient during work periods).

Many employees feel very strongly about the human relation factors. The money/benefits motive appears to satisfy the lower needs of Maslow's hierarchy, while job satisfaction appears to fulfill the higher needs. However, the power, responsibility, influence, and friendships that result from working with other people appear to be the strongest motives for most employees. When new systems threaten the human relations, the strongest resistance to change appears. These relations are threatened most when a new or changed system results in reorganization and shifts in responsibility and power. Changes in the content of a job can be dealt with if people's job goals are considered in the design of a new system.

New systems cause job changes

Industrial psychologists suggest that computer systems analysts be called "change makers" because their prime function in installing new systems is to change methods of doing work. New systems make people nervous because each change is a new test of their intelligence and capabilities. This attitude is to be expected, since the goals of many systems are diametrically opposed to the goals of the people they impact. Table 7-1 illustrates how the desires of people and the objectives of systems differ. These differences account for many of the problems that arise when new systems are installed.

Table 7-1. People's Goals Versus Systems Goals

People's Goals	*Systems Goals*
Steady employment	Eliminate people
Challenging job	Simplify tasks
Decision making	Preprogram decisions
Improvement of skills	Increase scope of system

Most people have a series of goals toward which they work. Some of these goals are:

- *Steady employment.* Work for a stable organization that offers job security.
- *Challenging work.* A job so diverse and interesting that the employee does not become bored and frustrated.
- *Decision-making responsibilities.* The opportunity to influence enough aspects of the job to feel they are making a contribution.
- *Improvement of skills.* A continual upgrading of one's abilities to both retain interest in the present job and prepare oneself for advancement.

To understand the threat people perceive from new systems, let's look at the common systems goals. The goals of systems analysts as they design systems tend to be the reverse of people's goals. Systems goals include:

- *Elimination of people* from their system (people want steady employment).
- *Making tasks as simple as possible.* The KISS (Keep It Simple, Stupid) method seems to be the guideline in designing many systems (people like challenging tasks).
- *Preprogrammed decision making* (people want to make the decisions).
- *Increase the system's scope of responsibility* (people want to increase the scope of their own responsibility and influence).

Both people's goals and systems goals are desirable. The problem is integration of the systems goals without dehumanizing people's roles in the system. This can be accomplished by letting the computer do the parts of the system it does best, and by letting the people do what they do best. Computers perform repetitive tasks well, whereas people handle unusual, isolated, one-of-a-kind situations well. For this reason, unusual and special processing procedures are best left to people, while the routine repetitive aspects of the system should be left to computers and business machines.

What is needed is for systems analysts to define clearly the role people will play in systems before they finalize the system specifications. Too frequently people are not considered until the end of the implementation phase. This results in chaos at start-up time for many systems because the employees have neither the training nor the desire to make the new system successful.

Computer Survival Rule #40

Computer systems change people's nice, happy, cozy world. Don't forget it, and do what is necessary to return them to their world.

Understanding change

Change is an interesting phenomenon. We generally recognize the effects of change but rarely understand the causes. We can best understand change by analyzing the results of change.

Because systems cause change, it is essential that systems designers be aware of how change affects people and organizations. Many large companies have industrial psychologists to help systems designers prepare the user for the coming change. If there were only one lesson you could remember from this book, it should be that change has a negative impact on people and organizations. Parties that cause change have a responsibility to prepare those affected by the change. To do this, the systems designer must understand the results of change. Figure 7-6 shows seven typical results associated with change. These results are explained below.

Change initially increases productivity

The Hawthorne studies of the 1930s showed that initially change, regardless of the type, causes an initial increase in productivity.

Figure 7-6. Results of Change

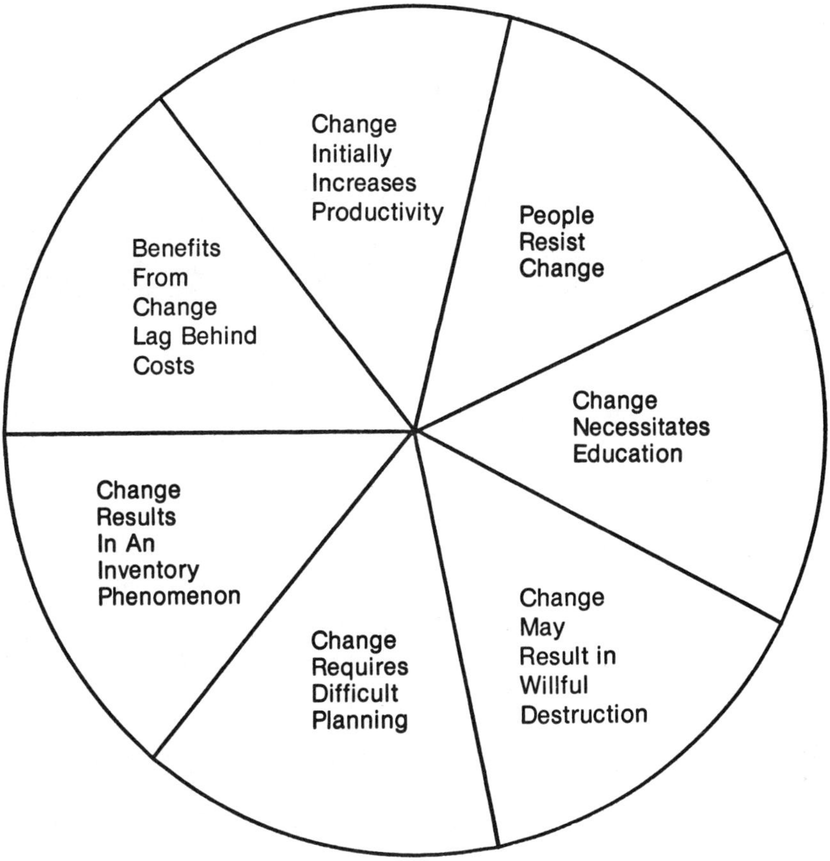

Experiments showed that, if the intensity of light was increased, productivity increased; similarly, if the intensity of light later was diminished, productivity increased again. However, the long-range effect of light change on productivity was negligible. Thus, if you measure productivity immediately before and after change, you can expect to see an immediate increase. If you understand this, then you will study the long-term effects of change to obtain meaningful data.

People resist change

Industrial psychologists state that people resist change of any type. Earlier in this chapter, we explained that successful implementation of change requires that the systems analyst consider people. If the goals and attitudes of people are considered fully, the negative effects of change can be minimized.

Change necessitates education

People cannot be expected to gain insight into change by osmosis. As much time should be spent educating people about the specifics of the change, how it affects jobs, and how people interface with new systems as is spent in development of the systems changes themselves. In many cases, the time and effort spent educating people will exceed that spent in changing the system.

Changes may result in willful destruction

If people are determined to resist change, they may willfully sabotage the system. This sabotage and resistance to change will be covered later in this chapter.

Change requires difficult planning

New systems force people to plan methods and procedures that may not be needed for years. Since the systems change will occur in the future, it requires that people do something they dislike: plan for the future. Therefore, when executive management authorizes systems changes, they also should authorize use of the necessary resources to educate the people involved and obtain commitments of support from them. Individuals involved in a systems change should be given the opportunity to provide input for the designer. Otherwise, systems designers will not have all the information and support they need to build a successful system.

Change causes cost/benefits lag

The cost/benefits lag states that benefits will not appear until long after costs are expended. Figure 7-7 shows that considerable time passes before benefits outweigh the cost of the change. Management usually understands this lag. What may not be understood, however, is the length of time involved. Since this aspect directly affects the return on investment, effort should be spent to reduce the time lag between the investment and the benefits.

Figure 7-7. Cost/Benefits Lag

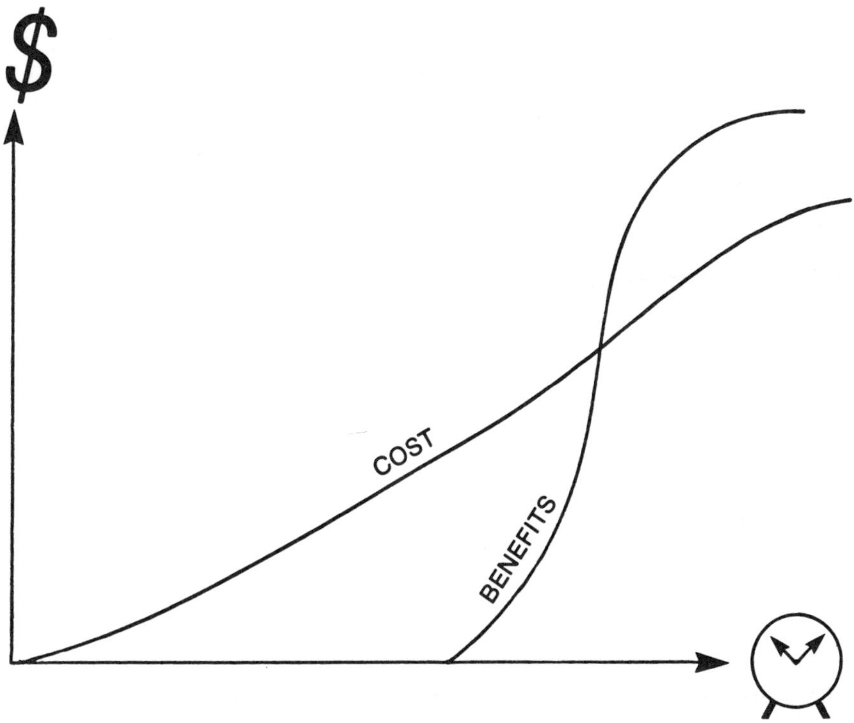

Changes result in an inventory phenomenon

Early designers built computer systems that converted inventory replenishment systems from manual to automatic. The automatic systems based replenishment on current usage data rather than on data that were several weeks or months out of date. The goal of these new systems was to reduce the volume of inventory on hand. The assumption was that continuous monitoring of sales and inventory movement would cause the computer system to reflect change more quickly; thus, smaller amounts of inventory would be needed. The planned result was a decrease in inventory. The actual result was that the inventory immediately increased (see Figure 7-8). Analysis showed that the computer system immediately ordered understocked items but could not correct for overstocked items. The result? Inventory increased. Since this phenomenon is experienced with many systems, it must be recognized by both systems designers

Figure 7-8. Inventory Phenomenon

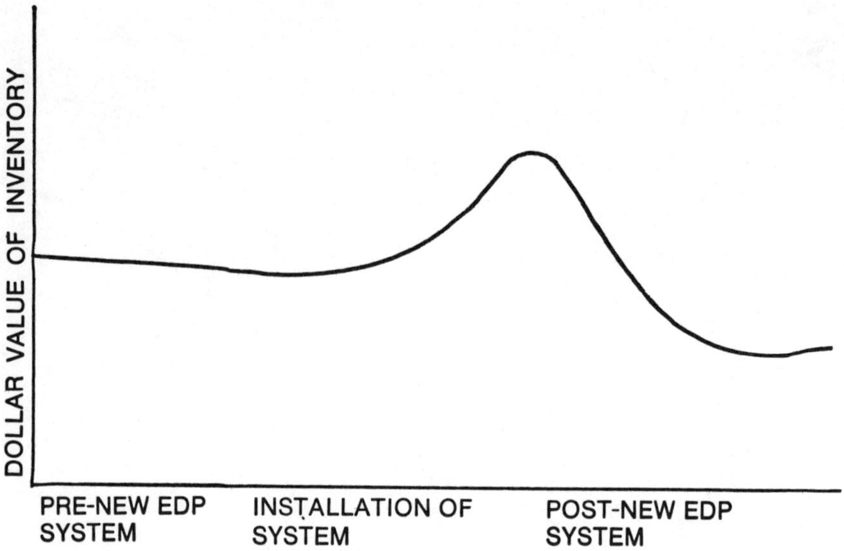

and management so that no one will be surprised when it happens.

Once we understand the results of change and how change affects people, we can begin to engineer systems for people to use.

Computer Survival Rule #41

Change should be managed like any other organizational function.

Engineering systems for people

Systems have to be built with the user in mind. A major cause of systems failure during the past decade has been the complexity of systems design. The knowledge required in order for clerical workers to operate these complex systems was beyond their training. Figure 7-9 illustrates this point. The figure shows that, when a computer application is very complex, the probability of success is very low. Conversely, when computer applications are very simple, the probability of success is very high. Failure

Figure 7-9. Systems Complexity/Success Ratio

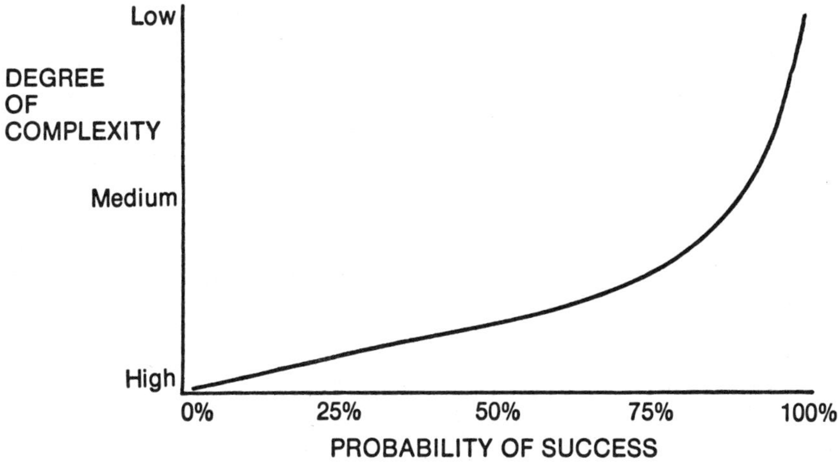

to learn this lesson has cost organizations hundreds of millions of dollars in aborted computer systems. Let's examine the common problems of computer systems in order to learn from the mistakes of others.

Systems problems

A sign often seen in computer rooms is, "If you must make a mistake, make a new one." The suggestion is that you should learn from your previous mistakes. The mistakes made in computer applications usually originate with people. Table 7-2 illustrates the computer application problems most commonly encountered. The segments of a computer system are input, processing, and output. Therefore, we will categorize the problems encountered in systems by these three segments.

A computer system's input data are prepared either by customers of the system or by the organization's clerical personnel. Customers encounter problems such as unavailability of data (e.g., forgetting passwords, customer or product number), failure to understand the system, or simply careless preparation of input data. Clerical personnel have many of the same problems. Although they should have all the data that are available to them, they are faced with the additional hazard of systems malfunctions (i.e., the input devices do not function correctly).

Table 7-2. Types of Systems Problems

Type	*Origin*	*Probable Cause*
Bad input data	Customers	Unavailability of data
		Doesn't understand system
		Carelessness
	Clerks	Doesn't understand system
		Carelessness
		Systems malfunction
Improper processing	User	Did not specify system correctly
		Requirements changed before system changed
		Failure to correct errors
	System designer/programmer	Misunderstanding of requirements
		Errors in implementation
	Computer operator	Used wrong data
		Errors in operation
Bad output	Various	Bad input data
		Improper processing
	User/customer	Failed to use data properly

Systems processing is affected by three groups of people: users, systems designers/programmers, and computer operators. The user is charged with the responsibility of specifying the system requirements. If this is not done correctly, the implemented system will reflect the improper specifications. In addition, the user may change the system requirements and notify the system's customers of the change, but fail to notify data designers and programmers in time for them to make the change before customers use the new procedures. A common systems failure is that the user is aware of problems but does not correct them. Another source of errors is that the systems designer/programmer misunderstands some of the user's requirements that they must implement. Programmers build systems according to their understanding of the specifications. In addition, the complexity of programming and computer applications makes at least some errors in implementation almost a certainty. Finally, the computer operator may use wrong data in operation of the system or make errors during the operation cycle.

The output of the system will be wrong if the input is bad or if the processing is erroneous. Any of the problems discussed above can cause such results. In addition, the user or customer of the system can misinterpret output and, as a result, fail to use the data properly. A computer system is less flexible than a manual system because the rules in a computer system must be decided *before* events occur.

Anticipating problems

A major difference between a computerized application and a manual application is that the computerized application must predetermine the action to be taken before it happens. The more competent the systems analyst is in anticipating problems, the fewer difficulties will be encountered during execution of that application. Here are some problems an analyst should anticipate:

- Entry of bad input data.
- Missing data in an input transaction.
- Failure of control personnel to act on error messages from the system.
- Incomplete or wrong systems specifications by the user.
- Failure to enter data at the proper time.
- Duplication of data entry.
- Misunderstanding of instructions by operators and customers.

However, anticipation is not enough. The analyst must build logic into the system in order to find these problems and then take positive action to correct the problem when it is discovered. Some of this logic can be programmed into the systems, while other logic must be directed at changing people's behavior. Over the years, data-processing personnel have learned many effective techniques to cope with the most common systems problems.

The systems analyst can cope with the problems discussed by using the following techniques during implementation:

- Perform extensive edit and audits of input data.
- Involve user personnel in testing the system.
- Work with user personnel throughout the development cycle.

- Prepare manuals and other educational programs on how to use the system.
- Implement sufficient internal controls to detect problems as soon as they occur.
- Provide for sufficient audit trail data to correct errors once they are detected.

Good techniques of systems development will go a long way toward ensuring successful systems. However, these techniques must take into account the fact that people work with systems. Thus, the systems analyst must know the caliber of personnel who will be using the system and build the system accordingly. Because jobs change, requirements change, and people are inconsistent at work, systems must be monitored continually to determine whether they are functioning correctly.

Feedback system

One aspect of computer systems is not orderly and systematic: people. People are highly volatile and often irrational. Where computers are precise and consistent, people are imprecise and inconsistent. This leads some people to conclude that computers perform tasks better than people. If you study systems problems associated with people, you will see that there are no easy solutions. People are both the problem and the solution. Even when systems are designed to take into account the inconsistencies of people, the inconsistencies will still surface in the form of unexpected problems.

Murphy's law states that, if things can go wrong, they will, and at the worst possible moment. No one will deny that Murphy's law applies to systems. However, when things go wrong with systems, a mechanism must exist to indicate where the problem is so that it can be corrected. This mechanism is called a feedback system (see Figure 7-10).

The three parts of a feedback system are:

1. *Performance criteria or standards* against which the system is to be evaluated. These standards and performance criteria must be reevaluated continually on the basis of the environment in which the system operates.
2. *Method of gathering data* from the system so that the actual performance of the system can be compared with the desired performance or standards.

Figure 7-10. Elements of a Feedback System

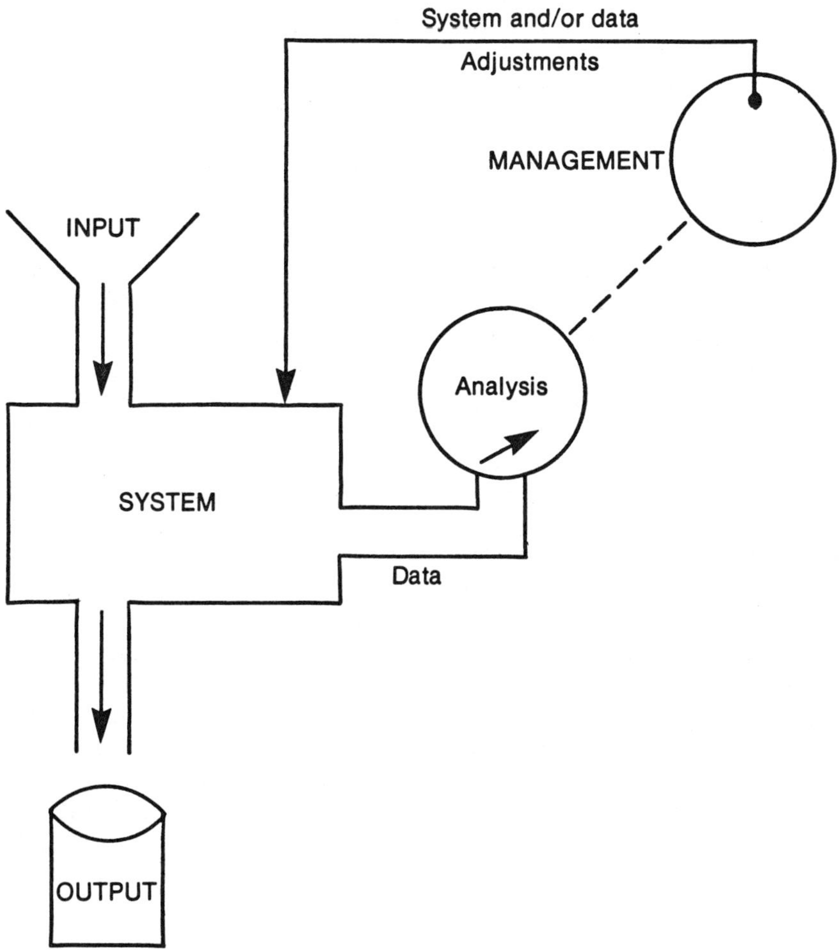

3. *Decision-making personnel* (management) who can review and act upon feedback data must be available. The corrective action results in adjustments either to data or to the system.

The purpose of feedback mechanisms is to evaluate performance. Because people are the system—that is, people design, implement, change, and use the system—feedback mechanisms really measure *people* performance. For example, if we measure the number of input errors, we can tell how well the input operators are performing. If we measure the length of time required to process an order, we can evaluate the performance of the order-processing people.

Evaluating people performance

Often overlooked in systems design is the development of criteria by which people will be evaluated. A simple axiom states that the performance of people usually conforms to the criteria by which they are evaluated. Unfortunately, in actual practice the evaluation criteria may have no relation whatever to desired job performance. However, in the systems world it is vital that desired performance and evaluation criteria be the same.

Systems analysts should be actively involved in the development of job descriptions for people who work on computer applications. It is only through restructuring of job descriptions that the systems analyst can include the desirable work characteristics by which people should be evaluated. Unfortunately, the systems analyst cannot make managers evaluate their personnel by the appropriate criteria; however, the system can provide the proper data for evaluation.

Job descriptions include the detailed characteristics of the job, such as what a person is supposed to do and, in many cases, exactly how the job is to be performed. Modern job descriptions also include the criteria by which to evaluate these characteristics. For example, if the job description states the employee is required to check all invoices to determine whether they have been properly authorized, the criteria for evaluation should be the accuracy with which the check is performed. However, if the job description says the individual must keypunch at a rate equal to or greater than 9,000 keystrokes per hour, then the criteria for evaluating that requirement is the operator's speed.

Jobs have many requirements. Logically, each requirement should be evaluated by different criteria. However, supervisors tend to assign greater importance to one characteristic than to others. Thus, if the supervisor is a stickler for accuracy, great operator speed is not an asset if the operator makes errors. In such a situation, the operator should concentrate on accuracy and disregard speed.

Most evaluation criteria can be classified into seven traits:

1. *Accuracy*. Performing work without error.

2. *Adherence to procedures.* Following the rules for performance of the job (plus verifying adherence with organizational policies and procedures).
3. *Speed.* Processing a high number of work units per day.
4. *Finding problems.* The ability to analyze transaction processing and select transactions that contain problems.
5. *Correcting problems.* Includes the ability to find problems and to be able to correct problem transactions appropriately.
6. *Freedom to operate.* This is an all-encompassing trait of independence that includes willingness to take responsibility for one's actions. It might also be described as a leadership trait. In order to be independent, people need the strong support of their supervisors for the actions they take. Freedom to operate implies freedom to perform tasks in the manner best suited to the individual.
7. *Hygiene factors.* This includes conformance to non-job-related factors, such as good attendance record, arriving at work on time, returning from lunch on time, leaving the office after closing time, and generally doing what the boss prefers in other non-job-related matters.

Table 7-3 shows what happens when a supervisor stresses certain traits in job evaluation. The chart demonstrates that unwise evaluation of personnel causes systems problems because people will perform in accordance with the traits by which they are evaluated.

The left-hand column of Table 7-3 shows the traits by which the worker is evaluated; the top row shows the desired work traits. The results listed in the matrix show how desired traits will be affected if the worker is evaluated by other traits. For example, evaluation of a worker on accuracy will enhance adherence to procedures. However, it also will tend to reduce the speed at which the worker operates. Thus, if speed is the desired trait, workers should be evaluated on their ability to produce a large number of work units, and accuracy should not be stressed overly.

When hygiene factors become the most important trait for evaluation, all other traits suffer. This is recognized as Maslow's theory X and theory Y of management. Flexible working hours is a new concept designed to bend the hygiene factors to the needs of the employee so that hygiene doesn't become a deterrent to performance. Flexible working hours enable an employee to work eight hours at their convenience within a ten- or twelve-

Table 7-3. Results of Work Evaluation

Traits Evaluated By Supervisor	*Desired Work Traits*						
	Accuracy	*Adherence to Procedures*	*Speed*	*Finding Problems*	*Correcting Problems*	*Freedom to Operate*	*Hygiene*
Accuracy		Helps	Reduces	Helps	Helps	No Effect	Reduces
Adherence to Procedures	Helps		Reduces	Helps	Helps	No Effect	Reduces
Speed	Reduces	Reduces		Reduces	Reduces	No Effect	Reduces
Finding Problems	Helps	Helps	Reduces		No Effect	Helps	Reduces
Correcting Problems	No Effect	No Effect	Reduces	Helps		Helps	Reduces
Freedom to Operate	No Effect	No Effect	No Effect	Helps	Helps		Reduces
Hygiene Factors	Reduces	Reduces	Reduces	Reduces	Reduces	Reduces	

hour work day. The worker need only be at the workplace during a certain segment of the day, called "core hours." Unfortunately, far too many supervisors and most managers overemphasize the hygiene factors, resulting in loss of the traits that are required for good job performance.

In the evaluation of performance, supervisors first should determine what traits are important and rank the traits in importance. For example, if accuracy and completeness are two very important traits for a job, the supervisor must decide which is most important and then both instruct and evaluate the worker accordingly. Classroom performance is no different. If most of your class grade comes from tests, you will emphasize studying for tests and not be too concerned about doing daily homework.

Earlier in the chapter, we briefly discussed people's resistance to change. Now that we have studied the results of change and how people are motivated and evaluated, we are ready to return to the subject of resistance to systems, both new and existing ones. People frequently take out their frustrations about working in an organization on the systems of that organization.

Computer Survival Rule #42

Build a system that is within the user's capability to operate. Systems built by Ph.D.s for Ph.D.s are useless to a non-Ph.D.

Resistance to systems

People resist new systems as well as existing ones, and this resistance is manifested in many ways. Whenever a change occurs, whether it be in a system, in a policy or procedure, in job rotation, or in duties, the change meets with resistance in one or more of the following ways:

- Misuse of the system through misunderstanding.
- Misuse of the system through carelessness.
- Sabotage by disgruntled employees.
- Fraud and sabotage by dishonest employees.

Some of these problems can be anticipated and planned for in the overall systems structure. Others must be detected through feedback mechanisms at the time they occur. Let's look at each form of resistance individually.

Misuse of system through misunderstanding

Most systems errors are caused by people who don't understand how systems work. This can result in bad input, failure to enter input, or failure to find or correct problems. The reasons for these misunderstandings include insufficient instructions; insufficient control over processing; nonexistent or unused feedback mechanisms; job requirements exceeding the capability of the individual; and inadequate supervision.

The errors that result from misunderstandings can provide valuable input for the systems analyst. Data-processing, control, and auditing personnel should monitor error rates continually to evaluate how well the system is working. Table 7-4 shows the relations between error rates and level of understanding of the system. Generally, the less people understand about the operation of the system, the more errors they make. Conversely, when people understand the system fully, error rates tend to be low. Much can be learned through analysis of errors over time.

Table 7-4. Correlation of Error Rate to Understanding of the System

Error Rate	*Understanding of System*
High	Poor
Average	Fair
Low	Complete

Analysis of errors and problems demonstrates trends that can be used to indicate corrective action. Figure 7-11 shows what an error-plotting graph looks like. The figure illustrates how to plot the number of errors per day over a given period. Analysis of the chart shows that something unusual happened on the fourth and fifth days of the time plotted. The error rate then returned to normal and, on the eighth day, began to rise at a steady rate.

Organizations that use such techniques usually can tell you that such a distribution shows that, on the fourth and fifth days, a new worker was assigned to the job or that the incumbent was sick and a substitute worker performed the task. The upward

Figure 7-11. Plotting the Frequency of Errors

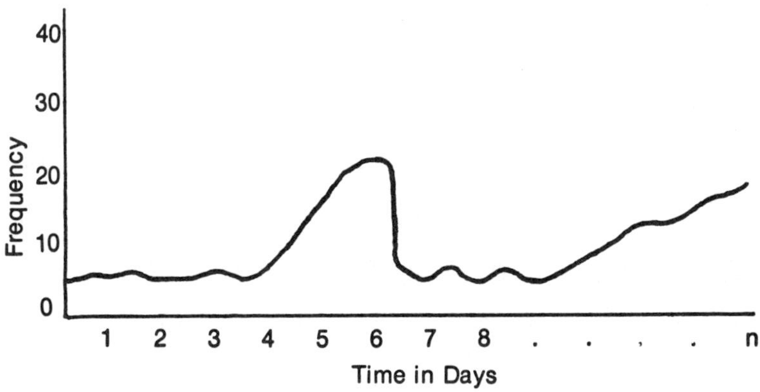

trend of errors beginning on day 8 indicates a serious systems problem. This frequently is due to the addition of something new to the system that the operators do not understand fully.

When such a trend appears, the procedure for correction of the problem is as follows: first, investigate the problem; second, when the cause is known, train the clerical workers who use the system if the problem is due to a misunderstanding; third, simplify the system if the problem is due to the complexity of the system.

Misuse of system through carelessness

Whether an employee is careless or misunderstands instructions, the effects on the system are the same. The difference is in how the problem is analyzed and corrected. Misunderstandings of the system result in drastic fluctuations in error rates or in error rates that are higher than normally would be expected. These problems can be corrected by educating the people who use the system or by simplifying the system itself.

When employees are careless, the error rate may not fluctuate so greatly. What generally happens is either slight fluctuations or a slow trend to a higher error rate. In such cases, the problem is more difficult to analyze. It involves looking at the work performed and determining whether the level of errors is consistent with the level expected. For example, no worker can be expected to be correct 100 percent of the time. A good keypunch operator will be 99 percent accurate. However, keypunch operators who are 99 percent accurate still make approximately 100 keystroke errors per hour. Even if keypunch operators are 99.9 percent accurate, they will make approximately 10 keystroke errors per hour.

Carelessness by employees can be handled best through proper supervision, which includes ascertaining whether the individual understands the job fully and evaluating the position by appropriate criteria.

Sabotage by disgruntled employees

Employees become disenchanted with their organization for many reasons, including failure to get a promotion or pay raise, dissatisfaction with the way the organization is treating them, and a desire to beat the system.

The disgruntled employee frequently takes out his or her frustrations on the system itself. Generally, employees know how to foul up a system, either by making errors intentionally or by doing something outside their job that will cause problems. The result of their act is sabotage of the system. However, sabotage is difficult to distinguish from unintentional errors or carelessness, since the effect on the system is the same. The only difference is intent.

The warning signs of sabotage (see Figure 7-12) are:

1. *Poor morale.* People complain about the system, the company, supervision, or the way things happen. Poor morale is manifested in decreased productivity.
2. *Frequent reruns.* Systems that must be run many times because it seems difficult to get the system to run correctly may have been sabotaged.
3. *Customers' dissatisfaction.* Customers complain that outputs from the system are inaccurate, incomplete, late, and irrelevant.
4. *Out-of-balance condition.* The details do not agree with the totals.
5. *Buildup ot pending files.* The number of transactions that cannot be processed continues to mount.
6. *High rate of systems changes.* Systems analysts are continually making changes to compensate for problems.
7. *Lost input.* Orders disappear and changes are not made because input is mysteriously lost.

Figure 7-12. Signs of Systems Sabotage

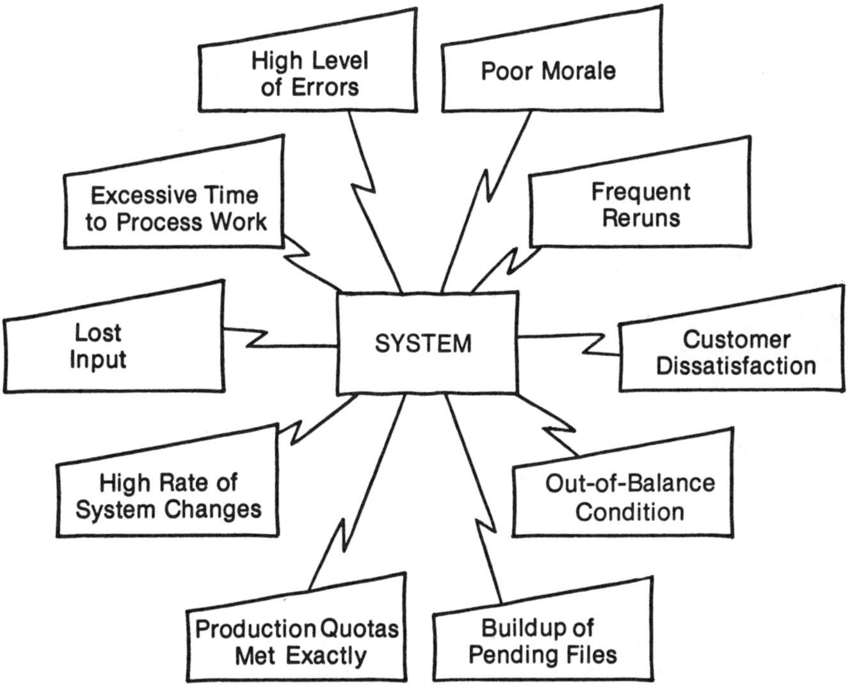

8. *Excessive time to process work.* Transactions take longer to process than they should.
9. *High level of errors.* The amount of incorrect data going into the system is excessive.
10. *Production quotas met exactly.* Employees always seem to produce the exact amount of work required. This is a form of sabotage because it tends to reduce the amount of work that could be obtained with maximal effort. Production workers frequently store excess production so that they can meet the next day's quota with little effort.

Auditors and control personnel should be alert for signs of sabotage because they indicate that people are having problems with systems. Feedback mechanisms that can detect these signs will enable management to make the necessary corrections. However, knowing when sabotage occurs is difficult because it looks the same as poorly performed work. Although sabotage seems to be a growing problem in organizations, this assertion is not supported by facts.

Systems misuse by dishonest employees

When fraud occurs, it is usually perpetrated by an employee of the organization. For example, more bank frauds are committed by employees than by any other group. Substantially more funds are lost through fraud and embezzlement by employees than through robbery.

If systems contain adequate internal controls, the probability of fraud can be reduced greatly. Some methods of control have been perfected over the years and are extremely effective if installed and used. The most frequent cause of fraud is a breakdown in control. For example, if a computer gives a status report but no one takes the time to analyze it and follow through, the controls will be ineffective.

Experience has shown that the best method of reducing problems of all types in computer systems is to have heavy user involvement in all aspects of systems design, maintenance, operation, and control.

Computer Survival Rule #43

If systems displease people, people will displease the system by not following or by breaking the system's rules. Be aware of this survival threat.

Involving users in systems designs

In order to ensure the success of a system, users must be involved in the design, maintenance, operation, and control of the system. Employees' suggestions systems have worked in production areas for years. However, many systems analysts have not yet learned how vital it is to involve clerical employees in the design of methods by which these employees perform their job. However, the systems designer first must identify the tasks within a system that require the involvement of people.

People's involvement with systems

Sixteen tasks can be identified in the transaction processing cycle. The system designer must determine how and where people can help with the system. Table 7-5 lists these tasks and

Table 7-5. People's Involvement with Systems

Processing Task	*People's Involvement*	*Example of Task*
1. Transaction initiation	Much	Receipt of a purchase order
2. Authorization	Much	Approval of a large credit
3. Input batch balancing	Much	Development of control number
4. Data entry	Average	Keypunching
5. Storage of input	Average	Filing purchase orders
6. Systems program edits	None	Program verifies customer number
7. Error correction	Average	Clerk corrects wrong customer number
8. Computer system set-up and operations	Some	Mounting tape, running programs
9. Data communication	Little	Telephone line call-up
10. File update and use	None	Programs interact with computer files
11. Computer processing	None	Application of system rules via programs
12. Storage of computer media	Some	Retention of tapes, disks, etc., for future use
13. Producing outputs	Little	Printing of reports
14. Systems balancing	Much	Verification of control figures
15. Use of output	Much	Use of data in job
16. Enhancements	Much	Suggestions for improvements

shows how people are involved in them. In order to explain what is meant by a task, an example of each task is given. For instance, processing task 1 (transaction initiation) requires "much" people involvement. The example for the task is an order entry clerk who receives a purchase order from a customer. Processing task 6 (systems program edits) has "none" involvement of people. This is a task performed automatically by a computer program. Processing task 9 (data communications) requires "little" people involvement and simply requires someone to be sure that the communication transmission lines are connected and appear to be functioning properly. From that point on, data are transmitted automatically.

When people are involved in one of these tasks, they should be given the opportunity to participate in developments or modifications to the method of performing that task. This can be accomplished by the following steps:

1. Call together the people involved.
2. Have the systems analyst explain the change, its impact, how it operates, and what is expected of the people involved in the system.
3. Let the people react to the explanation and make suggestions, recommendations, and changes.
4. When the systems analysts agree to these suggestions, recommendations, and changes, implement the methods.
5. When the systems analysts disagree with the reaction of the people, the analysts should explain to them why their suggestions, recommendations, and changes are not being implemented.

When to involve clerical personnel

It is important not only to involve the clerical personnel who will use the system in the design and enhancements of the system, but also to involve them at the most opportune time. Figure 7-13 shows nine phases in the system life cycle. It also shows at which phase the clerical personnel should become involved. The following are times at which clerical workers should be involved in systems design.

At completion of general systems specification

At this point, the analyst should explain the objectives of the system, what is hoped to be accomplished, and the general methods of operation. This will provide an opportunity for the clerical personnel to explain some of the problems they are encountering and to anticipate problems with the new system.

At completion of systems specifications

At this point, the system is fully specified. The systems analyst can explain in detail how the system will work and the part the

Figure 7-13. Involvement of Clerical Personnel in Design of System

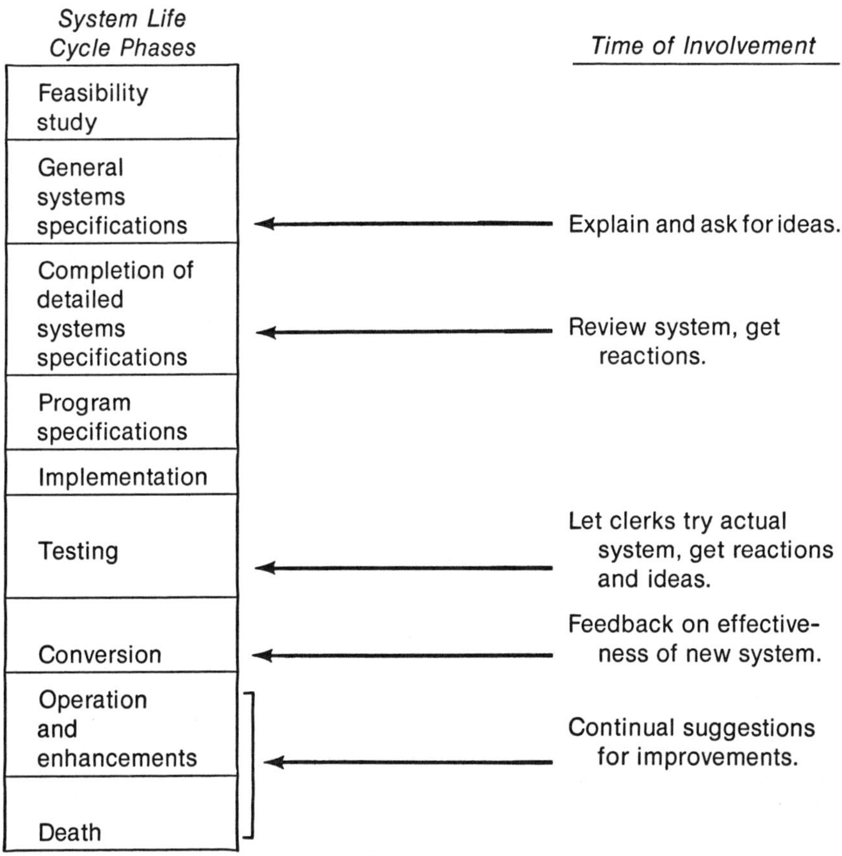

clerical personnel will play in the operation of the system. This step is quite important, since the analyst can become familiar with the clerical people's perception of the system.

During systems testing

At this point, the people who will use the system should become actively involved in testing. It is only by involving the users in systems testing that the analyst can understand fully whether or not the system meets the users' needs and can be implemented effectively by them. Problems can still be corrected at this time.

Immediately after operation

Within a few days or weeks after the system goes live, the systems analyst should discuss the system in depth with the clerical personnel. The problems that they are having with the system can then be analyzed to determine whether they are really systems problems or whether they indicate a need for further training.

During operations and enhancements

Employees should be encouraged to submit suggestions for improvements to the system at any time. When the system becomes unwieldy, the number of suggestions should increase. This can be one of the criteria for determining when a system should be revised.

Method of making suggestions

Employees should have a formalized method to provide input for the systems analysts. One method that has proved very effective is a form on which employees can explain problems they encounter. An example of such a form is given in Figure 7-14. Whenever a problem is found, it is entered on the form. Information should include the system in which the problem exists, the type of problem, the specific transaction, and suggestions about how to correct it.

The form is then submitted to the user and/or systems analyst who is responsible for the system. The problem must be evaluated in order to determine its seriousness, the amount of effort required to make the correction, the programs involved, and the individuals to be involved in making the correction. Once the analysis is complete, the change can be ranked by priority and placed in the normal process for changing systems.

Computer Survival Rule #44

Remember: A product you let others create for you will be a product that they *like, but one that* you *may not like.*

Figure 7-14. Request for Application Program Problem (RAPP)

DATES: Submitted ____________

Requested Completion ____________

REQUESTING DEPARTMENT

New Application ☐

Change to Existing Application ☐

Production ☐

PRIORITY:

☐ Critical (System Error) (Causing errors in daily operation)

☐ Normal (System request not causing errors)

☐ Future Requirement

*GENERAL SPECIFICATIONS:

____

____

____

____

____

*(Detailed specifications will be determined jointly between EDP and User Departments)

JUSTIFICATION: (Benefits to be derived)

____

____

____

APPROVALS: (Signatures)

____

Director of Requesting Department

____

Director of Computer Services

EDP DEPARTMENT USE ONLY

RAPP # ____________

Date Entered ____________

Estimated time to complete:

____

Date Completed ____________

Actual Time to Complete:

____

Effective systems design checklist

Data-processing systems usually are only as good as the people who develop and use them. If the system has not been designed on the basis of people's capabilities, its probability of success is significantly lowered. Too frequently computer systems are designed without consideration of how people will use the data in their day-to-day work. Industrial psychologists recommend that systems designers work closely during the design phase with the clerical personnel who will use the system.

The effective systems design checklist is to be used for assessment of the people factor in computer systems. A "yes" answer indicates that the people factor has been considered in designing the system, while a "no" answer indicates a potential people problem. The checklist can be used both in the design of new systems and in the assessment of a people problem in existing systems.

Checklist 7-1. Effective Systems Design Checklist

	Response			
Question	*Yes*	*No*	*N/A*	*Other*
1. Have the capabilities of the people in the user area been assessed as part of the systems design process?	____	____	____	________
2. Is the systems design based on the capabilities of those people?	____	____	____	________
3. Are the people who will use the computer system in their day-to-day work consulted during the design phase?	____	____	____	________
4. Is a formal effort made to explain to the people how the system will affect their job before installation of or change to the system?	____	____	____	________
5. Are all the people involved in a system consulted regularly as a part				

Checklist 7-1. Effective Systems Design Checklist (continued)

Question	*Response*			
	Yes	*No*	*N/A*	*Other*
of the systems design process?	___	___	___	___
6. Are the people threats to systems identified during the design phase?	___	___	___	___
7. If a new system or a change to a system will cause relocation of people, either physically or jobwise, are those people given the opportunity to interact with the systems development people during the design phase?	___	___	___	___
8. Have the scope and objectives of computer systems been explained to those who use the system?	___	___	___	___
9. If people need new skills to use the computer systems, have they been instructed in those skills?	___	___	___	___
10. Do supervisors work closely with people during the implementation phase of a new computer system or change to a system?	___	___	___	___
11. Are problems in computer systems analyzed to determine whether they are people problems?	___	___	___	___
12. Are people who use computer systems continually given the opportunity to make recommendations and suggestions for improvement?	___	___	___	___
13. If people make recommendations for improve-				

Checklist 7-1. Effective Systems Design Checklist (continued)

Question	*Response* Yes	No	N/A	Other
ment to computer systems, are those recommendations responded to promptly?	___	___	___	___
14. Is the system designed to optimize people's work wherever practical?	___	___	___	___
15. Do the people working with the computer system now have a job as challenging as it was before the new system or change was installed?	___	___	___	___
16. Have the people working with systems been taught how to identify problems?	___	___	___	___
17. Are the people working with systems told whom they should notify when they suspect a problem?	___	___	___	___
18. Are people working with the system notified when changes will occur so that they are alert to errors that might result from these changes?	___	___	___	___
19. Are people's jobs reevaluated to take into account the new computer functions so they can be properly rewarded and evaluated?	___	___	___	___
20. Has the type of error conditions that are indicative of systems sabotage been identified and are those conditions monitored?	___	___	___	___

Conclusion

By its nature, data processing is a systematic, orderly process. It is also a very detailed process that requires a standardized method of processing. Unfortunately, there are people and problems within that organized structure. One must recognize that systems cannot exist without people. People problems center around the amount of knowledge people have about the system and around their attitude toward the system. Systems analysts, auditors, and control personnel should know when problems arise so that they can be corrected. In order to know when problems occur, an analysis can be made to study error rates and other characteristics over time. These feedback mechanisms are essential in computerized applications.

If systems are to be successful, the people working with the system should become involved in its design and enhancements. Experience has shown that, when people who use the system work closely with the designers, three things happen: first, greater efficiency is obtained; second, job satisfaction is increased; and third, the probability of success improves dramatically.

8/ Verifying computer system results

The most important question

The question that should be on the mind of every user of computer systems is, "How do I know that my results are correct?" Picture yourself in an executive office when a 437-page report arrives from the data-processing department. At the bottom of the report it says that the total sales for the month are $467,382. How do you know that that $467,382 is correct?

Most people fail to contest the accuracy and completeness of computer-produced information. Ask yourself the following questions: Do I verify that the dollar amount of federal tax withheld from my pay each week is correct on my annual W-2 statement? Do I verify that the interest credited to my savings account is correct? Do I verify that the interest on my mortgage payment is correct?

If you are like most people, your answer to these questions was no. The reasons vary, including lack of time, lack of information, and simple acceptance of whatever the system produces. If people fail to take the time and effort to question their own personal finances, will they take the time and effort to verify the accuracy and completeness of any computer-produced result? The answer too frequently is no.

Many users of computer systems feel helpless. For example, they ask, "How can I verify that the interest on my savings bank account is correct? If I wanted to do it, could I?" The answer is yes, but you must want to do it. Perhaps a better answer would be first to learn what you can and can't do to verify the accuracy and completeness of computer data, and then make the decision as to whether it's worth the time and effort to perform those checks.

This chapter is about control and the risks those controls are attempting to reduce. Control is an essential ingredient to survival in the computer environment. On the other hand, control can be expensive and, unless properly constructed, ineffective. Although the design of control in a computer environment is a highly technical topic, users need to understand the concepts so that they can specify survival mechanisms.

What needs to be controlled?

Successful systems are built in a controlled environment that dictates individual work habits. Many factors comprise the environment in which a computer system operates. It is difficult to isolate an application system, such as payroll or accounts receivable, from the environment in which it operates. The individuals who design a system will conform to the environment in which they work.

Strong management support is the essential element for a well-controlled environment. Executive management of an organization is the primary motivator for establishment of administrative control, while operating management is the force behind development and implementation of application controls.

Planning goes hand in hand with control as a key to success in systems. This is particularly true of computerized systems. Computer applications do not have the same type of flexibility as manual systems. In a manual system, people can bend the rules to fit unusual circumstances; in computerized systems, this flexibility must be built into the system before implementation. Thus, situations that have not been predetermined cause systems problems.

Since the advent of the commercial computer, literally hundreds of thousands of systems have been built. These systems have achieved various degrees of success. Numerous authors have discussed why some systems succeed and others fail. Over time, a pattern has emerged that demonstrates the traits of a successful system.

Among the characteristics that most frequently appear in successful systems are the following:

- The system fits the needs of the user; that is, the user is not forced to adapt to the limitations of the computer.
- User personnel are enthusiastic about the forthcoming computer system.
- Information that is generated by the computer system will be timely, accurate, useful, complete, concise, and reliable.
- The system is designed to support, not supplant, the user.

- Measures are taken to ensure that turnover of systems personnel is low.
- The value of the system will be evaluated continually during the development stages.
- Measures are taken and controls are established to ensure that time schedules are met.
- Controls are established to ensure that budgets are met.
- Measures are taken to establish that changes to the computer system during the development stages are very infrequent.
- Measures are taken to ensure that the computer system is not unnecessarily elaborate.
- The system is built so that it can be adapted to changes in requirements.
- A good data security system is built hand in hand with the system.
- The application being built fits the organization's long-range systems plan.
- Criteria are established before building of the system to determine whether predicted benefits have been realized.

Analysis of systems that have failed also shows certain common systems characteristics. Failure can be defined as nonfulfillment of users' needs. Among the reasons for such failure are high development or operation costs, excessive complexity for the people who use the system, lack of the right data at the right time, and inability to change the system readily. It is important to analyze both successful and unsuccessful systems. Knowledge of the obstacles to success can help systems designers avoid these problems. The obstacles to effective computer systems are:

- Lack of knowledge by users about computer capabilities and limitations.
- Lack of computer personnel with adequate skills to specify the system.
- Lack of involvement by users.
- Users' fear about losing control of the system to the data-processing people.
- Ambitions of systems and user personnel being placed above the needs of the organization.

- Human resistance to change.
- Inadequate planning and developing of criteria for performance measurement.
- Lack of interest in the system by user management.
- Lack of interest in the system by executive management.
- Operations managers failing to use the information generated by the computer.
- High turnover of systems personnel during the systems development phase.
- Poor quality of systems design and project management.
- "It's not my system" syndrome.
- Inadequate testing of new systems.
- Computer system is overdesigned for the people who use it.
- Manual support system is underdesigned for the people who use it.
- Management fails to enforce adequate discipline in data preparation functions.
- Organizational barriers prevent smooth work flow.
- System floods a manager with too much information, making it difficult to use data effectively.
- Wrong applications (i.e., priorities) are developed.
- Late implementation of the system.
- Excessive development costs.
- Conversion from the old to new system is chaotic, causing people to lose (and never regain) confidence in the system.
- Frequent changes to new computer hardware.

If we know why systems succeed and why systems fail, we might logically ask why there are still so many systems problems. A two-year study on computer control funded by the IBM Corporation concluded that too little attention had been paid to controls. Most users know what can go wrong in systems but fail to specify avoidance of these problems as a systems requirement. Once reduction of problems is specified as a systems requirement, controls can be built to reduce those problems to an acceptable level.

Computer Survival Rule #45

The time spent on specifications, design, and implementation of controls should be considered an important part of the systems development process.

Using control in the business process

Management is responsible for ensuring an adequate system of internal control. Let us examine this responsibility. Management theory tells us that management has four functions: planning, organization, direction, and control. These functions are used to accomplish the objectives of the organization.

The objectives of an organization come from three sources: the organization's articles of incorporation and bylaws; the wishes of the owners as expressed through their board of directors and which comprise policies and procedures; and government regulations and public concern. The third area is growing in importance and is making a major impact on the thinking of management. No longer is profitability sufficient to assure management of success.

In this framework, management develops a series of programs for the organization. The business process, together with the system of internal controls, is illustrated in Figure 8-1. The management functions of planning, organization, and direction are related to the successful implementation of programs. In turn, these programs are used to achieve the organization's objectives. The fourth function of management (control) is used to ascertain that the programs are implemented according to the intentions of management. Again, bear in mind the increasing importance of outside influences, such as government and the public, on these programs.

Programs are controlled through both administrative and accounting areas. These controls monitor the programs and then feed information back to management. On the basis of evaluation of the program through controls, management is able to alter its planning, organization, and direction of programs. This is a repetitive cycle in which management continually must fine tune the operation of their programs.

One way to distinguish between administrative and accounting control is to consider administrative control as the "what" and accounting control as the "how." This means that, through administrative control, management tells the organization what to do in order to accomplish the organization's objectives; ac-

Figure 8-1. System of Internal Controls

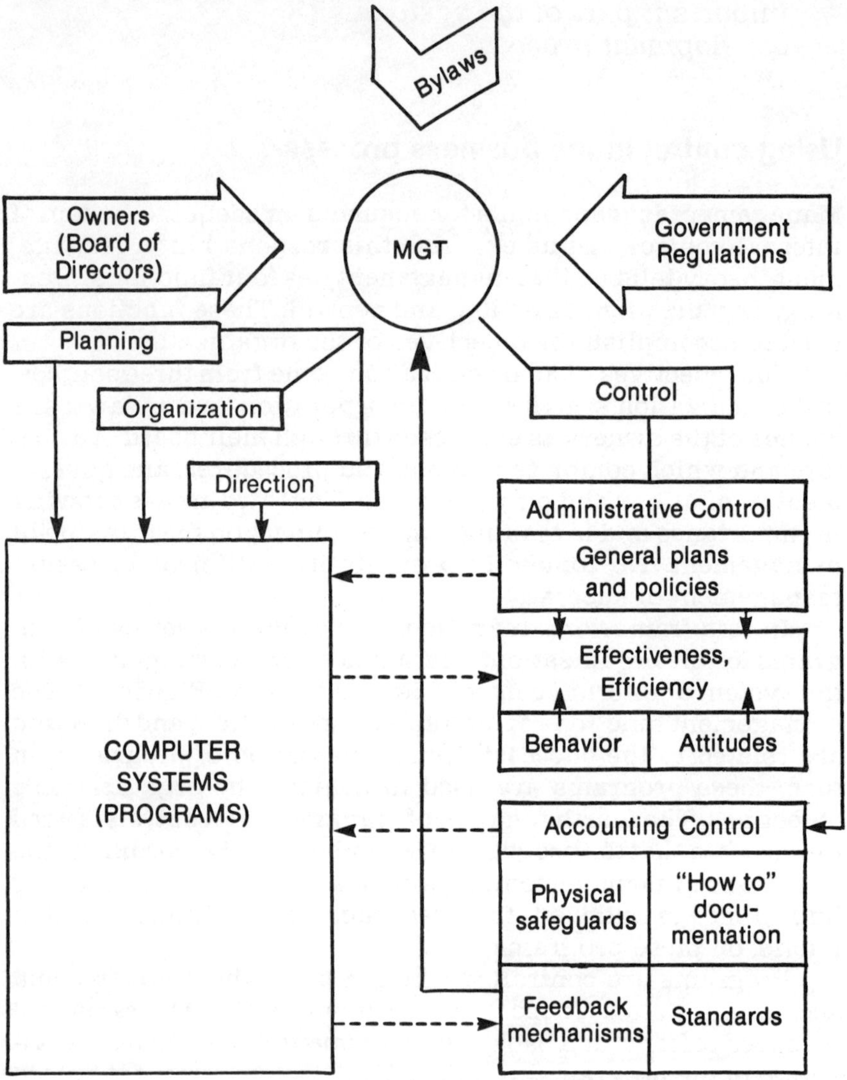

counting control determines they will do it. Perhaps this can best be explained by an example.

Organization X is in business to sell product Y. The organizational structure and environment are administrative controls. Management establishes a marketing organization to sell the product. The marketing organization is supported by a distribution department, which stores and distributes the merchandise. The accounting department is responsible for billing the customer and collecting funds. A pricing department is responsible for setting the price of the product. Sales personnel in the marketing group receive three months of technical training about the product before they begin to call on customers. Sales personnel are given a pricing manual that explains the organization's pricing policies and structure, as well as a manual on preparation of the paperwork required to complete the sales transaction. These all are administrative controls. They are management's methods of controlling the marketing process, and they explain to sales personnel what they can and can't do to sell the product.

The detailed methods used to accomplish the specific aspects of selling a product are the accounting controls. This "how to" aspect of marketing a product is basically the system that permits the organization to function. Accounting controls include the methods by which a customer is extended credit, the series of authorizations needed to accept an order or return of merchandise, the steps required to deviate from the pricing manual, the channels through which accounting information is recorded and processed, the steps by which the product is transported from the organization's distribution facilities to the customer's location, and so on.

The composition of accounting and administrative controls is illustrated in Figure 8-2. Note that administrative control could be considered a "soft" control in that measurement of the effectiveness of such controls is subjective. On the other hand, accounting controls tend to be "hard" controls in that measurement of their effectiveness is objective. For example, the steps taken to safeguard assets (accounting controls) are readily discernable, while the attitudes of security guards (administrative controls) can affect those physical safeguards, but are more difficult to quantify.

Accounting control is composed of four items:

- *Standards (goals and objectives).* In order to know whether a program is successful, management must set standards of achievement. These standards are measurable goals and objectives. For example, a standard can be production of a certain number of items per day, achievement of an error

Figure 8-2. Composition of Internal Control

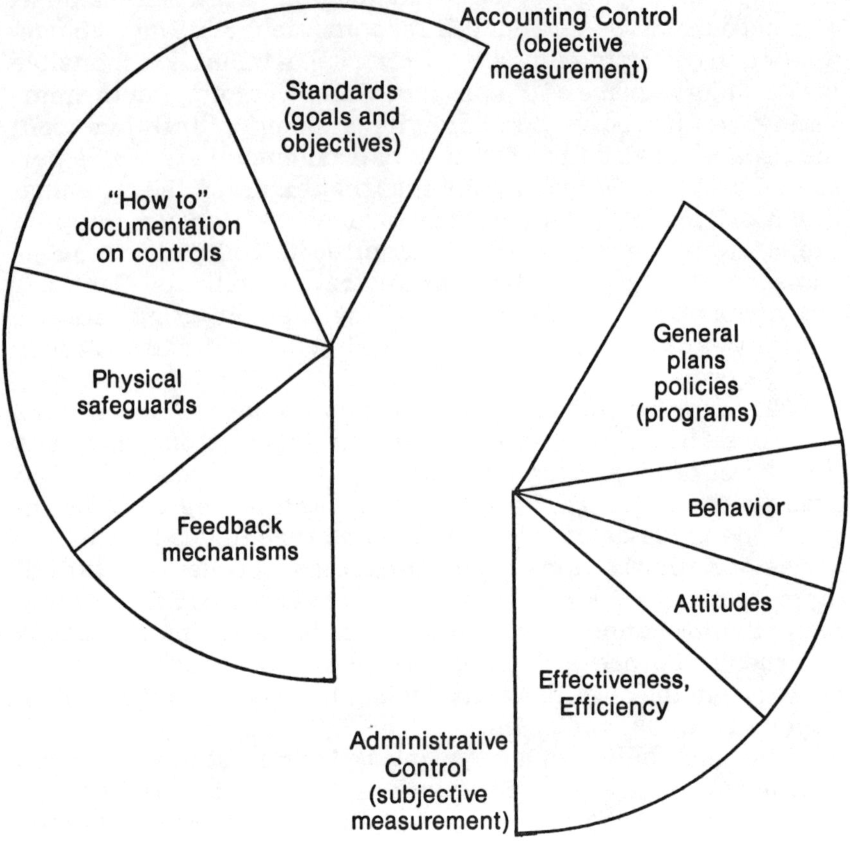

rate of less than X%, or employment of at least X% of minority groups in the organization.

- *"How to" documentation of controls.* These are the documented, detailed policies and procedures that explain how to perform particular functions. Examples of such documents may include an accounting manual on how to record transactions, a payroll manual covering which absences are paid and which are not, or a manual on how credit is extended to customers.
- *Physical safeguards.* These measures are designed to protect the assets of the organization. They include security guards, controlled access to designated areas, and periodic inventory of physical assets.

- *Feedback mechanisms.* These methods apprise management of the effectiveness of the internal control system. These mechanisms range from sensor devices, such as temperature and humidity control, to formal reporting mechanisms.

The composition of administrative controls is broad in scope. These controls determine the environment in which accounting control functions. Administrative control is comprised of:

- *General plans and policies.* The controls over programs to be implemented by the organization. For example, a program might be the installation of a new product, erection of a new facility, or addition of a new benefits plan. Administrative controls include the planning and implementation of procedures, budget, reports, and so on, all of which provide control over the use of the organization's resources.
- *Behavior.* Setting examples of control and conduct by the management of the organization. For example, if management fails to enforce controls, it has exhibited nonenforcement behavior. This affects employees compliance with controls.
- *Attitudes.* The outlook and ethics of the employees of an organization regarding control.
- *Effectiveness and efficiency.* A general measure of productivity of the organization in program implementation

Let us begin to explore how administrative and accounting controls are used to ensure the reliability, accuracy, and completeness of the programs of management. Table 8-1 illustrates

Table 8-1. Spectrum of Internal Control

Type of Control	*Concerned with Reliability of*	*Difficulty in Determining Reliability*
Administrative	Organizational objectives	Very difficult
Administrative	Effectiveness, efficiency	↑
Accounting	Internal data	Difficult
Accounting	External corporate reporting	
Accounting	External financial reporting	↓
Accounting	External financial statements	Less difficult

the two types of internal control, showing the difficulty in determining the reliability of their respective areas of concern.

Analysis of the table reveals internal control from the chief executive officer's top-down viewpoint. At the top, we can see that the chief executive officer's main concern is programs. Looking at controls from this view, we can begin to perceive how management controls the operation of an organization through the establishment of programs. It is at this high level that executive management interfaces with the organization's activities.

Thus, the highest level of internal control deals with control over the implementation of programs. For example, if executive management wishes to implement a program to expand production capacity by 20 percent, it first wants to know that the program will indeed be implemented. Working down the ladder of internal control, the second concern becomes the effectiveness and efficiency of programs. It is the broad spectrum of programs, effectiveness, and efficiency that falls under the aegis of administrative controls.

The third step down the ladder is the area of internal data. These are the data-producing procedures by which management can quantify the results of an operation. Some data are for accounting purposes, while others account for resources. It is just as important for management to know that it has 507 product Xs on the shelf as it is to know that the value of product X inventory is $2,535. The internal data become the basis for the final three areas on the spectrum of internal control. Again, the accuracy of a lower level of concern is related directly to the accuracy of a higher level. For example, if the internal data are incorrect, all accounting reports based on those data will also be incorrect.

External corporate reporting deals with nonfinancial data. This includes information such as the number of employees; percent increases between accounting periods; reports of policies, procedures, and plans; and a myriad of other data that the public and government use to analyze the stability, future profitability, and so on of organizations.

External financial reporting can include forecasts, projections, fair market value of assets, compensation of officers, proxy statements, and general information reported on Securities and Exchange Commission reports. The data with which accountants are most familiar are the external financial statements. The two most common of these statements are the balance sheet and the statement of income and expense.

If we analyze this spectrum of internal control, we will begin to see the relation between the objectives of the organization and the external financial statements. We then can see that it makes little sense to put the emphasis of our internal control on external financial statements and disregard the higher levels of control concern.

The lower the level of control concern, the easier it is to determine reliability. For example, if we accept the trial balance as correct, we can insert sufficient controls almost to guarantee accuracy from that point on. However, as we work backward and begin to talk of fair market value of assets, hours of work reported against a job, accuracy of budget data, and so on, control becomes much more difficult to specify and implement.

People who design systems usually can do little to affect administrative controls, since their area of control involvement is either accounting or applications. However, systems designers can either strengthen or weaken accounting controls, depending on how effective they believe administrative controls are in their organization. Let us step through the procedures a systems analyst should take in designing controls for a computerized application.

Means of achieving accounting control

Designing a system of internal control for an application system should be an integral part of the systems development process. Unfortunately, many data-processing personnel do not readily understand the concepts of control. While control to an accountant means accuracy and completeness, control to a data-processing person means control over the process. Thus, data-processing people are more concerned with the process itself than with the accuracy and completeness of the data being processed.

The design of the internal control system in a computerized application is a seven-step process. These steps need to be performed in conjunction with design of the computerized application. The process of developing a system of internal control should follow the same methodical and orderly process as does the specification of the application rules. A suggested process is illustrated in Figure 8-3.

Systems designers begin by defining the exposures that exist

Figure 8-3. Flowchart of Application Control Selection

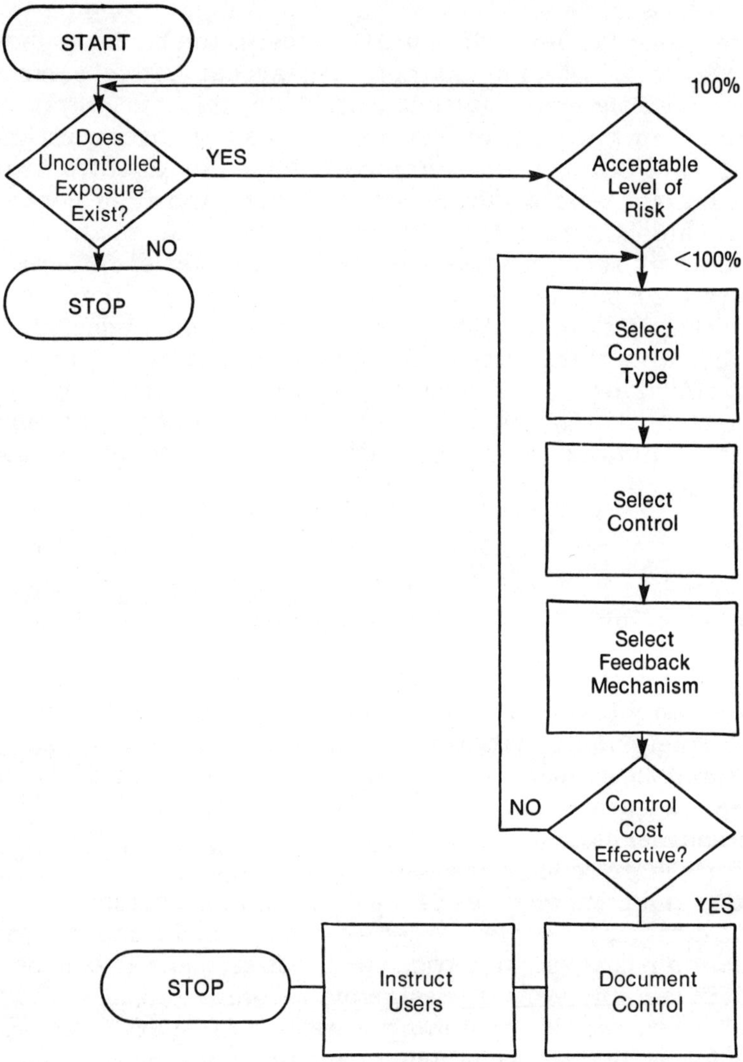

for their application. Remember that exposures are affected by the adequacy or inadequacy of administrative controls. Once the exposure has been identified, an assessment should be made of how much risk the organization is willing to accept. This is similar to the deductible coverage on automobile property damage. If you have a $100 deductible, you assume a risk of $100 on each accident that involves property damage. Once these two critical steps are completed, the selection process will be mechanical for a systems designer who is skilled in control. The seven steps involved in the specification of controls are described as follows:

Step 1: Definition of systems exposures

These are the exposures that are listed in chapter 7. However, they are defined in more detail in this step. For example, inaccurate contents on input is an exposure on all systems. In an accounts receivable system, the exposure could be that the cash receipts do not equal the amount due.

Step 2: Definition of acceptable risk level

Since it is impractical to expect 100 percent accuracy, the organization needs to define the variance from 100 percent accuracy that they are willing to accept. In the example of exposure in an accounts receivable system, an organization may decide that it will accept a variance of $5. This means that, if a payment is within $5 above or below the amount due, it will be accepted as payment in full. Thus, the organization is willing to accept a loss of $5 on each payment.

Step 3: Determination of type of control

The type of control should reduce the exposure, but within the risk tolerance defined. The organization can select a preventive, detective, or correct control or a combination thereof.

Step 4: Selection of specific control technique

Once the type of control has been determined, the organization can select a specific control technique (these will be discussed in the following section).

Step 5: Development of feedback mechanism

Techniques can be effective only when a feedback mechanism is used to measure the effectiveness of the control. For example, in our accounts receivable illustration, we indicated that the organization would accept a payment if it was within $5 above or below the amount due. A preventive control would reject payments only if they were more than $5 above or below the amount due. Thus, a payment of $4.99 less than the amount due would be accepted as payment in full. A feedback mechanism would provide management with information on the frequency of this occurrence and what this particular control was costing the organization. A feedback mechanism should periodically inform management of the difference between total payments and total amount due. This would enable management to adjust the variance on the basis of actual operating conditions.

Step 6: Determination of cost-effectiveness

The cost of operating the control should be less than the exposure which it is designed to reduce. Thus, cost-effectiveness becomes an important consideration in selecting the control technique.

Step 7: Documentation of technique and instruction for its use

Many systems failures are attributable to non-use of installed controls. Therefore, it becomes extremely important in any application to document the system of internal controls adequately and to instruct employees on how to use them.

Computer Survival Rule #46

Insist that your data-processing department develop a methodology for control development.

User's responsibility for EDP control

The primary responsibility for control in a computer system resides with the user. The user is responsible for the accuracy, completeness, and authorization of data. The data-processing department has a secondary responsibility for the design and implementation of controls to achieve the user's objectives.

As computer systems become more integrated and complex, the assignment of control responsibilities also increases in complexity. For example, in data-base management systems, many users share common data. In other systems, processing crosses organizational boundaries, causing confusion about which user has primary responsibility.

The first step in control design for the user, therefore, is the assignment of responsibility for control. This responsibility can be delegated as follows:

1. Responsibility for control over complete systems, such as having the payroll manager be responsible for the accuracy, completeness, and authorization of the payroll system.
2. Assignment of individual responsibility for control of a specific data element. For example, the personnel department may be held responsible for the accuracy, completeness, and authorization of the employee number data field.
3. Assignment of user's responsibility for a specific function in an application system. For example, the credit department may be assigned responsibility for establishment of credit limits and issuance of credit to customers of the organization within the billing application system.

The individual responsible for control should be held accountable for problems associated with that system, data element, or function. The responsible user needs to be provided with the tools and techniques to monitor the effectiveness of controls so that appropriate adjustments can be made. This involves notifying the user of problems and holding them responsible for both the short-term and the long-term solution to problems.

Computer Survival Rule #47

Make one person accountable for control at the lowest level possible.

Satisfying EDP control responsibility

The user needs to understand computer concepts and problems in enough detail to specify control needs. The computer has introduced some new methods of processing that require new means of control. Some basic EDP knowledge is necessary if we are to survive problems in the computer environment.

The user who is responsible for control should perform the following three actions: (1) define the acceptable level of risk; (2) implement controls over the non-EDP segment of the system; and (3) monitor the effectiveness of the controls.

The automatic inventory replenishment procedure that is incorporated in many computer systems introduces new risks to organizations that use it. These new risks require new controls. One organization decided to hold an open house for the families of their employees. In order to protect the facilities, the tour director decided to rope off areas where they did not want families to visit. This procedure required 20,000 feet of rope, which was taken from inventory. The automatic replenishment inventory algorithm required four months of stock on hand, and, since 20,000 feet were withdrawn, the system automatically issued a purchase order for 80,000 feet of rope. Since normal usage was 4,000 feet per month, the organization had a twenty-month supply on hand rather than the desired four-month supply. Had the user understood the characteristics of the computer system, a control could have been installed to monitor for unusual usages before issuance of purchase orders.

Defining an acceptable level of risk

The user is responsible for defining control needs. These needs should be expressed in terms of acceptable levels of risk. This is a two-part process that involves (1) definition of exposures (frequently referred to as risks), and (2) definition of the level of loss that is acceptable from that risk.

The identification of risk defines the areas in which controls may be needed. In an ideal environment, controls are unnecessary; everything will function according to specification. Controls are necessary only in an environment in which problems and errors can occur. Unfortunately, we have few, if any, ideal environments, thus making controls necessary.

The user must identify the risks associated with the application area. For example, in a payroll system, the user might define some of the risks in the following terms:

- A paycheck might be issued to unauthorized employees.
- Hours worked may be reported incorrectly.

- Year-to-date earnings might be totaled incorrectly.
- An employee might be paid according to the wrong pay rate.
- Unauthorized deductions might be made from an employee's pay.
- An employee might be given more vacation than he or she is entitled to.

Each of these risks should be described as a computer system need to the data-processing systems analyst. In addition to these application risks, there are technological risks, such as systems security; however, these should be the responsibility of the data-processing department. The user must define the degree of application risk that the user is willing to accept.

The risk must be quantified in order to determine the level that is acceptable. Some risks are completely acceptable, while others are only partially acceptable. For example, the user may accept the risk that a product description is entered incorrectly but may not be willing to accept the risk that a product number is entered improperly. The potential loss that would result from an inaccurate description may be minimal or absent, while the loss associated with the entry of an invalid product number could be substantial.

The risk can be quantified as a dollar amount, a stratum of risk, or a nondollar quantitative term. The following examples illustrate how a risk might be quantified by each of these three approaches:

1. The estimated loss from cashing bad checks in a bank is $38,000 per year (dollar amount).
2. The risk of fire is very high (stratum of risk).
3. Number of keypunch errors per thousand keystrokes is estimated to be five (nondollar quantitative).

The user then defines the acceptable limits for those risks, such as:

1. The loss from cashing bad checks in a bank should be no greater than $5,000 per year.
2. The risk of fire should be reduced so that it is no greater than in other areas of comparable size and function.
3. The number of errors per thousand keystrokes should not exceed two.

The acceptable levels of risk then become the control requirements for the data-processing personnel. This required level of control is necessary in order to design computer controls. Normally, data-processing personnel design and implement controls in only the automated segment of the application. It is the responsibility of the user, however, to design and implement controls for the nonautomated segment of the application.

Computer Survival Rule #48

The user must determine the acceptable level of risk as a computer systems requirement.

Implementing manual controls

One of the weaknesses of computer applications is the point of interface between the manual and the automated segments. This is the point where the baton is passed between the people who perform manual functions and those who perform automated functions. If communication fails at this crucial point, the integrity of the application can be lost.

The user is responsible for the manual segments of application systems. The automated segment can help to ensure that the manual segment has been performed properly, but the key word here is "help." That is, the prime responsibility resides with the user. For example, if the manual segment indicated that an individual wanted 1,000 of item X, all the computer system can do is question whether 1,000 is correct. If the individual really had wanted 100, it is the user's responsibility to be sure that 100 is entered into the automated part of the application. It is unreasonable to hold the data-processing personnel responsible for the 1,000 items if that number was entered (incorrectly) into the automated segment of the system.

There are manual controls over input, processing, and output. Each of these areas poses different risks to the integrity of applications as well as unique opportunities for ensuring the accuracy and completeness of processing. We will look at the three areas individually and discuss the types of controls that are effective.

Control of input

The user should be concerned with both the validation and the authorization of input into computerized applications. The user is responsible for ensuring that the data going into the computer are accurate, complete, and authorized. Some of the controls that users have installed for this function include:

- *Reasonableness checks.* User personnel are instructed to question items such as quantities, prices, and so on that appear to be abnormal.
- *Scanning.* User personnel scan input forms to ensure that all parts are complete and that the information provided is in compliance with the input rules.
- *Written procedures.* User personnel are provided with detailed step-by-step instructions on how to perform their tasks.
- *Levels of authorization.* The authorization as processed is graduated so that higher levels of management make higher authorizations. For example, a department head may be able to approve the return of products costing up to $1,000, but an assistant controller must approve returns of more than $1,000.
- *Anticipation criteria.* User personnel anticipate whether transactions of specific types or for specific individuals will fall within certain limits. For example, user X rarely purchases more than Y items, or employees in department A rarely work more than ten hours overtime per week.

Control of processing

The types of controls that users can implement to ensure correct processing in the automated segment include:

- *Simple accounting proofs.* The user maintains records that verify that the previous balance plus additions minus deletions equals the new balance produced by the computer.
- *File sequence checks.* The user uses sequentially numbered files or input data in order to verify that no data are missing and that a wrong version of a file has not been used for processing.
- *Exception reporting.* When the rules of the automated segment have been violated, a report is prepared to outline the violations.

Use of data

The user can initiate controls to help ensure that the data produced by computer systems are interpreted properly. The following controls are used:

- *Report explanations.* Each report contains a narrative description that explains the origin of the data, the date of the report, and the types of processing performed on the data.
- *Report recipient identification.* The person for whom the report is intended is listed on the report to ensure prompt delivery to the right individual.
- *Error message control.* A sequential number is assigned to error messages to ensure that no error message is lost and that all corrections are reentered into the automated segment of the application system on a timely basis.

These are examples of the types of controls that users can initiate for the manual segment of computer systems. The completeness and effectiveness of these controls may determine the value of the computer system to the organization. Control of the automated segment is limited to the determination that what is entered into the system is processed according to the system's rules. The automated segment cannot verify that the data have been recorded properly, authorized, nor can it verify that the users of the system results use that information properly. These become users' responsibilities.

Computer Survival Rule #49

If you forget to control the manual segment of a system, you've doomed the system to failure.

Monitoring the effectiveness of controls

Have you ever experienced being delayed by a traffic light in one direction, while there is little or no traffic in the other direction? You wait for three or four changes of the light in order to get through the intersection. Had you been coming from the other direction, you would have been through in one change of the light. What happened? The traffic light allotment of green-light time was not synchronized with the needs of the motorists. Not only does this waste people's time, but it also encourages traffic violations. In such instances, the first car races through too quickly and the remaining cars try to push their luck in getting through the intersection. This can cause accidents.

Controls in computer systems are equally as susceptible to becoming asynchronous with the needs of the organization. Unless these controls are monitored and adjusted continually, they can waste individuals' time and encourage them to violate the control procedures.

Users of computer systems should be assigned the responsibility of monitoring the effectiveness of both manual and automated controls. Fulfillment of this responsibility requires the establishment of feedback mechanisms. Feedback mechanisms are mini-report writers that provide information on the operation of controls (see Figure 8-4). As the controls function, the feedback mechanism should be collecting information about the functioning of those controls.

Let's look at an example of an accounts receivable system that is designed to accept as payment in full any payment that is within $.99 above or below the amount billed. A control is established to ensure that payments that deviate by more than a specified amount are not accepted. The user should monitor this control to determine the degree of customer variance in order to ascertain whether the control needs adjustment. The feedback mechanism tracks the number of customers and amounts underpaid and the number of customers and amounts overpaid. If the feedback mechanism shows that a large number of customers are underpaying by $.99, it may be necessary to adjust the control so that payments are accepted only if they are within $.09 above or below the amount billed.

The monitoring of controls requires the following three steps:

1. Feedback mechanisms are established to report to the user on the functioning of the control. Frequently, this must be done in the automated segment of the system. The information can be reported as lists of violations, summation of violations, bar charts, graphs, and so on. The method of presentation of feedback information is whatever is most practical for the user for monitoring the effectiveness of the controls.
2. The user must evaluate feedback information to determine whether the controls are functioning effectively and, if not, why not.

Figure 8-4. Feedback Mechanisms

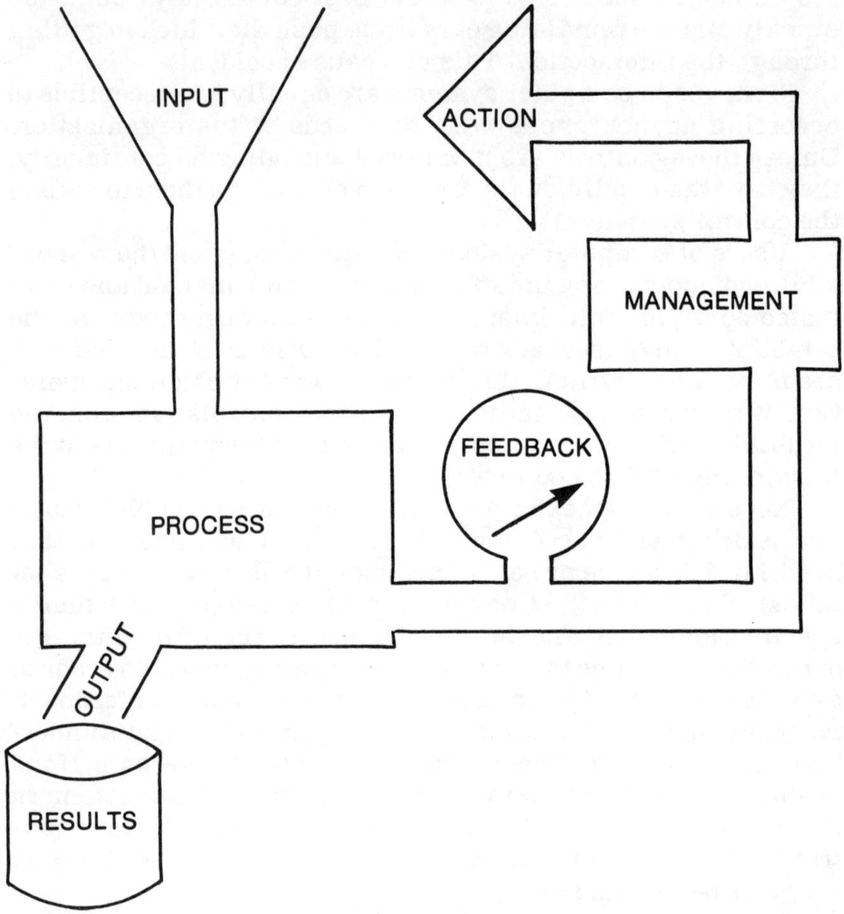

3. Whenever controls become ineffective, the user should take immediate steps to adjust the controls so that they do not affect employees' time or cause employees to circumvent systems controls.

Computer Survival Rule #50

An ineffective control may be worse than no control. Monitor controls continuously and adjust them whenever necessary.

Application system control checklist

Users of computer applications should assess the adequacy of controls for the application. Control is the responsibility of the user, and fulfillment of that responsibility requires that the user define, establish, and monitor the effectiveness of the controls.

Checklist 8-1 is designed so that "yes" answers indicate that control has been addressed adequately and "no" answers indicate potential control problems. Items that are answered negatively should encourage the user to investigate whether better methods or additional controls are needed to ensure the accuracy, completeness, and authorization of processing. This process should occur periodically throughout the life of the automated application.

Checklist 8-1. Application System Control Checklist

	Response			
Question	*Yes*	*No*	*N/A*	*Other*
1. Does your organization have a formal methodology for specification of controls in automated applications?	____	____	____	__________
2. Is the identification of risk an integral part of the systems development process?	____	____	____	__________
3. Have you, as the user of an automated system, described your control requirements to data-processing personnel?	____	____	____	__________
4. Does your organization have a procedure to determine whether or not controls are cost-effective?	____	____	____	__________
5. Do users of automated applications in your organization accept the responsibility for design and implementation of				

Checklist 8-1. Application System Control Checklist (continued)

Question	*Response* Yes	No	N/A	Other
controls in the manual parts of the application system?	____	____	____	____
6. Have you, as the user, accepted the responsibility for monitoring the effectiveness of computer controls?	____	____	____	____
7. Have feedback mechanisms been established for each control in the manual and automated segments of your computerized application?	____	____	____	____
8. Have the controls associated with each risk been identified and documented so that users can assess the adequacy of those controls?	____	____	____	____
9. Do problems occur that are not detected by controls in either the manual or automated segment of the application system?	____	____	____	____
10. Are feedback mechanisms monitored on a regular basis?	____	____	____	____
11. Are controls adjusted whenever they get out of synchronization with the organization's needs?				

Conclusion

This chapter has described the process of defining, implementing, and monitoring controls. Control is an essential and integral survival tool for users of automated application systems.

It is just as much a requirement of an application system as is any other user need. It is the user's responsibility to ensure that controls have been defined, implemented, and monitored adequately to determine their effectiveness.

In an ideal environment, controls are unnecessary; it is only when problems occur that controls should be installed. Controls should be cost-effective. That is, the cost of controls should be less than that of the problems they are designed to correct.

9/ People, not computers, make mistakes

Introduction

Discussions between users and data-processing personnel frequently fail to identify the true differences between the two groups. However, when the meeting is over, their actions are based more often on their deep-seated beliefs rather than on what they expressed during the meeting. This dichotomy manifests itself in unfulfilled needs and erroneous or inadequate results. There are ways to survive computer systems, but solutions cannot be found until people accept the fact that a problem exists.

Computerization is a disease—fortunately, a curable one. The final chapter in this book offers the medicine that will cure most of the maladies associated with computers. Some of the medicine may be distasteful, but it is far better than the disease of frustration and ineffective systems.

The communication gap

At last, the cause of computer problems has been identified. As with many of the more difficult problems, the solution is simple. The problem of holding a stack of papers together was solved by the paper clip and the staple. The problem of loading film into a camera was solved by the film cartridge. The solution to the computer system problem is communication.

The cause of problems with computer systems has been identified as a communication gap. Either people fail to talk, or they talk and fail to communicate. If you were to interview the two parties involved in an automobile accident, you would be convinced that they were not talking about the same event. Perhaps you have played the party game where person A tells a story to person B, who tells it to person C, who tells it to person D, and so on. Eventually, the last person in the line repeats the story to the group. If you haven't played this game, try it. The final version of the story usually bears little or no resemblance to the original story. Let's analyze some of the most common symptoms of communication problems.

Communication chain

As information is passed from person to person, it gets changed. This is the party-game syndrome described above. In data processing, this syndrome occurs when a user tells the systems analyst, who tells the data-base administrator, who tells the programmer, who tells computer operators, who tell the users what happened. The longer the chain, the greater the problem.

Language barrier

Communication is an imprecise art. The meaning of words is colored by experience, background, and education. The phrase "audit program" means something completely different to an auditor than the phrase "audit program" means to the data-processing person. When communication is coupled with technology, the language barrier increases. The greater the barrier, the lesser the communication.

Structured deadlock

People are taught or required to perform jobs in a certain manner. For example, you may be told to complete a change request form before data-processing people will talk to you about making a change. But you may not be sure what you want and might wish to discuss it before you fill out the form. The situation is now deadlocked because neither party will budge before the other does. This stalemate can lead to inaction, frustration, and outright hostility.

Expectation gap

Two parties frequently overestimate what they expected from each other. The non-data-processing professional may live in awe of technology and believe that the data-processing professional can solve all problems. On the other hand, the data-processing professional wants a precise definition of needs so that he or she can fulfill the service function of translating the needs into computer technology. When one party fails to deliver, the other party feels disappointed.

Point of order

Many participants in data-processing communications are acknowledged parliamentarians. As such, they recognize that each party must operate within predetermined bounds. For example, if the user begins to discuss how solutions might be implemented on the computer, the data-processing person will cry, "Point of order!" and explain that the Rules of Order on Technological Discussion prohibit users from involvement in technology.

"Up to your ass in alligators"

A common saying states that it is difficult to concentrate on draining the swamp when you are "up to your ass in alligators." This concept blocks communication in many conversations. Either the data-processing person or the user is heavily overloaded during such discussions. For example, the user may request a certain type of change, but because the data-processing person is working sixteen hours a day to catch up on backlog, the prevailing attitude of the latter is, "No, I don't want to do it." The reason has nothing to do with what's actually being discussed but, rather, with factors external to the conversation.

Handshaking hassles

Most conversations begin with a "handshaking dialogue." This involves a discussion of topics such as the weather, sports, or other irrelevant topics. However, these handshaking tactics can divert one from the real discussion or result in a hassle. For example, a fight over whose team won can preclude communication.

Legalistic arguments

Many individuals adopt the attitude that it is necessary to correct errors in diction, grammar, relevant facts, or the like. For example, one person may say that the temperature in the room is 78°, but the legalist will correct them by stating that the temperature actually is 77°.

The above are symptoms of communication problems. Most likely you have identified some of them in your everyday conduct of business. They are all symptoms that disrupt communication between people. This communication gap can be traced as the culprit in computer catastrophes.

Advanced stages of "communication gap-itis"

"Communication gap-itis" can occur in various stages. Have you experienced some of the following advanced states?

1. You go to the data-processing systems analyst to request what appears to be a minor but highly desirable change. After dialogue, documentation, analysis, and estimate, you are quoted a price for the job that is equal in amount to that for which you would sell your house.
2. You are expecting some reports from computer operations and they do not arrive on time. You call computer operations and they tell you they don't know the status of the reports but that they will get back to you. Time passes and nothing happens. You call back and are told that the individual you spoke to originally has gone home for the day, and that the person you are speaking to doesn't know what happened but that they will get back to you.
3. Part of your job or the information needed to do your job is computer assisted. Suppose you want to make some type of change (e.g., you want to obtain a certain type of information), and you approach the guardian of the computer with your request. The guardian tells you that he or she would love to honor your request but the computer won't allow it. In other words, the computer is the bad guy.

These and a million and one other war stories lead us to believe the computer is the root of all problems. However, computers don't feel; computers don't make our lives miserable. What happens is that people fail to communicate either the need or the result in the terms that foster harmony between people and machines. Thus, survival suffers significantly.

Survival solutions

People cannot live by computers alone. When people and the computer are in harmony, all is good. However, when disharmony occurs, problems are sure to follow.

In a perfect environment, harmony exists between people and a computer. Unfortunately, a relentless search has failed to discover the perfect environment. Therefore, some medicine is needed to cure the problems inherent in imperfect environments.

This chapter offers nine survival solutions to aid in the quest for high-quality computer systems. These are real-world solutions that work and are immediately implementable in most computer operations. Some of the solutions must be implemented in the data-processing area, while others are external to the data-processing function.

Solutions are designed to get at the heart of computer problems—that is, the communication gap. This gap exists, not only between users and data-processing people, but also independently in the data-processing user areas. It also exists between senior management and data processing management. In other words, all the parties involved in EDP may have a communication gap. The solutions can be instigated by any party, regardless of the area in which the problem is centered.

The survival solutions are divided into two categories: short-range and long-range. Short-range solutions address day-to-day problems, while long-range solutions are designed to avoid the repetition of problems over time. For example, improved communication may alleviate the problems associated with late delivery of a report, but it does not identify the cause of the late delivery. This problem may require a long-range solution.

Short-range solutions

Installation of a short-range survival solution today can bring immediate relief from the pains of computer problems. Short-range survival solutions aid in the identification of problems, so that people can address these problems before serious consequences occur.

Solution #1: Knowledge

In the computer field, there is nothing to fear but fear of ignorance. People who believe that a computer is a black box and who stand in awe of it tend to accept whatever the box produces. In many cases, such people do not know what to expect from a computer or how to ask the right questions to get what they need. Although this book is designed to be one small step toward education in these areas, the task may require more.

Data-processing personnel may need more knowledge in areas such as user processing and requirements, organizational policies and procedures, government requirements, audit requirements, control development methodologies, and business risk analysis. Similarly users of data-processing services may need knowledge in areas such as computer terminology, computer operation procedures, systems development methodologies, computer concepts, and data definition concepts.

Solution #2: EDP customer service

You walk into the store with a problem. If you walk up to one of the sales clerks and say, "The product I ordered has not arrived. Can you help me?", the sales clerk probably will look at you with a blank face and say, "No." Perhaps that sales clerk could make a call, perhaps you could make a call, perhaps something could be done, but that's not the way it works. The sales clerk asks you to go to the customer service department, which has the facilities and resources necessary to solve your problem.

Similarly, when you have a problem with the computer department, you may go to the individual who sold you the data-processing project. Unfortunately, the individual you dealt with initially in the data-processing area may not be able to help you. The example of a user who calls to find out the status of a job and is told that the person who was to give the information has left for the day has happened to me, and all too frequently.

The EDP solution is to establish a function within the data-processing department whose major mission is to make users happy. This is a data-processing customer service section that will attempt to serve customers' needs. With such a function, it is the only telephone number the user needs for the data-processing department. What a relief that could be!

One of the questions that frequently arises about survival solutions is, "Can my organization afford it?" The answer is, "Can you afford *not* to have it?" It's a pay-now or pay-later dilemma. Isn't it costly to have a senior systems analyst chasing problems in the computer room? Survival solutions should pay their own way.

The type of issues that should be addressed to a data-processing customer service department include status of production jobs, status of systems changes, queries on charges for services, availability of services, clarification of data-processing procedures, and instructions on how to complete forms.

Solution #3: User EDP service section

Users suffer a dual dilemma regarding data-processing information services. People in the user department have problems with computer systems and are uncertain to whom they should complain. On the other hand, data-processing people have problems with user requests and systems and are not sure whom to go to for the appropriate information.

This lack of the right "phone number" results in what data-processing people call "thrashing." Thrashing is a computer term that refers to the large amounts of time spent on administrative overhead. It tends to degrade computer service and consume computer resources.

The solution to thrashing is establishment of a central clearing point for requests and answers. The focal point in the user area should be a data-processing services coordinator. This is the individual to whom both user and data-processing personnel go for answers. The position is not intended to eliminate direct communication when appropriate channels are opened. Rather, the function of the coordinator is to eliminate the frustration of not getting the appropriate answer.

One large organization cited that their business philosophy was an "IWIN" philosophy. IWIN stands for I Want It Now. Before the computer, people relied heavily on written memos and letters. Today, people employed in industry are not willing to wait the time it takes for correspondence to turn around when they can get an immediate response on the telephone. However, they also don't want to have to call several people. They want to call one individual and get the answer. The customer service solution in both data-processing and user areas helps to provide the answer *now*.

Solution #4: Cost/benefit analysis

Many computer decisions are, in reality, "seat of the pants" decisions. Of course, few managers admit to using the approach of wild-guess decision analysis. However, it really is a very common way of approaching decision analysis in data processing.

Large funds can be expended on new systems, technology, and methodologies. Many such expenditures are made in an effort to cover one's tail, although some are made to satisfy the quest for new technology. However, in reality, many EDP decisions result simply from poor business judgment.

The solution to many computer problems is knowledge of the facts. These are not the technological facts or the facts about what people want; these types of facts are known already. The type of facts that frequently are missing are those related to the economics of taking or not taking a particular action.

Let's evaluate the situation of fire in a computer room. Years ago, organizations installed carbon dioxide gas in computer rooms, to be activated in the event of fire. Unfortunately, carbon dioxide gas not only puts out the fire but "extinguishes" the operators. Along came OSHA, (Occupational Safety and Health Act) and it no longer was in vogue to kill employees. Therefore, a new solution was needed.

The solution that appeared most obvious was Halon gas. Unfortunately, Halon gas is a very expensive solution to fire, and corporate controllers were loath to spend $15,000 to $20,000 to put out an operator's cigarette. In order to avoid this situation, the controllers decided to install delay switches on the wall of the computer room to delay the release of Halon should a less expensive alternative, such as a fire extinguisher, be acceptable. In large fires, Halon gas extinguishes flames but is not a coolant. Therefore, if oxygen returns to the computer room before the combustible area cools, it will reignite and destroy the computer room.

The Halon solution, which frequently is made without appropriate consideration of the economics, is a solution that may not be cost-effective for either small or large fires. Knowledge of the cost/benefit facts may have enabled data-processing people to look for other solutions to extinguishing fires. One of the reasons the facts of cost/benefit have been used so sparsely is the difficulty of quantifying many data-processing-related benefits, along with the lack of commonly accepted procedures for cost/benefit estimation.

This survival solution requires organizations to take the following steps:

1. Develop a methodology for identifying the costs and benefits associated with data-processing risks.
2. Develop a cost/benefit methodology that facilitates the production of consistent cost and benefit amounts.
3. Delay decisions until the appropriate cost/benefit analysis has been performed and the results are accepted by the parties involved.

Solution #5: Independent assessment

Areas of concern should be reviewed periodically by independent experts. For example, periodic reviews by a financial analyst helps to pinpoint weaknesses in financial planning, insurance, and other programs. Properly used, this low-cost review not only identifies weaknesses, but also provides solutions.

Independent assessment is directed at the problem frequently described as not being able to see the forest for the trees. That is, people who work too intimately in a particular area begin to believe that whatever they do is correct. Industrial psychologists have called this phenomenon the self-fulfilling prophecy. People believe that what they do is right and thus develop a rationale that proves their belief.

Review by independent experts should be rewarding, even if the verdict is that what you are doing *is* the best thing to do. Such reviews can eliminate doubts, not only in the minds of the parties directly involved, but also in the minds of senior management.

Independent reviews of computer solutions can be performed by any or all of the following groups: senior management, user management, auditors, and consultants.

Long-range solutions

Data processing in the business world is a relatively new concept. Much of the effort in data-processing has been expended in mastery of technology. However, as data processing matures, the discipline needs to be modified to smooth out the rough edges.

Short-range solutions deal with the symptoms, while long-range solutions are designed to cure the underlying disease.

Solution #6: Computer systems discipline

Visualize masons, plumbers, carpenters, and electricians assembling in a vacant lot. You, the prospective homeowner, come by and tell them that you are a family of four, that you like to play ping pong and pool, that you own two cars, and that you want them to build you a house. You tell them that you want living quarters appropriate to the size and needs of your family.

The group of technicians forms a committee to discuss your requirements. Each technician adds ideas and suggestions, and then they all start to work. The masons begin to pour concrete and lay block, the carpenters start to put the frame together, the plumbers run the pipes, and the electrician lays the wires. If the process sounds somewhat disorderly, it is. The solution is to orchestrate the construction of a home with a plan and a builder. With such orchestration, an unstructured, chaotic process becomes an orderly, step-by-step methodology in which all the pieces fit together in the appropriate sequence.

To the uninitiated, the planning process for building a home seems to take an endless amount of time during which no progress seems to occur. In our first example, the technicians started work on the very first day. The age-old argument continues to be, Which method is faster? Do planning, methodology, and structure slow progress? Experience and studies have shown that they do not.

Entire methodologies have been developed to improve the building of complicated computer systems. Among the methodologies that have proved helpful in avoiding problems, delays, and cost overruns in the building of data-processing applications are: SDLC, structured design, structured programming, data dictionaries, and project tracking.

Solution #7: Information management

Information is a resource of the organization and belongs to the organization. This fact rarely is disputed in theory but is disputed widely in practice. In fact, people believe that they own computer data. For example, most organizations have established a chargeout procedure for computer services. In other words, the departments who use the services are charged for the services.

Let's look at how a payroll manager might view data-processing services. The payroll manager wants an automated payroll system. In order to obtain this, the manager must go through an elaborate procedure of cost justification to develop the cost for implementation and operation of the system, together with the benefits to be gained from the system. The data-processing manager pays for the system as it is being developed. When the system is operational, the data-processing manager still pays to use it. The manager also pays for any changes that are made in the system. How, then, can the payroll manager view data-processing as anything other than something he or she has bought and paid for? If you buy and pay for something, you own it. Since data are part of data processing, the purchaser owns not only the processing, but the data as well.

Thus, if we say that data is a resource of the entire organization, is owned by the organization, and should be shared by all involved parties, the payroll manager says, "Not so. I bought and paid for my data. If someone wants to use it, they must either get my approval or pay me for the right to use it."

The solution to this problem is for senior management to administer and arbitrate the use of data from an organizational perspective. This situation usually necessitates a change in organizational structure. The two solutions proposed for this change concern data-base technology and necessitate the establishment of one of the following two functions:

1. *Data administrator/data-base administrator.* This change makes one individual responsible for the definition of data for the organization. Should disputes arise, this individual arbitrates or decides the course of action the organization should take.
2. *Information record management.* Information as a resource of an organization requires the same type of management as any other resource. Personnel is managed by a personnel administration section. Inventory is managed by an inventory control, and frequently a committee oversees the acquisition of fixed assets. Information record management applies the same principles to ensure that information is properly safeguarded and used in the organization.

Solution #8: Quality assurance

Quality, like beauty, is in the eyes of the beholder. One person's junk is another person's treasure. In data processing, there are wide discrepancies throughout an organization in the meaning and definition of quality in data processing. At the same time, many users of data-processing systems are unhappy with the service they get from data processing. Much of this conflict is due to a failure to agree on the quality of the product expected.

When a person buys a new automobile and problems occur with that automobile, the buyer has a feeling of disappointment and frustration with the manufacturer. The consumer is led to believe that they will receive a perfect product, while the manufacturer recognizes that there will be a certain percentage of defects in the products they manufacture. However, most manufacturers fail to inform the public that they have X percent chance of getting a defective product. This situation illustrates a quality expectation gap.

The function of quality assurance in data processing is to make one group responsible for the definition and measurement of quality. This group attempts to develop procedures and an environment in which users and data-processing people agree to a "contract" that defines the level of quality desired. The quality assurance function then attempts to ensure that the delivered product has achieved this level of quality.

Solution #9: Tell it like it is

The purpose of computer systems documentation is twofold: to enable people to develop a computer system, and to maintain the system. This picture resembles the documentation required to build a home. The builder needs the blueprints and wiring diagrams to construct the house, while the homeowner needs the appliance guarantees, deed, and so on to prove ownership and keep the home in proper order.

The question in data processing has never been whether or not documentation is needed. Rather, the question has been what type of documentation and how much. Documentation is an integral part of the computer survival kit. There are many aspects of documentation, some of which are of vital concern to the user, while others are primarily for the data-processing systems analyst and programmers. The user's concern, obviously, is with user documentation.

In determining whether documentation is sufficient, the user must ask the following questions:

- How will I know how to use the types of reports and other information provided by the data-processing system?
- What types of decisions will I need to make about computerized activities? Will I know where to find the information to make those decisions?
- How will I know what types of information I should be receiving and when I should be receiving it?
- How will I know what the system is doing so that I will know how to change it?
- How will I know the capabilities of the system so that I will know what more the system can provide than I am currently getting?

The answers to these questions determine the type and extent of documentation that are needed. If the documentation available can provide satisfactory answers to these questions, the documentation should be considered complete. However, if the documentation fails to answer the questions, survival problems may arise. Good documentation should provide the road map for helping you survive your crossing of data-processing country.

Is that all there is?

A janitor walked into a washroom to mop the water from the floor. A spigot had been turned on, causing water to drip slowly onto the floor. With great skill and finesse, the janitor mopped up the water quickly and efficiently. When the floor was clean, the janitor left the washroom, leaving the spigot open and the water dripping onto the floor. A short time later, the water again covered the floor, and the janitor returned and repeated the task. The janitor repeated this exercise time and again without ever turning off the spigot. Why? The reason is that cleaning the floor was the janitor's job, but turning off the spigot wasn't.

Whose job is it to ensure that computer systems are economical, efficient, and effective and that they meet the needs of the organization? Too frequently the answer to that question is, "Not me." In reality, it must be everybody's problem, or else the water will keep dripping onto the floor and the janitor will keep cleaning up the mess. The bystanders all will say, "What a terrible operation," but they will neither clean the floor nor turn off the water.

That's all there is to it. It means involvement of users in the computer process, involvement of data-processing people in the users' needs and concerns, and the creation by senior management of an environment in which communication can flourish.

Too frequently, senior management "executes" those involved in data processing and promotes the innocent. This survival guide was designed to help you avoid lying wounded on the data-processing battlefield when management starts shooting.

Appendix A
Computer Survival Rules

1. Even simple tasks are complex for a computer to perform. Don't overestimate the ease with which the computer can perform simple tasks.
2. Define all terms in such a manner that each term can be distinguished from all others.
3. Supply the precise times when a given action should be performed, along with any special variations that accompany these times.
4. Specify exact locations, physical or relative, that are pertinent to a given action.
5. Explode multistep operations into simplified, step-by-step procedures.
6. Devise routines that will minimize losses attributable to error conditions and permit completion of the task under any circumstances.
7. There are a lot of methods for accomplishing the same task. Leave the methods to the data-processing personnel; you concentrate on the tasks.
8. Verify that appropriate steps are taken to ensure the accuracy and completeness of input data.
9. Verify that procedures are adequate to ensure that input data will be placed in the proper location.
10. The same attention to control of people-readable documents should be expended on machine-readable data.
11. Evaluate the risk of inconsistent processing in a computer application, and develop controls that are commensurate with the risk.
12. Don't permit processing to become more complex than people can understand.
13. Spend the time necessary to anticipate all the unusual conditions that might occur in an application system. Then

include in the system instructions on what to do if those conditions occur.

14. Build a computer system a little larger than necessary in order to accommodate future needs. Installation of extra capabilities during construction usually are nominal in cost.
15. The integrity of output from computer systems should always be questioned.
16. Know what information is contained in the computer system but is not routinely printed.
17. Verify that procedures are adequate to ensure that codes can be verified properly.
18. Determine whether the data-processing department has adequate procedures to protect information on reusable magnetic storage media.
19. Recognize the risks of making instantaneous decisions.
20. Pennies spent on controls usually reap dollar savings through fewer systems problems.
21. A crucial check in computer systems is verification of the accuracy, completeness, and proper authorization of data that are to be entered into the computer system.
22. Don't err in the placement of data in a computer system.
23. Don't work with computer data unless you are friendly with those data.
24. The definition of data should be delimited by the people whose needs must be satisfied by those data.
25. Verify that all parties involved have contributed their requirements to the data definition process.
26. If you want to be sure data are accurate and complete, check, recheck, cross-check, and back-check. Even then, things may go wrong.
27. The category of information will give you the same insight into the information as does the table of contents in a book.
28. A piece of data should be entered into an organization's computer system only once. Then it should be checked sufficiently to ensure its accuracy and completeness.
29. If your organization chooses data-base technology, it also should choose a member of senior management to administer the data.

30. Determine how you want to use data, and *then* determine the best method to organize data to achieve your objective.
31. GIGO: Garbage in, garbage out. This means that, if the data going into the computer are no good, then the data coming out will be no good.
32. Organizations need an individual who is responsible for overseeing the currentness and usability of data in the organization. (This individual frequently is called the data administrator or data-base administrator.)
33. If the rule states that employees are not allowed access to a certain part of a building, a clerk would rather let them be cremated in a burning building than allow deviation from a rule over which that clerk has enforcement authority. In other words, argue your case in the right court.
34. If you wouldn't pay $50 an hour to hear yourself talk, do some additional preparatory work before you begin discussions with data-processing personnel.
35. Data processing is too important a function to be left entirely in the hands of data-processing personnel.
36. Of all the systems development approaches, the best one is the one with heavy user involvement.
37. Systems are not works of art; they require blueprints. The SDLC is the blueprint for a successful system.
38. Computer system users should be prepared. Systems survival means installation of procedures during the SDLC that will minimize the probability of failure.
39. Systems are built by people for people. If systems don't serve people, they are useless.
40. Computer systems change people's nice, happy, cozy world. Don't forget it, and do what is necessary to return them to their world.
41. Change should be managed like any other organizational function.
42. Build a system that is within the user's capability to operate. Systems built by PhDs for PhDs are useless to a non-PhD.
43. If systems displease people, people will displease the system by not following or by breaking the system's rules. Be aware of this survival threat.
44. Remember: A product you let others create for you will be a product that *they* like, but one *you* may not like.

45. The time spent on specification, design, and implementation of controls should be considered an important part of the systems development process.
46. Insist that your data-processing department develop a methodology for control development.
47. Make one person accountable for control at the lowest level possible.
48. The user must determine the acceptable level of risk as a computer systems requirement.
49. If you forget to control the manual segment of a system, you've doomed the system to failure.
50. An ineffective control may be worse than no control. Monitor controls continuously and adjust them whenever necessary.

Appendix B
Computer Survival Solutions

Number	*Solution*
	Short-range
1	Knowledge
2	EDP customer service
3	User EDP service station
4	Cost/benefit analysis
5	Independent assessment
	Long-range
6	Computer systems discipline
7	Information management
8	Quality assurance
9	Tell it like it is

Glossary

Address (1) An identification, represented by a name, label, or number, for a register, location in storage, or other data source or destination; for example, the location of a station in a communications network. (2) Loosely, any part of an instruction that specifies the location of an operand for the instruction.

Alphanumeric characters In programming, usually the characters A through Z, digits 0 through 9, and #, $, and @.

American National Standards Institute An organization sponsored by the Business Equipment Manufacturers Association (BEMA) for the purpose of establishing voluntary industry standards. Abbreviated ANSI.

Assembler language A source language that includes symbolic machine language statements in which there is a one-to-one correspondence with the instruction formats and data formats of the computer.

Auxiliary storage (1) Data storage other than main storage; for example, storage on magnetic tape or direct access devices. Synonymous with external storage, secondary storage. (2) A storage that supplements another storage. Contrast with *main storage*.

BASIC An algebralike language used by engineers, scientists, and others who may not be professional programmers for solving problems.

Binary code A code that makes use of exactly two distinct characters, usually 0 and 1.

Blocking Combining two or more records into one block.

Bug A mistake or malfunction.

Byte (1) A sequence of adjacent binary digits operated on as a unit and usually shorter than a computer word. (2) The representation of a character. (3) In System/360 and System/370, a sequence of eight adjacent binary digits that are operated on as a unit and that constitute the smallest addressable unit in the system.

Catalog An ordered compilation of item descriptions and sufficient information to afford access to the items.

CE Customer engineer.

Channel A path along which signals can be sent; for example, data channel, output channel.

Compiler A program that converts programmers' statements into machine language.

Control total A sum that results from the addition of a specified field from each record in a group of records, used for checking machine, program, and data reliability.

Core storage A form of high-speed storage that uses magnetic cores.

CPU Central processing unit.

Data base A collection of data that are fundamental to an enterprise.

Data management A major function of operating systems that involves organizing, cataloging, locating, storing, retrieving, and maintaining data.

Data set The major unit of data storage and retrieval in the operating system that consists of a collection of data in one of several prescribed arrangements and is described by control information to which the system has access.

Debug Locate and remove errors from a computer program. Synonymous with troubleshoot.

Default value The choice among exclusive alternatives made by the system when no explicit choice is specified by the user.

Device A mechanical, electric, or electronic contrivance with a specific purpose.

Digital Pertaining to the use of discrete integral numbers in a given base to represent all the quantities that occur in a problem or a calculation.

Direct access (1) Retrieval or storage of data by a reference to their location on a volume, rather than relative to data retrieved or stored previously. (2) Pertaining to the process of obtaining data from or placing data into storage, where the time required for such access is independent of the location of the data obtained or placed in storage most recently. (3) Pertaining to a storage device in which the access time is effectively independent of the location of the data.

Directory In direct-access storage, an index that is used by a control program to locate one or more blocks of data that are stored in separate areas of a data set.

Disk Loosely, a disk storage device.

Disk pack A removable, direct-access storage volume that contains magnetic disks on which data are stored. Disk packs are mounted on a disk storage drive, such as the IBM 2311 Disk Storage Drive.

Disk storage Storage on direct-access devices that record data magnetically on rotating disks.

EDP Electronic data processing.

Emulation The use of programming techniques and special machine features to permit a computing system to execute programs that are written for another system.

Field In a record, a specified area used for a particular category of data; for example, a group of card columns used to represent a wage rate or a set of bit locations in a computer word that is used to express the address of the operand.

Field-developed program A licensed program that performs a function for the user.

File A collection of related records that are treated as a whole unit and organized in a specific manner. For example, a payroll file (one record for each employee, showing rate of pay, deductions, etc.) or an inventory file (one record for each inventory item showing the cost, selling price, number in stock, etc.).

Flowchart A graphic representation of a solution to a problem.

Generate To produce a program by selection of subsets from a set of skeletal coding under the control of parameters.

Halt instruction A machine instruction that stops the execution of the program.

Hard copy A printed copy of machine output in a visually readable form; for example, printed reports, listings, documents, summaries.

Hash total A summation for checking purposes of one or more corresponding fields of a file that ordinarily would not be summed.

Header label A file or data-set label that precedes the data records on a unit of recording medium.

Header record A record that contains common, constant, or identifying information for a group of records that follow.

Hexadecimal Pertaining to a number system with a base of 16; valid digits range from 0 through F, where F represents the highest units position (i.e., 15).

Host computer The primary or controlling computer in a multiple computer operation.

Index An ordered reference list of the contents of a file or document, together with the keys or reference notations for identification or location of those contents.

Indexed sequential organization A file organization in which records are arranged in logical sequence by key. Indexes to these keys permit direct access to individual records.

Input Pertaining to the insertion of data.

Inquiry A request for information from storage; for example, a request for the number of airline seats available, or a machine statement to initiate a search of library documents.

Instruction A statement that specifies an operation and the values or location of its operands.

JCL Job control language.

Job A specified group of tasks prescribed as a unit of work for a computer. By extension, a job usually includes all necessary computer programs, linkages, files, and instructions to the operating system.

Job control language A programming language used to code job control statements. Abbreviated JCL.

Job scheduler The part of the control program that reads and interprets job definitions, schedules jobs for processing, initiates and terminates processing of jobs and job steps, and records job output data.

Job step The execution of a computer program explicitly identified by a job control statement. A job may specify that several job steps be executed. Also, a unit of work associated with one processing program or one cataloged procedure and related data. A job consists of one or more job steps.

Label One or more characters that are used to identify a statement or an item of data in a computer program.

Library A collection of organized information used for study and reference; collection of files related to such information.

For example, one line of an invoice may form an item, a complete invoice may form a record, the complete set of such records may form a file, the collection of inventory control files may form a library, and the libraries used by an organization are known as its data bank.

List An ordered set of items; to print every relevant item of data.

Load module The output of the linkage editor; a program in a format suitable for loading into main storage for execution.

Load-module library A partitioned data set that is used to store and retrieve load modules.

Lockout In multiprocessing, a programming technique used to prevent access to critical data by both central processing units at the same time.

Machine code A language that a machine is designed to recognize.

Machine language A language that a machine is designed to recognize.

Macro instruction An instruction in a source language that is equivalent to a specified sequence of machine instructions.

Main frame Central processing unit.

Main storage (1) The general-purpose storage of a computer. Usually, main storage can be accessed directly by the operating registers. Contrast with *auxiliary storage.* (2) All program-addressable storage from which instructions may be executed and from which data can be loaded directly into registers.

Mass storage (on-line) The storage of a large amount of data that also are readily accessible to the central processing unit of a computer.

Memory Storage.

Merge To combine items from two or more similarly ordered sets into one set that is arranged in the same order.

Message An arbitrary amount of information with a beginning and an end that are defined or implied.

Message switching A telecommunications application in which a message received by a central system from one terminal is sent to one or more other terminals.

Microsecond One-millionth of a second.

Millisecond One-thousandth of a second.

Module A program unit that is discrete and identifiable with respect to compiling, combining with other units, and loading; for example, the input to or output from an assembler, compiler, linkage editor, or executive routine.

Multiplexing The division of a transmission facility into two or more channels, either by splitting the frequency band transmitted by the channel into narrower bands, each of which constitutes a distinct channel (frequency-division multiplexing), or by allotting this common channel to several different information channels, one at a time (time-division multiplexing).

Multiprocessing (1) Pertaining to the simultaneous execution of two or more computer programs or sequences of instructions by a computer or computer network. (2) Loosely, parallel processing. (3) Simultaneous execution of two or more sequences of instructions by a multiprocessor.

Multiprocessor (1) A computer that uses two or more processing units under integrated control. (2) A system consisting of two or more central processing units that can communicate without manual intervention.

Multiprogramming system A system that can process two or more programs concurrently by interleaving their execution. Abbreviated MPS.

MVT Multiprogramming with a variable number of tasks.

Object program An assembled program that is ready to be loaded into the computer.

Off-line Equipment that is not under control of the central processing unit.

On-line Equipment that is under control of the central processing unit.

Operating system Software that controls the execution of computer programs.

Output Data delivered from a device or program.

Page (1) In virtual storage systems, a fixed-length block of instructions or data, or both, that can be transferred between real storage and external page storage. (2) To transfer instructions or data, or both, between real storage and external page storage.

Parallel operation Pertaining to the concurrent execution of two or more operations.

Partitioned data set In direct access storage, a data set that is divided into partitions, called members, each of which can contain a program or part of a program.

Password (1) A unique string of characters that a program, computer operator, or user must supply to meet security requirements before gaining access to data. (2) In systems with time-sharing, a one- to eight-character symbol that the user may be required to supply at the time he or she logs on the system. The password, in contrast to the user identification, is confidential.

Permanent storage Fixed storage.

Pointer An address or other indication of location.

Polling A technique by which each of the terminals that shares a communications line is interrogated periodically to determine whether it requires service.

Printer A device that writes output data from a system onto paper or other media.

Privileged instruction An instruction that can be executed only when the central processing unit is in the supervisor state.

Processor (1) In hardware, a data processor. (2) In software, a computer program that includes the compiling, assembling, translating, and related functions for a specific programming language; for example, COBOL processor, FORTRAN processor.

Program A series of actions designed to achieve a certain result.

Program library A collection of available computer programs and routines.

Programmer A person involved in the designing, writing, and testing of computer programs.

Programming language A language that prepares computer programs.

Prompting In systems with time-sharing, a function that helps the user of a terminal by requesting the user to supply operands necessary to continue the processing.

Queue (1) A waiting line or list formed by items in a system that are waiting for service; for example, tasks to be performed or messages to be transmitted in a message-switching system. (2) To arrange in or form a queue.

Random access Direct access.

Random processing The treatment of data without respect to their location in external storage, and in an arbitrary sequence governed by the input against which they are to be processed.

Reader (1) A device that converts information in one form of storage to information in another form of storage. (2) A part of the scheduler that reads an input stream into the system.

Real time Pertaining to an application in which response to input is fast enough to affect subsequent input, such as a process control system or a computer-assisted instruction system.

Record A collection of related data that are treated as a unit.

Record layout The arrangement and structure of data in a record.

Recovery Restarting of a system after a problem has destroyed the integrity of the system.

Redundancy check An automatic or programmed check based on the systematic insertion of components or characters, used especially for checking purposes.

Remote job entry Submission of job control statements and data from a remote terminal, causing the jobs described to be scheduled and executed as though they were encountered in the input stream.

Remote terminal An input/output control unit and one or more input/output devices attached to a system through a transmission control unit.

Report program generator A processing program that can be used to generate object programs that produce reports from existing sets of data. Abbreviated RPG.

Response time (1) The time between the submission of an item of work to a computing system and the return of results. (2) In systems with time-sharing, the time between the end of a block of user input and the display of the first character of system response at the terminal.

Restart To begin processing from a point of known integrity.

RPG Report program generator.

RPQ Request for price quotation.

Scheduler See *job scheduler.*

Secondary storage Auxiliary storage.

Security Prevention of access to or use of data or programs without authorization.

Seek time The time that is needed to position the access mechanism of a direct-access storage device at a specified position.

Sequence (1) A specified arrangement of items. (2) In sorting, a group of records whose control fields are in either ascending or descending order, according to the collating sequence.

Sequencing Ordering in a series or according to rank or time.

Signed field A field containing a character that designates its algebraic sign.

Simulation The use of programming techniques alone to duplicate the operation of one computing system on another computing system.

Simultaneous transmission Transmission of control characters or data in one direction while information is being received in the other direction.

Software Programs and procedures involved in the operation of a data-processing system.

Sort A routine that orders data.

Source program A computer program written in a language other than machine language.

Source statement A statement written in symbols of a programming language.

Storage A device in which data can be held.

Storage protection Control that prevents unauthorized access to storage for reading or writing.

Systems analysis The analysis of an activity to determine precisely what must be accomplished and how to accomplish it.

Systems programmer (1) A programmer who plans, generates, maintains, extends, and controls the use of an operating system with the aim of improving the overall productivity of an installation. (2) A programmer who designs programming systems and other applications.

Telecommunications Data transmission between a computing system and remotely located devices via a unit that performs the necessary format conversion and controls the rate of transmission.

Telecommunications lines Telephone and other communications lines that are used to transmit messages from one location to another.

Teleprocessing The processing of data that is received from or sent to remote locations by way of telecommunication lines.

Terminal A device, usually equipped with a keyboard and some kind of display, that is capable of sending and receiving information over a communications channel.

Throughput The total volume of work performed by a computing system over a given period.

Time-sharing A method of using a computing system that allows several users to execute programs concurrently and to interact with the programs during execution.

Trailer label A file or data-set label that follows the data records on a unit of recording media.

Trailer record A record that follows one or more records and contains data related to those records.

Translator (1) A device that converts information from one system of representation into equivalent information in another system of representation. In telephone equipment, the device that converts dialed digits into call-routine information. (2) A routine for changing information from one representation or language to another.

Turnaround time The time elapsed between submission of a job to a computing center and the return of results.

Unit record A card that contains one complete record; a punched card.

User Anyone who requires the services of a computing system.

User exit A point in a vendor-supplied program at which a user-exit routine may be given control.

Utility program A problem program designed to perform an everyday task, such as transcribing data from one storage device to another.

Variable-length record A record whose length is independent of the length of other records with which it is logically or physically associated.

Virtual storage Addressable space that appears to the user as real storage, from which instructions and data are mapped into real-storage locations. The size of virtual storage is limited by the addressing scheme of the computing system (or virtual machine) and by the amount of auxiliary storage available, rather than by the actual number of real-storage locations.

Index